W9-CCB-416

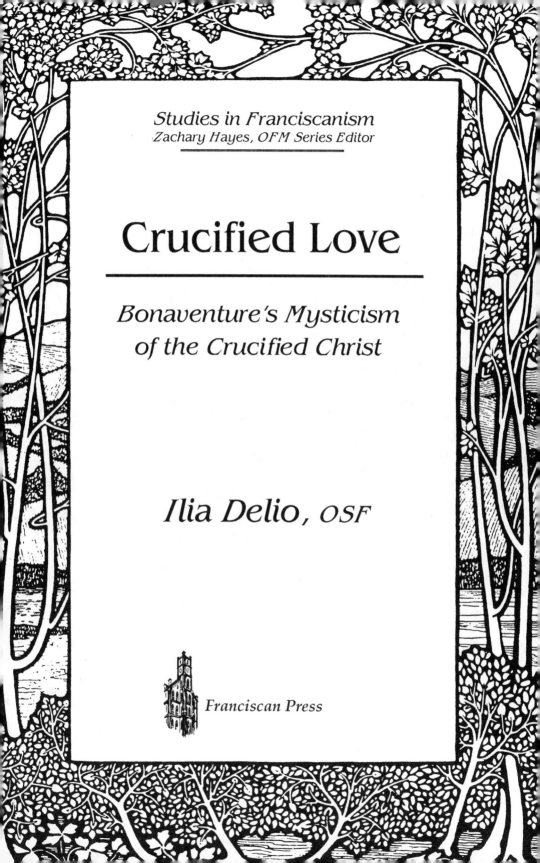

Studies in Franciscanism
Zachary Hayes, OFM Series Editor

Crucified Love

*Bonaventure's Mysticism
of the Crucified Christ*

Ilia Delio, OSF

Franciscan Press

Crucified Love: Bonaventure's Mysticism of the Crucified Christ
Ilia Delio, OSF

Franciscan Press
Quincy University
1800 College Avenue
Quincy, IL 62301
PH 217.228.5670
FAX 217.228.5672
http://www.quincy.edu/fpress

© 1998 Franciscan Press

All rights reserved.

Book design and typesetting by Laurel Fitch, Chicago, IL.
Cover: Icon of the Crucified by Judy Coles, 1997

Printed in the United States of America
First Printing: October 1998
     2   3   4   5   6   7   8   9   0

Library of Congress Cataloging-in-Publication Data available upon request.

I would like to dedicate this book to Professor Ewert Cousins,
a true friend and mentor,
and to my mother who embodies the meaning of crucified love.

"Via autem non est nisi per ardentissimum amorem crucifixi."
Bonaventure, *Itinerarium Mentis in Deum* prologue 3

Contents

Acknowledgements

This book grew out of my dissertation on Bonaventure's Christ mysticism written under the direction of Professor Ewert Cousins of Fordham University. I would like to express my sincere thanks to Ewert for his support and encouragement. I would also like to thank Ingrid Peterson, O.S.F. for graciously reading the entire manuscript and offering helpful suggestions, and the staff of the Franciscan Institute where I first wrote my dissertation. The final text could not have been made without the diligent efforts of several students of the Washington Theological Union: Karla Manternach, Jessica Wormely, and Carol Ludwig. A heartfelt thanks to Karla, Jessica, and Carol for proofreading the chapters and preparing the index. I also thank Dr. Terrence Riddell of Franciscan Press for seeing this work come to completion.

Preface

In recent decades interest in Bonaventure has continued to acceler-
ate. The foundation for this was laid in the last century through
the impetus given in 1879 by the encyclical *Aeterni Patris* of Pope
Leo XIII, which launched the Neoscholastic revival. Although this
movement focused primarily on the thought of Thomas Aquinas,
overshadowing that of Bonaventure, nevertheless it stimulated
Franciscan scholars to edit the critical Latin text of Bonaventure in
ten volumes, 1882-1902, which has been the foundation of all subse-
quent Bonaventure scholarship. Following the trend of the time,
though, the editors of this critical edition tended to interpret
Bonaventure from the perspective of Thomas. In 1924 a major turning point came when Etienne Gilson published his *Philosophy of Saint
Bonaventure*, which clearly distinguished the thought of Bonaventure
from that of Thomas, establishing it as a distinct vision in its own
right.

BONAVENTURE REVIVAL

In the 1960s, as the seventh centenary of the death of Bonaventure approached, a new wave of Bonaventure scholarship was
launched by Jacques-Guy Bougerol, O.F.M. He organized two conferences in France and orchestrated international collaboration which
issued in the publication of five volumes containing articles from
almost a hundred scholars from Europe and America. This was followed by an international congress on Bonaventure in Rome, organized in the centenary year 1974, by Alfonso Pompei, O.F.M. Conv.,

which produced three volumes of scholarly articles. These projects drew many scholars to direct their attention to Bonaventure, thus providing a broad base of interest in Bonaventure's thought. Since then there has been a steady flow of works on Bonaventure that have continued to explore the many aspects of his theology, philosophy, spirituality, and mysticism as well as his role as Minister General in the history of the Franciscan Order. Parallel with this in the twentieth century there has been an impressive flow of scholarship on Francis of Assisi and more recently on Clare.

In the present book, Sister Ilia Delio builds on this scholarship and makes a distinctive contribution to what I have described as the on-going Bonaventure revival. With the skill of an artist, she has woven a beautiful tapestry reflecting the complexity and nuances of this rich array of scholarship. Although she draws a picture of Bonaventure's thought that is grounded in this scholarship, the highlights and brush strokes are distinctly her own. But to say this is not enough. Her real achievement lies not in her masterful control of the vast corpus of Bonaventure's texts and the on-going tradition of scholarly interpretation. Rather it lies in her penetrating insight into the very heart of Bonaventure's vision. She sees that crucified love is at the center of Bonaventure's theological vision and spiritual teaching, as it is in the mystical experience of Francis at La Verna, and at the center of the *Itinerarium Mentis in Deum*. Her book is not merely another study of a theme in Bonaventure, for she claims that crucified love is the door to all other aspects of his thought. Through this prism of crucified love she sees the fountain-fulness of love in the inner life of the Trinity, that self-diffusive love which flows out in creation, and which in the incarnation enters, in poverty and humility, into the suffering of the world.

In the light of her insight into crucified love, Sister Ilia interprets the twofold aspect of Bonaventure's teaching on mysticism: the ultimate union of the soul with God described in the final chapter of the *Itinerarium* and the mysticism of the historical event, so richly explored in Bonaventure's meditations on the life of Christ in the *Lignum Vitae*. It is not merely meditation on the divine manifestations in creation—rich though this is—but the crucified love on Cavalry that leads to the glory of the resurrection, as Bonaventure says in the prologue to the *Itinerarium:* "There is no other path but through the burning love of the Crucified."

In the light of the depth and comprehensiveness of her insight into crucified love, it would not be an exaggeration to say that her book can provide a vision and a catalyst for the on-going Franciscan revival of our time.

Ewert Cousins
June, 1998

Introduction

There are two qualities of the human person that cry out for meaning in our time—love and suffering. Every person desires to love and to be loved; every human person suffers. We might say that love and suffering are existentials of the human condition. To the modern mind, love and suffering are contrary, the person who loves must not have to suffer and the person who suffers finds no reason to love. We seek love that will bring joy, happiness and freedom from suffering. We free ourselves from suffering so that we may enjoy the delights and satisfaction of love. In this daily struggle to love and to be freed from suffering, we encounter conflict and dead ends. Rather than attaining our true desire, to love, we end up suffering and, sometimes, we suffer to such an extent that we become apathetic or indifferent to love.

It is because the questions of love and suffering in our modern age are not readily resolved by modern thought that we turn to the past to try to glean the wisdom of some of the great theologians and saints. I became interested in the Franciscan theologian, Saint Bonaventure of Bagnoregio, as a doctoral student at Fordham University while studying under Professor Ewert Cousins. I discovered in Bonaventure not only a brilliant theologian who appealed to the heart but, moreover, one who united love and suffering in a stunning vision of the world with Christ Crucified as its center. Bonaventure had the gift to understand love and suffering not as opposites but as complements in the cross of Jesus Christ. Through his insight to the mystery of the Crucified, he envisioned the harmony of all reality—God, humanity and creation—united in the cross, their center.[1] My thesis is that Christ Crucified forms the synthesizing principle of Bonaventure's theology, drawing humanity and creation together into the unity of God. The basis of this unity is the suffering or crucified love of Christ which Bonaventure perceived as the diffusion of God's goodness in the world.

Bonaventure's mysticism of the Crucified Christ is influenced by the Stigmata of Francis of Assisi. The Stigmata have, historically, been a source of contention and debate among scholars.[2] Spiritually, however, they signify the transformation of Francis into the Crucified whereby love (in this case ecstatic love) and suffering are joined together. The Franciscan emphasis on the primacy of love helps us to understand the meaning of the suffering and death of Jesus not so much as a reversal of sin but as the explicit manifestation of divine love in the created world. It is the resurrection and ascension of Jesus *crucified* and glorified that transforms the world in divine love—"through his wounds we are healed" (1 Pet 2:24). It is precisely because Jesus ascends into glory in his crucified humanity that his wounds become our wounds, and our wounds become the doors to divine love. Our capacity to be united to God rests not so much on our ability to love God, since our love can never equal God's, but on our ability to suffer as a way of expressing our love for God. Bonaventure grasped this completely when he wrote: "There is no other path [to God] than through the burning love of the Crucified."[3] In Jesus Christ, suffering and love are united. This is an unfathomable mystery that fails the test of human reason alone. It is the mystics such as Francis, Bonaventure, and others, especially women mystics, who grasped the meaning of Jesus's passion and death as the personal expression of divine love. They came to value the suffering of their lives as a way to be united to Christ and thus to the fullness of divine love.

Several scholars have suggested that the pivotal point of Bonaventure's thought took place in 1259, two years after he was elected Minister General. At this time he went up to the mountain of La Verna, where Francis had received the Stigmata, in search of peace. While there meditating on the event of the Stigmata, he had a sudden insight to the meaning of this event. He "saw at once that this vision represented our father's rapture in contemplation and the road by which this rapture is reached."[4] True to the spirit of Francis, Bonaventure realized that one could make the journey to God only through Christ Crucified. After this time, Bonaventure directed his writings, particularly his spiritual writings, to the mystery of the Crucified Christ. While in his earlier writings he perceived the Crucified to be the center of the soul and the path to interior peace, by 1274, the year of his death, he understood the Crucified to be the center of the world, of all history and time, and the path to eschatological peace. After the La Verna experience, the Crucified captivates his thought and becomes the model of authentic human existence, of divine love and unity in the world.

Ewert Cousins claims that Bonaventure took two elements found in Francis: his imitation of Christ, and his sense of the universal presence of God in nature, and fused these into a doctrine of Christocentricity.[5] With Francis in mind, Bonaventure not only considered the love of God in himself but how that love is expressed in the created world. The figure of Francis stamped with the mystical wounds of Christ indicated to Bonaventure that mystical union with the Crucified Christ is the basis of spiritual transformation and the realization of the new creation in Christ.

Francis was a true lover of Christ, according to Bonaventure, because he was perfectly conformed to the Crucified Christ both in spirit and in flesh. The stigmatized Francis signifies to Bonaventure that if one desires happiness and peace, one must contemplate God and strive for mystical union through conformity to Christ Crucified, the Word of God. Bonaventure maintains that from the beginning of creation we were ordained to contemplate God but we lost this grace with sin. The whole person was placed in paradise, he states, to contemplate God, but the whole person fell through sin. The soul and flesh entered into spiritual pride and physical gluttony.[6] Bonaventure's "holistic" view of the human person as body and spirit underscores the unity of the human person created in the image of God. Since Christ is the true image in whom we are created, he is our model of what it means to be authentically human.

Bonaventure places a positive emphasis on the humanity of

Christ—that is, the earthly life of Christ—in his birth, public life and passion, highlighting the significance of the humanity of Christ as that which enables us to attain to God. The significance of the humanity of Christ corresponds to Bonaventure's theology of the Word who is *medium* of the Trinity (the center between the Father and Spirit) and the *medium* of creation (the center between the Father and the created world).[7] The Seraphic Doctor perceives that the journey to God and the entering into divine love can be realized only by following the incarnate Word, Jesus Christ. Imitation of and conformity to Christ is the path that leads to mystical union, a path that may be called the "mysticism of the historical event,"[8] since it is through participation in the earthly life of Christ that one attains to God. While Bonaventure describes the journey to God in "stages," it is not a linear progression but a spiral process. Rather than moving unidirectionally to God as if one were climbing a ladder, leaving the world behind, imitation of Christ leads to a progressive transformation of the person in Christ, leading to a deepening of love in union with Christ. It is this union which enables one to embrace the world with compassionate love, following the example of the Crucified.

For Bonaventure, love is integral to the human person because we are made in the image of God and therefore are capable of being united to God. Although we are images of God, we are in fact an image of the Son who is the perfect image of the Father. Just as in the Trinity the Father and Son are joined together by an eternal dynamic spirit of love, so too, in the created world, the human person is called into a dynamic spirit of love with the divine. Francis became a true image of Christ through imitation of and conformity to Christ. In spirit, Francis "burned" with compassionate love for God and neighbor and for all created things including the lowly things of creation; in his flesh he was marked with the mystical wounds of the Crucified. For Bonaventure, Francis not only became the exemplary Christ mystic but the exemplar of divine goodness in the created world. Through his conformity to Christ, Francis was opened up to transcendent goodness expressed in compassionate love, a love that was so ardent that he longed for the grace of martyrdom in perfect imitation of Christ.[9]

The stigmatized Francis is the model that Bonaventure constantly places before us as one who attained peace and happiness in this world by uniting himself to the Crucified and becoming one in love with the suffering love of Christ. Francis' integration into Christ or rather the integration of the Crucified into the life of Francis enabled him to be fully integrated in the world, not standing over the world in power and position but standing "under" the world in humility and servanthood, united to all creatures. Through his conformity to Christ Crucified, Francis lived in a spirit of compassionate love and, through this love, healed broken relationships and transformed the world around him.

There is no doubt that Bonaventure perceived in Francis, particularly the stigmatized Francis, something powerful and mysterious. He saw realized in Francis the potential of the human person created in the image of God and what the human person can become in relation to God. We might say that Bonaventure perceived in Francis the "mysticism of the human person," the mystery of God hidden in the human person in whom the capacity to be united to God not only transforms one in God but transforms the world around the human person. Since this potential for God is rooted in our nature as image and since our true image is Christ Crucified, it is only in conformity to the Crucified that the human person can become authentically human, rightly ordered to God, neighbor and the created world. Just as the Crucified unites all that is separated from God through his compassionate love, so too, the human person conformed to the Crucified helps to unify God and creation through the spirit of compassionate love.

In light of the stigmatized Francis, Bonaventure suggests that consummation of the world can take place only when the human person is in union with Christ and, specifically, Christ Crucified, who is the perfection of divine love in the world. This means a constant spiritual program of conforming one's life to the Crucified, imitating Christ in word and deed, entering into the events of his life and allowing this experience to open one up to the presence of God hidden in Christ. The opening up to God in Christ is, at the same time, the opening up of the world to God, for Christ is the center of the world. Bonaventure sees that Francis was so rightly ordered to God through his conformity to Christ that he called even the lowliest of creatures brother and sister because he recognized that they had the same primordial source as himself (*LM* 8, 6). Union with Christ Crucified, as Francis's life reveals, leads to the truth of all reality created by God and the interrelatedness of all reality in God.

The task of this book is to elucidate Bonaventure's theology of the Crucified Christ, based on Francis's spirituality, and to show how he develops his theology into a Franciscan Christocentric world view grounded metaphysically in the self-diffusive good of the Trinity. In order to accomplish this task, I begin with the central inspiration of Bonaventure's thought, namely, Francis of Assisi. Although Bonaventure was influenced primarily by the stigmata of Francis, an examination of Francis's writings indicate that the principal ideas that form the basis of Bonaventure's Christ mysticism are already present in Francis. The central themes of his writings include, the Trinity, Christocentricity, the poverty and humility of the cross, the humanity of the Crucified Christ, and the role of the Spirit. Understanding Francis's spirituality, therefore, enables one to appreciate Bonaventure's Christ mysticism as one that is distinctly Franciscan.

While the close spiritual relationship between Francis and Bonaventure has raised questions, particularly in view of Bonaventure's biography of Francis (the "Franciscan Question"),[10] there is no doubt that the poor man of Assisi was deeply influential on the learned theologian. Chapter two examines the influence of the stigmatized Francis on the thought of Bonaventure, and how meditation on the Stigmata of Francis impelled Bonaventure to embark on a new theological direction, one focused on the crucified humanity of Christ. This relationship is examined in light of the *Itinerarium Mentis in Deum* in chapter three and concludes with a discussion of a metaphysics of the good emerging in Bonaventure's thought in chapter four. Using the *Itinerarium* as a "turning point," I try to show that from this work on, Bonaventure's writings are devoted to understanding the mystery of the Crucified Christ as center, and mystical union with the Crucified as the way to God. In this respect, it is not surprising that his principal spiritual works which concentrate on the Crucified are composed within a year of each other: the *Itinerarium Mentis in Deum*, the *Lignum vitae*, the *Triplici*

via, and the *Legenda Major*.[11] After 1259, Bonaventure focuses primarily on the mystery of the Crucified Christ and devotes his theologial
gifts to elucidating this mystery.

Chapter five examines the method Bonaventure uses to attain
union with God through conformity to the Crucified based on the
Lignum vitae. It is a method that employs the senses and imagination
and calls for participation in the life of Christ. The *Lignum vitae*, a
popular medieval work, provides the most apt illustration of
Bonaventure's way to union with the Crucified. Conformity to the
Crucified leads one into the profound mystery of God hidden in
Christ. Union with the Crucified leads not only to personal transformation but to cosmic transformation, since Christ Crucified is both
the center of the soul and the center of the world. In chapter six, the
mystery of Christ Crucified as the center of the world is examined in
light of cosmic Christocentricity. The first *collatio* of the
Hexaëmeron forms the basis of this vision. The Christocentrism that
emerges in this *collatio* shares similarities with the contemporary
Christocentric vision of Pierre Teilhard de Chardin. A brief comparison between Bonaventure and Teilhard is made at the end of chapter
six.

The core of Bonaventure's thought is that mystical union with
the Crucified Christ is the key to personal and cosmic transformation. Because God who is love is relational, everything that takes
place in this world depends on our relationship to God, and this relationship is fully realized in union with Christ Crucified. We cannot
hope for a "new creation" unless we first become that new creation in
Christ, burning in love with the same spirit as the Crucified. This
central idea forms the basis of Bonaventure's world view which is elucidated in chapter seven. Following the theme of the Crucified in
Bonaventure's spiritual writings enables us to construct a world view
based on his theology of the Crucified Christ. Comparing it to the
world view of the monastic world, we see that Bonaventure's view
with Christ Crucified as center is an integrated one. The material
world is not transcended or left behind as in the Neoplatonic ascent
(see Appendix One); rather, as one ascends to God, one descends to
neighbor and the created world. As one is transformed in Christ
Crucified, one is transformed in relation to neighbor and creation. As

Bonaventure writes of Francis in chapter eight of the *Legenda Major*: "He was drawn up to God through devotion, transformed into Christ through compassion, attracted to his neighbor through condescension, and universally reconciled with each and every thing."[12] Thus, in union with Christ Crucified, we are not only transformed personally and brought into the mystical relationship of love between the Father and Son but the whole world is transformed and moves toward what Teilhard de Chardin called the Omega point, the final consummation of all things in Christ.

The last chapter discusses the importance of Bonaventure's theology for the contemporary world. The dynamic character of his theology marked by its profound Christocentrism can help elucidate some of the major concerns in our time, the concern for non-violence, holism and integration, and orientation toward the world through compassionate love. Bonaventure's theology is not only relevant to questions in liberation theology and Postmodern spirituality but can address many aspects of contemporary Christian life in a meaningful way.

I have included Appendix One as a supplementary chapter to illuminate the background of mysticism, beginning with the metaphysics of Plato. This Greek structure of reality so influenced Christian thought that it still forms, to a large extent, the foundation on which we formulate theological doctrine. Bonaventure was familiar with Neoplatonism, especially as it filtered through the university curriculum and circulated among spiritual writers, providing the structural framework with which to describe the spiritual journey. Scholars still debate the degree to which he was a Neoplatonist in light of the Augustinian and Aristotelian principles which are found in many of his writings.[13]

The Christian Neoplatonic ascent to God was developed by monks both in the East and West. Examination of the principal themes in monasticism and the role of Christ in the journey to God show that contemplation is an anticipation of the eternal vision of God in the heavenly Jerusalem. Although devotion to the humanity of Christ arises in monastic circles in the Middle Ages, the focus remains oriented to the eschatological future of the heavenly Jerusalem. Union with God, even as Bernard of Clairvaux maintained, is union with the ascended and glorified Christ. An understanding of the ascent to God in the monastic tradition helps us to appreciate the original contribution Bonaventure makes by his radical Christocentricity.

Bonaventure's mysticism of the Crucified is the mystery of God in the world, the mystery of love and suffering united in the embrace of Jesus Christ on the cross. He offers us an authentic Christian metaphysics and calls each of us to discover Christ Crucified as the center of our lives and of our world. Although it is a medieval doctrine developed in a medieval culture, its profound significance should not be denied by the boundaries of time and place.[14] Some people may find it difficult to embrace suffering as an expression of love, especially in our century which has seen all too much suffering. Others may say that it is precisely the acceptance of Christ's suffering as a way of life that has supported the oppression of women, third world people, various ethnic groups, and creation itself. While there is historical truth to this, I would suggest that oppressive suffering persists because we fail to love by way of suffering. The model of Christ Crucified that Bonaventure illuminates indicates to us that love and suffering cannot be dualistic, that the triune God of love has loved us and all creation precisely through the wounds of suffering. We fail our brothers and sisters in love when we fail to love by suffering in and for them.

As we approach the dawn of the twenty-first century, I believe that Bonaventure's Christocentric vision will find its place at the center of Christian theology. As Etienne Gilson once noted, it is so systematically complete that no one part can exist in isolation.[15] God, humanity, and the created world are a unified whole in the Crucified Word, Jesus Christ. It is my hope that Bonaventure's theological vision will be grasped by the world as an authentic Christian vision of relationship with God, with one another, and with the non-human created world. It is a vision that can impel us to become truly Christian and truly human by turning toward the other, to Christ and our neighbor, in a spirit of compassionate crucified love. It is a vision of true relationship, a response to God's grace in Christ and a continual progression on the spiritual journey to union with the Crucified Christ. If we are willing to enter into relationship with the suffering Christ, to enter his wounded side, then we will find our peace and happiness in the perfection of love. For from his wounded side, Bonaventure indicates, the new creation has already begun.

Ilia Delio, OSF
Washington D. C., 1998

Abbreviations

KEY TO FRANCIS' WORKS

Adm.	*Admonitiones*
EpCler	*Epistola ad clericos*
1 EpCust	*Epistola ad custodes (recensio prior)*
2 EpCust	*Epistola ad custodes (recensio posterior)*
1 EpFid	*Epistola ad fideles (recensio prior)*
2 EpFid	*Epistola ad fideles (recensio posterior)*
EpOrd	*Epistola toti ordini missa una cum oratione: omnipotens, aeterne*
EpRul	*Epistola ad populorum rectores*
LD	*Chartula Fr. Leoni data*
OffPass	*Officium passionis Domini*
RegB	*Regula Bullata*
RegNB	*Regula non Bullata*
RH	*Regula pro eremitoriis data*
Sal. virt.	*Salutatio virtutum*
Test	*Testamentum sancti Francisci*

KEY TO BONAVENTURE'S WORKS

Apol. paup.	*Apologia pauperum*
Brev.	*Breviloquium*
Coll. Jn.	*Collationes in Evangelium Joannis*
Comm. Lc.	*Commentarius in Evangelium S. Lucae*

Comm. in Joan.	*Commentarius in Evangelium Joannis*
De perf. vit.	*De perfectione vitae*
De reg. anim.	*De regimine animae*
De Sp. sti.	*Collationes de septem donis Spiritus sancti*
De tripl. via	*De triplicia via*
Hex.	*Collationes in Hexaëmeron*
I, II, III, IV, Sent.	*Commentarius in I, II, III, IV, librum Sententiarum*
Itin.	*Itinerarium Mentis in Deum*
Lig. vit.	*Lignum vitae*
LM	*Legenda maior*
Lm	*Legenda minor*
M. Trin.	*Quaestiones disputatae de mysterio Trinitatis*
Q. evang. perf.	*Quaestiones disputatae de perfectione evangelica*
Q. Sci. Chr.	*Quaestiones disputatae de scientia Christi*
Red. art.	*De reductione artium*
Solil.	*Soliloquium de quatuor mentalibus exercitiis*
Tract. de plant.	*Tractatus de plantatione paradisi*

Francis of Assisi:
Mystic in the World

In order for one to truly appreciate the richness of Bonaventure's mysticism of the Crucified Christ and its implications for our world, it is necessary to explore the root of his mystical doctrine. While he was undoubtedly a learned theologian, being trained at the University of Paris, his most profound inspiration did not come from books but from the model of Saint Francis of Assisi, the little poor man who loved Christ with such an ardent love that he received the Stigmata, the mystical wounds of Christ. Eric Doyle entitled his book of Bonaventure's sermons on Francis, the *Disciple and the Master,* a most appropriate title that underscores the profound interconnectedness between these two great saints.[1] The spirituality of Francis provides a solid foundation on which to construct the theological vision that Bonaventure formulates. Paul Rout has shown a defined spiritual relationship between Francis and Bonaventure that can be described as mutual, insofar as we understand the one more clearly in light of the other.[2] However, I would suggest that Bonaventure's theological vision is not circumscribed by his relation to Francis but rather springs from his life, entering into the mystical depths of God's love in the Crucified Christ.

There is perhaps no saint in history who has been subject to more historical critical analysis than Francis of Assisi. Born in 1181 or 1182 (sources are unsure of the exact date), Francis was the son of a wealthy middle class merchant, Pietro di Bernadone. The sources describe him as gentle, likable and fun-loving. Although his education was limited, he learned to read and write at the local St. George's church-school and was taught French by his father. Influenced by the romance of chivalry, Francis joined in battle between Assisi and Perugia and became a prisoner for a year at Spoleto. While recuperating from his injuries, he received a divine revelation urging him to serve the Lord rather than man. Afterwards, he began to help poor priests as well as the needy and to associate with the poor. Around the year 1206 when Francis was about twenty-five years old, he publicly renounced his father to follow Christ, put on a hermit's cloak, and began to live a life totally dedicated to God.[3]

The way of life that Francis embraced was not entirely new since, in the early part of the thirteenth century, many groups were forming with the goal of returning to an authentic gospel life, a revival of the *vita apostolica* and *ecclesia primativa*. The desire for a spirituality focused on the humanity of Christ, especially in his poverty and suffering, impelled men and women to live in conformity to Christ through a life of extreme poverty. Examples of this type of life can be found in groups such as the mendicants (Franciscans and Dominicans), Waldensians, and Humiliati.[4] While many took up this new life in the midst of commercial cities, others chose the eremetical life as a way of following the poor Christ, combining contemplation and poverty, while still others went to the Holy Land to fulfill their desire to be conformed to Christ in poverty, humility and suffering.

The first biography of Francis by the friar Thomas of Celano was written between 1228 and 1229 at the request of Pope Gregory IX. Because Thomas did not have a chance to study all the sources, a second biography was requested by the Minister General Crescentius of Jesi and composed by Celano between 1244 and 1247. In the later biography, Celano used material provided by the companions of Francis. The second major biography was composed by Bonaventure at the request of the General Chapter at Narbonne in 1260 (or Rome in 1257). The text was approved in 1263 and in 1266 defined by the Franciscan Order as the only canonical text. A minor life of Francis was also composed by Bonaventure although without attaining official status in the Order.[5]

While the biographies have provided a description of Francis' life and spirituality since the time of his death, a retrieval of authentic sources, that is, works composed by Francis himself, has taken place in this century with the result of shedding new light on the spirituality of the Poverello.[6] What is of interest is that a perusal of Francis' own writings gives little evidence of concentration on the humanity of Christ; further, the mystical element in Christianity, either of the monastic *contemplatio* model, or of the ecstatic contemplation of the Beguines or other visionaries is virtually absent in his writings.[7] Although the hagiographical tradition (biographies and legendary sources) emphasizes Francis' ecstatic visionary experiences and imitation of Christ, the saint's own writings make no mention of these.

Bernard McGinn claims that it is exceedingly difficult to present any single synoptic view of Francis' theology based on his writings. Deceptively simple at first glance, the seeming verbal poverty of his writings hides unusual theological riches. What is most striking is the distance between Francis the writer and Francis the saint as portrayed by the hagiographers. Yet, many themes are common to both, such as his insistence on poverty and emphasis on the virtues of humility and obedience. But in Francis' works these themes take on their own complexity because they appear within a rather different theological perspective than what is found in the writings of his followers. Some of the hagiographical aspects of Francis such as his role as the perfect imitator of Christ, and his emphasis on the concrete visual presentation of the mysteries of Christ's life, while not without historical evidence, are not found in any explicit way in his own writings.[8]

A Life of Solitude?

The breadth of difference between Francis' writings and those of his biographers make the search for authentic Franicscan spirituality, and more specifically, Franciscan mysticism, a challenging one. Most of the hagiographical sources describe Francis at the beginning of his spiritual journey as a solitary, spending long periods of time in the woods and mountains, dedicating himself to a life of prayer.[9] Thomas of Celano recounts the early life of the friars at the

Portiuncula as withdrawn from the world, meditating on heavenly truths and rendering unceasing praise to the Lord: "Those who dwelt in this place were occupied with the divine praises without interruption day and night, and fragrant with a wonderful odor, they led an angelic life."[10] However, the sources further indicate that Francis wavered between a life totally dedicated to prayer and an active life of service. After consultation with some of the brothers and the lady Clare, Francis purportedly decided that he should not embrace the contemplative life but should "preach as the herald of Christ."[11]

Francis composed a *Rule for Hermitages* rather late in his career, either in 1217 or 1222, at approximately the same time that the regular *Rule (Regula bullata)* was composed.[12] He begins the *Rule for Hermitages* not by establishing it as a rule for those who wish to live as hermits but for "those who wish to live religiously in hermitages." The appellation of the "Rule" suggests that hermitages were already in existence within the early fraternity prior to the writing of this *Rule* by Francis. It was not presented as an innovation but rather instructions as to how religious life should be lived out in the hermitage. Thus, it does not set up another set of legislation for friars living in the hermitages, that is, with the intent of superceding the approved *Rule* of the friars minor. In the critical edition of the *Rule*, Kajetan Esser entitles the work, *Regula pro eremitoriis data*; it is a rule given *for* hermitages. It is a voluntary life not necessarily undertaken permanently nor for prayer alone, since there is the opportunity for both service and prayer in the hermitage.[13] The *Rule for Hermitages* indicates, however, that solitude of prayer is an important aspect of the Franciscan spiritual life.

God in the Writings of Francis

Although the radical life of Francis has always been intriguing and attracted followers, the more important question is, I believe, not how Francis envisioned the life that he embraced but how he envisioned God. How did he, who was considered a second Christ in the Middle Ages, relate to God? Who was God for Francis? If we examine Francis' writings and compositions we see that his theological vision is deeply Trinitarian and Christological. He does not speculate on the mystery of the Trinity but concentrates on the presence of the Trinity in the three great acts of the history of salvation: creation, redemption, and final consummation. For Francis, the terms "Creator, Redeemer, Savior" apply to the whole Trinity. For example, in *RegNB* 23, 9 he writes: "Let us desire nothing else, let us wish for nothing else, let nothing else please us and delight us save our Creator and Redeemer and Savior, alone true God, who is the full good, the whole good, the total good, the true and highest good."

Thadée Matura has shown that for Francis, the Father is the object of his love.[14] Despite the fact that he is remembered historically as a second Christ (*alter Christus*), he shows almost no personal relationship to Christ in his writings. However, he does refer to the Father personally as, "my holy Father," or "Holy Father." In his Office of Psalms he changes the word "God" to "my holy Father." Similarly, in one of his Holy Week psalms he writes, "My holy Father, King of heaven and earth, do not leave me."[15] According to Matura, Francis uses the word "Father" in an explicitly trinitarian context more than twenty times.[16] It is interesting that while the Father is personal to Francis he is at the same time the "heavenly Father," transcendent, glorious, and distant. Francis perceives the Father as the Creator, the Most High, yet the Father as Creator is known only through the Son and Spirit. The Father is never separated from Son or Spirit. In the *Regula Non Bullata* Francis writes:

> All-powerful, most holy, most high and supreme God, Holy and just Father, Lord, King of heaven and earth, we thank you for Yourself for through Your holy will and through Your only Son with the Holy Spirit, You have created all things spiritual and corporal . . . And because all of us wretches and sinners are not worthy to pronounce Your name, we humbly ask that our Lord Jesus Christ Your beloved Son . . . give You thanks as it pleases You and Him for everything.[17]

This passage underscores the key to Francis' thought, namely, that there is no direct contact with the Father other than through the Son, since the Father is totally transcendent. He refers to the Son of the Father as "Your Beloved Son." For example, in the Our Father he prays: "And forgive us our trespasses through your ineffable mercy through the power of the passion of *your beloved Son*."[18] The father-hood of God, therefore, is rarely placed in direct relationship with humans. Rather, God is Father because of the mystery of Trinity and because of the Son and his relation to him. In two of Francis' prayers we can detect the relation between the Father and Son. The first is before the San Damiano Crucifix where Francis, praying before the Crucified, hears a voice beckoning him to "repair my house which is falling into ruin." Afterwards, Francis prays, "Most High Glorious God enlighten the darkness of my heart, and give me Lord a correct faith, a certain hope, a perfect charity, sense and knowledge, so that I may carry out Your holy and true command."[19] Although Francis hears the voice coming from the cross, he does not direct his prayer to Christ but to the "Most High," the Father. Similarly, after receiving the Stigmata, Francis does not pray to Christ but rather praises the Father: "You are holy, Lord, the only God, You do wonders, You are strong, You are great, You are the Most High, You are the almighty King. You, holy father, the king of heaven and earth."[20]

The primacy of the Father is revealed in the fact that he sends the Son who descends from his heavenly riches to take on our human fragile nature. In his second version of his *Letter to the Faithful* Francis writes: "The most high Father in heaven announced this Word of the Father—so worthy, so holy and glorious—in the womb of the holy and glorious Virgin Mary, from which he received the flesh of humanity and our frailty."[21] Thus, the Father is Father of the Son and is present in the Son in the incarnation. Everything belongs to the Father and is given to the Son who receives and transmits everything in turn to the Father.

The Son

Understanding the Father in Francis' writings helps us gain a clearer understanding of who Jesus Christ is for him. The most thorough study to date on the role of Christ in Francis' theology is that by Norbert Van Khanh.[22] According to Van Khanh, Christ is the Son of the Father, the "beloved Son." Christ is the "true wisdom" of the Father, the "Word of the Father." He is given to us "from on high" by the Father and comes to be with us as "light." Although the words "God" and "Lord" are often found alone in Francis' writings, the names Jesus, Jesus Christ or Christ are never found alone; rather, Francis always uses Lord Jesus, Lord Jesus Christ, Our Lord Jesus Christ or the Lord God. Expressions such as "my Jesus" or "my Lord Jesus Christ" which convey a personal relation to Christ are absent in the writings of Francis. Conversely, the word "Father" is often prefaced with a personal pronoun. The Father is referred to as: "my most holy Father," "my holy Father" or "my Father."[23] It is not without significance that the prayer Francis considers *par excellence* and the first one he teaches the friars to pray is the Our Father. Because the Father lives in "inaccessible light" (1 Tim 6:16) Francis sees the way to the Father through the Son: "The Father and I are one" (Jn 10:30). It is the Father, the Creator God, who has revealed himself in the Son.

The originality of Francis, according to Van Khanh, is his note of exclusiveness. Christ alone is the One in whom the Father takes delight. He is obedient to the Father and wishes to be submissive in all things to the will of the Father. This notion of the obedient Christ predominates over the image of the poor Christ in Francis' writings.[24] The Son satisfies the Father in everything and reveals the Father to us. Throughout his writings, Francis makes it clear that Christ reveals the Father not only through his words but also by his life and example, leading us to the Father. Indeed, the deepest reason to cling to Jesus is that he reveals the Father. He is "the Son of the Most High" (*LOrd* 4). According to Francis, the Father has no need of anyone's love save the Son's nor the worship of any sinful human. That is why he does not offer a prayer of thanksgiving directly to the Father but rather turns to Christ as the representative of humanity, since the Son alone can thank the Father in a fitting way. The Father accepts our offering of thanks in and through the Son.

Word of the Father

Francis often uses the expression "Word of the Father" when speaking about the person of Christ. In the second version of his *Letter to the Faithful* he states that he is setting before them in this present letter and message the words of Our Lord Jesus Christ, who is "the Word of the Father and the words of the Holy Spirit, which are spirit and life."[25] In this letter Francis does not propose to announce the precise words of Christ recorded by the Evangelists but to speak of the person himself, the Word of the Father. Thus he writes in the following verse: "Through his angel, Saint Gabriel, the most high Father in heaven announced this Word of the Father, so worthy, so holy and glorious, in the womb of the holy and glorious Virgin Mary from which he received the flesh of humanity and our frailty."[26] Francis highlights the intimate union between the Father and the Son by saying that it is the Father who announces the coming of the Son to the Virgin Mary; the Archangel Gabriel plays an intermediate role. This is a note of originality that reflects his own theological understanding of the Son as the Word of the Father who descended into the poverty of humanity to do the will of the Father.

In his second *Letter to the Faithful* he recounts the principal episodes in the life of Christ, his coming in mortal flesh, the last scene with the disciples, his prayer in the garden of Gethsemane, his death on the cross and his presence in the Eucharist. This is one of the few places where he describes the life of Christ, although his description is laconic. It is precisely in this context, however, that he inserts the Christological expression, "Word of the Father," an expression which has profound theological significance. By doing so, he establishes a comparison between the divine Word which is entirely worthy, holy and glorious, and the Incarnate Word which assumed our fragile human nature. He draws attention to the Word of the Father who left his divine riches in order to take on the poverty of humanity. The Incarnation, therefore, is an actual movement of descent (*synkatabasis*) undertaken by the Word of the Father. This movement of descent effected by Christ is again expressed by Francis when he speaks to his brothers about the Son of the Father who is given to us in Christ the human person and now in the Eucharist:

> See, daily he humbles himself as when he came from the royal throne into the womb of the Virgin; daily he comes to us in a humble form; daily he comes down from the bosom of the Father upon the altar in the hands of the priest.[27]

Francis highlights the two extreme aspects that characterize Christ: the royal throne where he was from all eternity with the Father and the womb of the Virgin where he has taken human flesh: the bosom of the Father and then the altar and the hands of the priest. His thought therefore is directed from one extreme to the other, along the path of God to humankind.

The descent of the Word into humanity underscores the humility of God. Humility here is not designated by the poverty of the earthly life of Jesus, rather, it is simply another name for the divine love for humankind, a love which always has its source in the Father Most High. This love is called humility because Francis perceives the love of the Father in the descent of the Son to humankind, that is, in the Incarnation. Humility is not a virtuous attitude but an act; it is an act of the Father by which he gives of himself to humanity in the incarnation of his Son. The humility of the human person will be the total gift of him or her self to God in response to that first act of divine love: "Therefore, hold back nothing of yourselves for yourselves so that he who gives himself totally to you may receive you totally."[28]

The vision of the humility of God which has its source in the eternal Father and is manifested in the Incarnation of the Son is, according to Alexander Gerken, the source of Bonaventure's theology of the Incarnation.[29] For Bonaventure, as for Francis, the humility of God is expressed in the descent of the Word of the Father whose incarnation is both the expression of the Father's will and the manifestation of the humble Trinity. Humility and poverty are essential to the nature of God.

The Holy Spirit

The lack of emphasis on the earthly life of Christ in Francis' writings is surprisingly replaced by the profound emphasis on the role of the Spirit. The Spirit makes us "children of the heavenly Father, spouses, brothers, and mothers of our Lord Jesus Christ"[30] (2 *EpFid* 50). The renowned Franciscan scholar, Kajetan Esser, indicates the importance of the Spirit for Francis by saying:

> With St. Francis it is not simply a question of an external following of the life of Christ, but rather first of all that the spirit of Christ must become alive and active in the would-be follower. This doctrine of the spirit of the Lord . . . may be called the very center of St. Francis' thinking and Christian behavior.[31]

Sebastián López sees chapter ten of the *Rule* in which the Spirit of
the Lord is described, as the "theological center" of Francis' thought.
The expression, "to have the Spirit of the Lord," arises out of a comprehensive formulation of the Franciscan life, the culmination of
which consists in attaining to the unity of Father and Son, communi-
cated to us in the Holy Spirit. This is an indication that the Spirit of
the Lord is the key to contemplation in Francis insofar as it is the key
to the inner life of the Trinity.[32] The Spirit of the Lord leads the
individual into depths of the following of Christ and to intimate
union with the triune God. In Spirit we are able to adore the Father
and give him thanks. The Spirit permits us not only to see and adore
God but also unites us with him. The Spirit unites the faithful to
Jesus to become mothers and brothers and children of the Father.

The following of Christ depends radically on the Spirit. Only by
first possessing the Holy Spirit can we follow the footprints of the
Son and come to the Father: "Inwardly cleansed, interiorly enlight-
ened and inflamed by fire of the Holy Spirit, may we be able to follow in the footprints of your beloved Son and . . . may we make our
way to You, Most High."[33] The journey back to the Father takes
place in reverse order: from the Holy Spirit through the Son to the
Father. Everything begins with the Spirit. The following of Christ,
therefore, does not mean imitation of an external model but attention
to the Spirit of the Lord. The following of Christ means living like
Christ, totally dependent on the Father, in unceasing adoration of the
Father, like the beloved Son, and in union with him. One may ask, if
the Spirit is central to Francis's theology, can his theology be truly
characterized as "Christo-centric?" Yes, but Christ is always in relation to the Father and Spirit. Francis' path takes us through the
Spirit, in Christ, to the Father. Thus while he is "Christocentric" he
is at the same time "Trinicentric." Those who bear the Spirit of the
Lord are children of the heavenly Father and spouses, brothers and
mothers of Jesus Christ (1 *Ep Fid* 5-8).

In his *Rule*, Francis distinguishes himself from the *Rule* of Saint
Benedict by prefacing his teaching on prayer with the "Spirit of the
Lord," a change that underscores his whole program of life.
Concerning the role of the Spirit with regard to prayer Benedict
writes:

> We must know that God regards our purity of heart and
> tears of compunction, not our many words. Prayer should
> therefore be short and pure, unless perhaps it is prolonged
> under the inspiration of divine grace.[34]

Whereas Francis states:

> Instead let them pursue what they must desire above all
> things: to have the Spirit of the Lord and his holy manner of
> working, to pray always to him with a pure heart and to have
> humility, patience in persecution and weakness.[35]

Francis indicates that three things are necessary for prayer: to have
the Spirit of the Lord, to pray unceasingly, and to pray with a pure
heart. The call to unceasing prayer is found four times in the writings of Francis. He associates unceasing prayer with the Spirit of the
Lord and purity of heart: ". . . to have the Spirit of the Lord and its
holy manner of working, to pray always to him with a pure heart."[36]
From this injunction it can be said that Francis associates unceasing
prayer with good works and that such prayer is possible only in one
who has the Spirit of the Lord.

The significance of unceasing prayer is closely associated with
purity of heart. In the earlier *Rule* Francis exhorts all the brothers to
serve, love and adore the Lord God with a clean heart and a pure
mind, for he desires this above all things: "And let us adore him with
a pure heart, because we should pray always and not lose heart; for
the Father seeks such worshipers. God is spirit, and those who worship him must worship him in spirit and in truth."[37] The same theme
is found in the second version of the *Letter to the Faithful* where he
uses the expression "spirit of truth" to suggest that it is the Spirit of
the Lord who produces in us the act of praying with a pure heart.

In the *Regula non bullata* Francis indicates that the heart is the
dwelling place of the spirit, that is, of an energy or force that
influences the activities or movements of the human person. In this
respect, it is the place where the Spirit of the Lord struggles with the
spirit of the flesh: ". . . let us be very much on our guard so that we
do not lose or turn away our mind and heart from the Lord under
the guise of achieving some reward or doing some work or providing

some help... adore the Lord God with a clean heart and a pure mind for this is what he desires above all things."[38]

The meaning of the words, "Spirit of the Lord," can be elucidated in more detail by examining the passage in which they are contained.

> I admonish and exhort the brothers in the Lord Jesus Christ that they beware *of all* pride, vainglory, envy, avarice, cares and worries of this world, detraction and complaint. [And those who are illiterate should not be eager to learn] Instead let them pursue what they must desire above all things: to have the Spirit of the Lord and his holy manner of working, to pray always to Him with a pure heart and to have humility, patience in persecution and weakness.[39]

Francis prefaces his teaching on prayer with the words: "I admonish and exhort." After "I admonish," the text contains two parts: the first is negative, introduced by "that they beware" and followed by "should not be eager" thus indicating vices and sins to be avoided. The second part is positive with the exhortation, "let them endeavor" to have above all the "Spirit of the Lord and its holy activity."

Francis reflects a Pauline understanding of the flesh and spirit here. In the letter to the Galatians, Paul opposes the works of the flesh to those of the spirit; in the *Rule*, Francis does the same. He believes that the human person is essentially good, being created in the image of God. However, the flesh is weak and is both an enemy and deceiver.[40] Francis speaks negatively of those caught up in the flesh and those who live carnally. In Gal 5:19-23 Paul speaks of the vices of the flesh; similarly, in the *Rule* Francis lists them as "pride, vainglory, envy, avarice, cares and worries of this world, detraction and complaint."[41] He warns against these "spiritual sins of the heart" as well as the sins of the flesh, the body and self-love. To overcome the spirit of the flesh he exhorts the friars to have above all the Spirit of the Lord and its holy activity. This underscores a life of penance. In his first *Letter to the Faithful*, Francis describes the life of penance as the total gift of heart, soul, mind and strength to God (1, 1), the love of neighbor as self (1, 2a) and the hatred of the body with its vices and sins (1, 2b). The significance of the penitential life with the subjugation of the flesh to the spirit indicates that the life of the spirit is of paramount importance for Francis, an idea which is borne out in his understanding of Christ.

Francis also associates purity of heart with adoration of God and unceasing prayer, made possible in the person in whom the Spirit of God dwells: "And let us adore him with a pure heart, because we should pray always and not lose heart (LK 18:1) . . . . God is spirit and those who worship him must worship him in spirit and in truth (cf. Jn 4:23-24)."[42] He uses the Gospel passage of the seed (Lk 8:11) to indicate that only the pure of heart have the proper soil to receive the Word of God which is the spirit of truth and brings forth spirit and life (Jn 6:64). Only the person with a pure heart receives the Word of God and, in receiving the Word, has the Spirit of the Lord; and where the Word and Spirit dwell, so too does the Father who abides with the Word: "If anyone loves me he will keep my word, and my Father will love him, and we shall come to him and make our home with him" (Jn 14:23).

We see the same emphasis on the Spirit in his exhortation on the Divine Office. In his *Letter to the Entire Order,* Francis indicates how the Office is to be recited. Clerics are to say the Office with devotion before God, not concentrating on the melody of the voice but on the harmony of the mind, so that the voice may blend with the mind, and the mind be in harmony with God: "Let them do this in such a way that they may please God through purity of heart and do not charm the ears of the people with sweetness of voice."[43] For the Benedictines, the Office has an eschatological focus since in his *Rule* Benedict writes: "In the presence of the angels I will sing to you. Let us consider, then, how we ought to behave in the presence of God and the angels, and let us stand to sing the psalms in such a way that our minds are in harmony with our voices."[44] Whereas Benedict speaks of "minds in harmony with voices," Francis advocates that "the voice may blend with the mind, and the mind be in harmony with God."

Benedict links chanting of the Office with the angelic life. By suggesting that hearts must be in tune with words, he implies a liturgical celebration of unceasing praise before the throne of God in the heavenly Jerusalem. Through the Divine Office the monks partake of the angelic life of divine heavenly praise in anticipation of the future glory in the heavenly Jerusalem. Francis does not associate recitation of the Office with the angelic life. His prescription that the harmony of the voice and mind must blend with the heart devoted to God seems to refer to something different. It corresponds to his spiritual program of a pure heart in which the Spirit of the Lord dwells, and this corresponds to adoration of God: "Let us . . . adore the Lord God with a clean heart and a pure mind, for this is what he desires above all things."[45] The Office, therefore, essentially serves the same function as the spirit of interior prayer. The spoken word must be an outward expression of what fills the inner mind and spirit.

It is not without significance that Francis prescribes recitation of the Divine Office in the Later *Rule* in the same chapter in which he discusses fasting and the sending of the friars on mission (*RegB* 3). He distinguishes himself from the monastic tradition by prescribing a monastic practice, recitation of the Divine Office, with missionary activity, preaching the word of God. Vocal prayer is to serve a similar function as private prayer, that is, to enable one's mind and spirit to be attentive to the Lord so that wherever the friar is in the world he may adore the Lord.

Francis and the Humanity of Christ

Francis had a special love of God in the "mysteries of divine humility," those mysteries which express the poverty and humility of the incarnation: the birth of Jesus, the passion and death of Jesus, and the blessed Eucharist.[45] Although the Holy Spirit has a prominent role in his spirituality, Francis's mysticism can be distinguished by his devotion to the humanity of Christ. If we examine the context of the humanity of Christ in his writings, we see that it is precisely Christ's humanity that enables us to understand what contemplation is for Francis. We can identify three ways in which the humanity of Christ is expressed in Francis' writings: Scripture, the Body and Blood (Eucharist), and the image of the good shepherd.

Francis discovers in Scripture the living presence of Christ, and he approaches the Scriptures as he would the person of Christ. In his

Letter to Clerics he associates the Word with the body and blood of Christ indicating that the holy words are a corporeal sign of the Son of God just as in the Eucharist. Thus, Scripture is sacramental. In his second *Letter to the Faithful*, Francis writes: "And let all of us firmly realize that no one can be saved except through the *holy words* and *blood* of our Lord Jesus Christ which the clergy pronounce, proclaim and minister."[47] Here he indicates that the holy words and the body of Christ, that is, the humanity of Christ, are the same source of spirit and life. Just as the Spirit gives meaning to the letter, so too, the Spirit gives meaning to the humanity of Christ. For Francis, the letter and the spirit are inseparable. Once the letter is rooted it gives rise to the spirit of life. The so-called literalism of Francis, therefore, is not directly associated with a literal and historical interpretation of Scripture. Rather, it is an attitude of faith, a profound respect for all the words of Scripture because they are the words of the Spirit. The words of Scripture which impart the spirit of life, therefore, hold the same significance as the humanity of Christ:

> And if the most holy body of the Lord is very poorly reserved in any place, it should be placed in a precious location. . . . In a similar way the written words of the Lord, whenever they are found in an improper place, should be gathered together and kept in a becoming place.[48]

In his *Regula Non Bullata* Francis indicates that the presence of God's words express the presence of God, whereas the absence of God's words express the presence of Satan. For Francis, Christ dwells in his disciples until the end of the world through his holy words, which are spirit and life. As he writes in his *Rule*: "My words remain in you; I am with you until the end of the world. My words are spirit and life; I am. . . the life."[49] To keep the word of Christ means to abide in Him. The reception of the Word of God creates a bond of love between the faithful and the Trinity. Francis establishes a link between reception of the "fragrant words of the Lord" and the coming of the Holy Spirit who is the principle of union between the faithful and the Trinity.

While Francis encounters Christ in the Scriptures, it is in the Eucharist that the humanity of Christ is supremely evident because it is here that the presence of God can be seen. Francis speaks of God's presence in the Eucharist in seven out of ten letters that he composed.[50] The underlying theme in his letters is reverence for the body and blood of Christ; for only by partaking of the body of Christ can one enter the kingdom of God. It is significant that Francis never uses the word "Eucharist." Instead he uses the expression, "the body and blood of our Lord Jesus Christ." Van Khanh suggests that these words evoke in a special way the human nature of Christ, identifying the Eucharistic body with that of the humanity of Jesus Christ.[51] In the humanity of Christ, the body and blood sacrificed on the altar, the "all-powerful" comes upon the earth. In his *Letter to the Order*, Francis indicates that in the humanity of Christ the humble God is revealed: "That the Lord of the universe, God and Son of God, so humbles himself that for our salvation he hides himself under the little form of bread. Look, brothers, at the humility of God."[52] The revelation of God in Christ, signified in the Eucharist, means that the only way to be united to God, to glorify the Father and to do the will of the Father is to be conformed to Christ *in his humanity.*

Francis brings this idea to light in his *Admonition One* which is entitled "On the Body of Christ." Here, he indicates that conformation to Christ is entirely the work of the Spirit. In this *Admonition* he speaks of the body and blood of Christ, the humanity of Christ, by opening with the passage from John's Gospel in which Jesus tells his disciples that he is the way to the Father:

> The Lord Jesus says to his disciples: *I am the way, the truth and the life; no one comes to the Father except through me. If you had known me, you would also have known my Father; and from now on you will know him and have seen him. Philip says to him: Lord, show us the Father and it is enough for us. Jesus says to him: Have I been with you for so long a time and you have not known me? Philip, whoever, sees me, sees also my Father* (Jn 14:6-9).[53]

Francis presents here his trinitarian understanding of God and the revelation of the Trinity in Christ. Jesus is the Way to the Father who lives in "inaccessible light" (1 Tim 6:16). However, since "God is spirit" (Jn 4:24) and "no one has ever seen God" (Jn 1:18), it is only in the Spirit that one can come to the Father through the Son. Thus, while it is by means of the humanity of Christ that the Father is made known to us, it is only by way of the Spirit that we can see the Father in Christ and thus know the true presence of God hidden in Christ. This underscores the significance of the Spirit of the Lord which Francis exhorts in his *Rule*. He explains this significance in *Admonition One* when he states:

> He cannot be *seen* except in the Spirit since it is the Spirit that gives life, the flesh does not offer anything (Jn 6:64). But neither, inasmuch as he is equal to the Father, is the Son *seen* by anyone other than the Father or other than the Holy Spirit. Therefore all those who *saw* the Lord Jesus according to his humanity and did not *see* and believe according to the Spirit and the Godhead that he is the true Son of God were condemned. . . . Therefore it is the Spirit of the Lord, who lives in his faithful, who receives the most holy body and blood of the Lord. All others who do not share in this same Spirit and who presume to receive him eat and drink judgment to themselves (cf. 1 Cor 11:29).[54]

Norbert Van Khanh points out that in verses 6 to 14 of this *Admonition* the word "spirit" occurs nine times and the word "see" six times. Similarly, the second section is constructed around the phrase: "Philip, whoever *sees* me *sees* my Father as well. The key words from the Johannine passages that Francis quotes in this admonition are: way-truth-life; see, come, know, show, spirit. Among these, the most important are "spirit" and "see". The latter is situated within the group: see, believe, contemplate, appear, manifest, eyes, insight.[55] The intimate link between vision and spirit indicates that, in the Spirit, one can see the true divinity hidden in the humanity of Christ. For Francis, this is the meaning of "spiritual vision," to behold the divine presence.

Although the Son brings us to the discovery of the Father, the Son cannot be known in his deepest being except by the Spirit who enables one to "see" the Father in the Son. It is the Spirit, Francis says, that unites us to Christ by making us a spouse of Christ: "We are spouses when the faithful soul is joined to our Lord Jesus Christ by the Holy Spirit . . ."[56] Union with Christ in the Spirit leads us to the Father: "Thus . . . inflamed by the fire of the Holy Spirit, may we be able to follow in the footprints of Your beloved Son, our Lord Jesus Christ and, by Your grace alone, may we make our way to You, Most High."[57] This Johannine understanding of Christ as intimately united to the Trinity suggests why Francis does not focus on the detailed circumstances of the earthly life of the Incarnate Word. Christ is the manifestation of God revealed only to those who see with spiritual eyes. The desire "to see" expressed in *Admonition One* underscores the importance of spiritual vision, the vision of God present in the Incarnate Word. God enters into the concrete reality of our world through the Word made flesh and Francis exhorts us to see the wonder of God made manifest. It is always the person of Christ who stands at the center of Francis' thought. That the Word of the Father is sent from on high means that the humanity of Christ is always in union with the divinity.

Francis' understanding of God is relational: the Father is made known by the Son, the Son is made known by the Holy Spirit. Since God is spirit (Jn 4:24), he cannot be seen except in the Spirit since "it is the Spirit that gives life" (Jn 6:64). Therefore, it is important to *see* the Eucharist with the eyes of the spirit and to recognize there the presence of the Son of God. In *Admonition One*, it is the Spirit who gives divine life, the life of the Father in the Son. Francis concludes that all those who see the Lord Jesus only as human and do not also see and believe in him as God are lost.[58] It is interesting to note that Francis uses the word "contemplate" in this admonition alone and in no other writings. He states: "As they saw only his flesh by means of their bodily sight, yet believed Him to be God as they contemplated Him with their eyes of faith, so, as we see bread and wine with our bodily eyes, we too are to see and firmly believe them to be his most holy Body and Blood living and true."[59] We see here what contemplation means for Francis: to see God in Christ with the eyes of the spirit. Perhaps that is why he frequently refers to the presence of God rather than of Christ in others (for example *Adm.* 8, 3). For Francis, it is precisely the *humanity of Christ* that enables one to see God with the "eyes of the spirit." Physical sight is integrated with spiritual sight. It is not a stimulus to look beyond this world (i.e., transcend it) to seek truths but rather to open up to the truth of this world which is permeated with the divine presence.

The Good Shepherd

If the humanity of Christ is significant for Francis, he indicates in several places that it is the Crucified who is preeminent. The Crucified is the glory of the Father and the love of the Father expressed in the Son. To love the Father completely is to become like the Son, crucified in love. Francis indicates this in his image of the good shepherd, the one who laid down his life for his sheep. In *Admonition Six*, he discusses the imitation of the Lord as the following of the good shepherd; those who wish to glorify God must be willing to follow the good shepherd who laid down his life for his sheep:

> Let all of us, brothers, look to the good shepherd who suf-
> fered the passion of the cross to save his sheep. The sheep of
> the Lord followed him in tribulation and persecution, in insult
> and hunger, in infirmity and temptation, and in everything else,
> and they have received everlasting life from the Lord because
> of these things. Therefore, it is a great shame for us, servants of
> God, that while the saints actually did such things, we wish to
> receive glory and honor by merely recounting their deeds.[60]

The image of the good shepherd is significant for Francis because it shows the great love of God for us in Jesus Christ; through the sacrifice of the shepherd we are brought into union with the Father. It is an image of contemplation for Francis because it represents the union of the Son with the Father and submission to the will of the Father out of love and obedience. Christ's love impelled him to voluntarily choose death by submitting to the will of the Father; in doing so, he glorified the Father. The good shepherd, therefore, is one who is in union with the Father in all things and this union leads him to the cross. To be in union with the Father, therefore, means to follow the way of the cross. These are the "footprints we must follow" Francis states. We must love to the point of martyrdom and death if we wish to attain eternal life. The desire to be united to the Father and to glorify the Father is also the desire for martyrdom, a desire fulfilled in union with Christ in the Spirit.

In his first and second *Letter to the Faithful*, Francis associates the image of the good shepherd with Jesus Christ as spouse, brother and mother. To be a spouse is to be joined to Christ in such an intimate way (*coniungitur*) that one's whole life becomes an imitation of Christ insofar as one has the spirit of Christ; this is the fruit of prayer. One who desires union with God, and who is conformed to Christ in the Spirit, will be led to the cross; contemplative union is also the expression of the desire for martyrdom. In chapter 22 of the earlier *Rule*, Francis summarizes his thoughts on following the good shepherd, underscoring union with Christ. This particular chapter, according to David Flood, was his last will and testament prior to his sojourn among the Saracens where Francis hoped to obtain the reward of martyrdom:

> And let us have recourse to him as *to the shepherd and guardian of our souls,* who says: "I am the good shepherd who feeds my sheep and I lay down my life for my sheep." *All of you are brothers. And do not call anyone on earth your father, for one is Your Father, the One in heaven. And do not let yourselves be called teachers for your teacher is the One Who is in heaven . . . .* Let us, hold onto the words, the life, and the teaching and the Holy Gospel of him who humbled himself to ask his Father for us and to make his name known to us, saying: *Father, glorify Your name and glorify Your Son so that Your Son may glorify You.. . . I am not asking that You remove them from the world, but that You protect them from the evil one. . . . I pray not only for these, but also for those who because of their words will believe in me, so that they may be completely one, and the world may know that You have sent Me and that You have loved them as You have loved Me* (Jn 17:17-23).[61]

Francis unites the imitation of the good shepherd with the priestly prayer from John's Gospel to indicate to the friars that the essence of their life is to be conformity to the Crucified, their spouse and brother, to the glory of the Father. Here we see the significance of the passion in Francis' spiritual vision. To mount the summit of God's love is to follow the good shepherd, to lay down one's life as he did and thus to glorify the Father. He expresses the same thought in the *Letter to the Order*: "He has sent you into the entire world for this reason that in *word and deed you may give witness* to his voice and bring everyone to know that there is no one who is all-powerful except him."[62] The path of the good shepherd is the path of martyrdom and, yet, it is the same path to union with God. For to be conformed to Christ in the Spirit, and to love as he loved, brings one to the cross and to union with him in whom the Father is revealed. Francis indicates that preaching the Gospel is as much a part of contemplative union with God as a life of asceticism and imitating Christ: "I pray . . . for those who because of their words will believe in me" (Jn 17:20). Thus we see that his desire for martyrdom by preaching the Gospel among the Saracens and his union with Christ on the mountain of La Verna are part of the same contemplative movement. The contemplation of God in Christ leads one to union that is both mystical and active. To preach the Word one must have the Spirit of the Lord and it is the same Spirit that joins one to Christ; and to love Christ as Christ loved means to follow him to the cross. Thus, union with Christ and preaching the Word of God are two poles of the same contemplative movement.

La Verna: The Mystery of Union with Christ

Francis' desire for martyrdom in imitation of the good shepherd, his following of the humble and poor Christ, and his desire to glorify the Father leads him to union with Christ. On the mountain of La Verna (1224), while praying, he encounters a six-winged Seraph in the form a man crucified, his hands and feet extended in the form of a cross and fastened to a cross. The La Verna event is not described by Francis but is recounted in the biographies. Because it is part of the hagiographical tradition, it has been the subject of detailed historical critical analysis, particularly by Octavian Schmucki.[63] However, historical criticism should not deter one from examining the deeper spiritual significance of this event in light of Francis' own writings.

Francis' encounter with the Crucified is told by both Celano and Bonaventure. The account by Bonaventure is as follows:

> On a certain morning about the feast of the Exultation of the Cross, while Francis was praying on the mountainside, he saw a Seraph with six fiery and shining wings descend from the height of heaven. And when in swift flight the Seraph had reached a spot in the air near the man of God, there appeared between the wings the figure of a man crucified, with his

hands and feet extended in the form of a cross and fastened to a cross. Two of the wings were lifted above his head, two were extended for flight and two covered his whole body. When Francis saw this, he was overwhelmed and his heart was flooded with a mixture of joy and sorrow. He rejoiced because of the gracious way Christ looked upon him under the appearance of the Seraph, but the fact that he was fastened to a cross pierced his soul with a sword of compassionate sorrow. . . . As the vision disappeared, it left in his heart a marvelous ardor and imprinted on his body markings that were no less marvelous. Immediately the marks of nails began to appear in his hands and feet just as he had seen a little before in the figure of the man crucified.[64]

Bonaventure shows that he is familiar with Francis' thought by making ample use of the noun "vision" and the verbs "appeared" and gazed" underscoring the notion that spiritual vision is to behold the true presence of God in Christ. While Francis is praying on the mountainside, he *sees* the Seraph approaching. When it comes closer to him, the Seraph *appears* to be a crucified man. Bonaventure uses these categories of sight, one active, the other passively received, in relation to the divine and human dimensions of the crucified Seraph.[65] By repeating the use of the sense of vision in this event, Bonaventure indicates that Francis is actively engaged in the event both physically and spiritually. Upon receiving the vision, Francis is filled with a *marvelous ardor* (*LM* 13, 3) indicating that love is the consummation of contemplative prayer. Through the fire of love Francis is transformed into the image of Christ. In the *Itinerarium* Bonaventure states:

> On the height of the mountain . . . he passed over into God in ecstatic contemplation . . . this, however, is mystical and most secret . . . no one receives except him who desires it and no one desires except him who is *inflamed* in his marrow by the fire of the Holy Spirit whom Christ sent into the world . . . this *fire* is God and his furnace is in Jerusalem; and Christ enkindles it in the heat of his burning passion.[66]

To be "inflamed by the Holy Spirit" is the same expression Francis uses to describe union with Christ: "And *inflamed* by the *fire* of the Holy Spirit may we be able to follow in the footprints of Your beloved Son, our Lord Jesus Christ." Bonaventure describes Francis' union with Christ as an ecstatic union enkindled by the love of the Holy Spirit. To be inflamed with the Holy Spirit means to be conformed to the crucified humanity of Christ. Here we see Francis' understanding of the triune God come to fruition. To see Christ is to see the Father (Jn 14:9) and "to see" for Francis is to behold with the eyes of the spirit; it is to participate in the life of Christ in union with the Spirit. In this way, one beholds the true divinity in Christ by seeing that he is truly God and Son of God, the way to the Father and the glory of the Father. Thus, Bonaventure describes Francis' contemplative experience of God as a mysticism of the historical event, a participation in the passion of Christ, leading to union with God.

According to Bonaventure, the union between Francis and the crucified Word is like the indelible impression of a seal. Through the fire of love Francis is forged into the likeness of Christ and the wounds of the Stigmata are the marks of the seal.[67] He presents the episode of the stigmatization as a sacramental celebration. The result is that Francis is transformed into a living likeness of Christ crucified. Bonaventure refers to the Stigmata as the *Sacramentum Domini* (*LM* 13,4), using the word *sacramentum* in the same sense as *mysterium*. Francis becomes the sacramental presence of Christ in his suffering and glorification.[68] The mysticism of the historical event on La Verna, the contemplation of God in Christ, fulfills Francis' desire for martyrdom. Bonaventure writes: "He was to be totally transformed into the likeness of Christ crucified, not by the martyrdom of his flesh, but by the fire of his love consumming his soul."[69] In his own humanity, Francis becomes a living witness of the Gospel message; conformed to Christ in body and spirit, he becomes the true image and likeness of God (*Adm.* 5).

For Francis, to be in union with Christ means to be inflamed with the Spirit of the Lord. Since the highest love of God is manifested in the cross, union with God means to be united to the Crucified in the Spirit, to follow the good shepherd, and thus to be in union with the Father. The desire to see the Father and be united with him is at the same time the desire for martyrdom. It is not without significance that, in the later *Rule*, Francis included a chapter on going among the Saracens (*RegB* 12). For the spiritual state formed by prayer and contemplation looks to union with Christ through the cross but also outside itself to the neighbor who does not yet love God or share in the faith. Thus, union with God through the crucified Christ is both interior and exterior, mystical and active. It demands the growth of a love that directs one at once toward God and one's neighbor. One must long to die for the sake of Christ and those whom Christ suffered to redeem.[70] The desire for martyrdom corresponds to the fact that one who is filled with the Spirit of the Lord will attain union with God through the cross. The height of union is the willingness to offer one's life for the sake of Christ crucified as he himself offered it for the world. Bonaventure views Francis' union with the Crucified as the passover into peace which means to be in union with the Father. Peace is to mark the final age in this world.

Bonaventure:
Theologian and Mystic

The spirituality of Francis, centered on Christ and the Trinity, provides a basis for exploring Bonaventure's doctrine. As we have seen, Francis urges his brothers and sisters to follow in the footprints of the Crucified Christ as the most perfect means of attaining union with the Father. This idea, in essence, is the foundation of Bonaventure's mysticism of the Crucified Christ, although he develops it theologically by probing the mystery of Christ as the Word of God. In doing so, Bonaventure shifts the focus from the Father, which predominates in Francis' spirituality, to Christ, and elucidates a thoroughly Christocentric mystical doctrine. The task from here on in is to explore this doctrine in its multiple dimensions. This chapter will examine Bonaventure's understanding of God as Trinity and the fundamental relationship of Jesus Christ to the Trinity.

Born in 1217 in Bagnoregio, a small town near Orvieto, Bonaventure, son of the physician, John Di Fidanza, seemed predestined to follow the Poverello of Assisi.[1] As a child he contracted a serious illness and was cured through the intercession of Saint Francis, a factor, he writes, which enabled him to experience the power of Francis in himself.[2] It is because of this cure that he accepted the request at the Chapter of Narbonne to write a new life of Francis.

Bonaventure entered the University of Paris in 1236 and studied under Alexander of Hales, a renowned theologian who had moved his chair to the Franciscans when he entered the Order in 1231. Bonaventure himself entered the Franciscan Order in 1243, and it is quite possible that his entrance was inspired by the example of his mentor. He progressed through the various levels of study, ultimately becoming a Master of Sentences in 1253 and recognized by the Chancellor of the University as a Doctor and Master of Theology. From 1253 to 1254 he taught as a Master at the Franciscan School at the University of Paris.

As an academician, it is unlikely that Bonaventure ever planned to be an administrator; however, trouble in the Franciscan Order led to his appointment as Minister General of a rapidly expanding Franciscan Order in 1257, at the age of forty years old. His appointment was made under difficult circumstances since the incumbent Minister General, John of Parma, was forced to resign because of his affiliation with radical Joachites.[3] The rise of Bonaventure to Minister General opened up a new horizon of theology, perhaps inspired by the conflicts of human affairs, a factor not always considered within the confines of the university. His training as a theologian, however, is evident, throughout his writings. Ewert Cousins describes three major genres of Bonventure's works: 1) scholastic writings, including his Commentary on the *Sentences* and Gospel commentaries; 2) spiritual writings; and 3) lectures or *collationes*.[4] The scholastic works were composed between 1243 and 1257, and the spiritual writings and lectures comprise the period 1257 to 1274. These latter works are distinguished by their personal nature and their almost exclusive focus on the suffering humanity of Christ.

Much of Bonaventure's mystical theology is traditional, influenced especially by Augustine, Dionysius, Gregory the Great, the Cistercians, and the Victorines. Bonaventure's most important influence, however, is that of Francis, particularly the stigmatized Francis, and it is this influence that rescues him from being a prosaic interpreter of the tradition. In his insightful study on Bonaventure, Hans Urs von Balthasar writes:

> The Stigmata are the living, organizing center of Bonaventure's intellectual world, the thing that lifts it above the level of a mere interweaving of the threads of tradition. His world is Franciscan, and so is his theology, however many stones he may use to erect his spiritual cathedral over the mystery of humility and poverty. . . . And yet, when we have established

that the Franciscan mystery is the center that crystallizes all, we have not yet uncovered the ethos that is peculiar to Bonaventure. For Bonaventure does not only take Francis as his center: he is his own sun and mission.[5]

Balthasar captures the essence of Bonaventure's thought as that which is creatively shaped by the life of Francis. Doyle, too, has stated that Bonaventure saw realized in Francis everything he was striving for: gospel perfection and contemplative peace.[6] He approached St. Francis as a theologian and, for that matter, as a mystic himself.

The influence of Francis on Bonaventure's thought is suggested by Bonaventure himself where, in the prologue of the *Itinerarium Mentis in Deum*, he describes his insight to the meaning of the Stigmata. In 1259, two years after his appointment as Minister General, Bonaventure went up to La Verna to seek peace. While there meditating on the Stigmata of Francis he discovered, in a "flash of insight," (*statim visum*) the meaning of Francis' vision of the fiery Seraph in the form of the Crucified. He writes:

> I withdrew to Mount La Verna seeking a place of quiet and desiring to find there peace of spirit. While I was there reflecting on various ways by which the soul ascends to God, there came to mind, among other things, the miracle which had occurred to blessed Francis in this very place: the vision of a winged Seraph in the form of the Crucified. While reflecting on this, *I saw at once* that this vision represented our father's rapture in contemplation and the road by which this rapture is reached.[7]

Bonaventure understood, in a sudden moment, the significance of the Crucified Christ. He encapsulates his thought by saying: "There is no other path than through the burning love of the Crucified."[8] The path to ecstatic wisdom and peace, that path which Francis marked out through his conformity to Christ Crucified, underscores the structure of the *Itinerarium*. Based on the Stigmata of Francis and his vision of the fiery Seraph, Bonaventure composed the *Itinerarium*. Francis is the inspiration for this profound mystical work, but Bonaventure is the author. Since there is no historical account of Bonaventure's experience on La Verna, it is difficult to say whether or not he himself mystically encountered the Crucified, but from this time on, his writings are firmly oriented to union with the Crucified Christ. The number of scholars who have identified this "shift" is not surprising. Eric Doyle has stated that Bonaventure came down from the mountain of La Verna signed interiorly with the marks of the Crucified, that is, "spiritually stigmatized."[9] Similarly, Joseph Ratzinger claims that the *Itinerarium* is "a first sign of a new intellectual direction. From this book onward, the figure of Saint Francis enters ever more into the center of his thought."[10] Noel Muscat, in his dissertation on the *Verbum Crucifixum*, states, "It is a concrete and specific image of Francis that dominates Bonaventure's writings in the period of 1257 to 1274, namely that of a Francis who is a living icon of Christ Crucified."[11] And Marigwen Schumacher states, "I, personally, am certain that the experience—vision—'happening' on Mt. Alverno in October of 1259 was deeply significant. . . It is in this light of revelation-realization that the incredible number of mystical opuscula which Bonaventure writes in the year immediately after 'Alverno' should be read."[12] The Stigmata enable Bonaventure to discover the key to contemplation, to wisdom and peace. The burning love that transforms Francis into the perfect image and lover of Christ, transforms him not only spiritually but corporeally. This is the key to Franciscan contemplation as it unfolds in Bonaventure's mysticism of the Crucified Christ.

It is striking that the Stigmata form the basis of Bonaventure's sermons on Francis and is discussed by Bonaventure in all five sermons on Francis. Zachary Hayes identifies the significance of the Stigmata as: 1) the supreme experience of Francis, 2) a pre-eminently ecstatic, contemplative experience; 3) eschatologically significant and 4) a validation of Francis' way of life.[13] As the supreme experience of Francis, the Stigmata represent the spiritual martyrdom of Francis whereby he becomes the perfect example of contemplation and the example of the Seraphic Order. As an ecstatic-contemplatve experience, the Stigmata represent the power of burning love. According to Hugh of St. Victor, the power of love is a communion that transforms the lover into the likeness of the beloved.[14] The Stigmata symbolize the love mysticism of Francis. The transforming power of love is symbolized by the heat of fire. The way to Christ, therefore, is only through the most burning love. This interior fire of love is expressed outwardly in the flesh. Francis is the exemplar that integrates nature and grace, body and soul, action and contemplation. As the vindication of his way of life, Bonaventure states that God imprinted the Stigmata at the time when Francis sought approval for Rule.[15] The eschatological significance of the Stigmata is given in the interpretation of Francis as the angel of the sixth seal, the new Elijah, the one who ushers in the final age. The Stigmata establish Francis as a potent apocalyptic figure who seals God's chosen ones with the tau mark of crucifixion. Francis has attained the final age of peace. Those who desire to reach this age must, like Francis, be impressed and expressed with the mystical wounds of Christ. E. Randolph Daniel states that Francis is the exemplar of those who desire to restore evangelical perfection in this last age before the end of history.[16] Similarly, Zachary Hayes states that Francis is the head of a new exodus. He is the model of the spiritual journey for all Christians: friars and laity.[17]

Francis' spiritual journey is oriented toward a profound, grace-filled contemplative experience in history and the anticipation of an eschatological consummation of eternity. As model of the spiritual life, Francis shows us that the ultimate goal of the spiritual journey is a final, loving union between God and creation in which creatures will find their ultimate fulfillment. Yet, despite the fact that Francis forms such a significant part of Bonaventure's thought, the spirituality of the two saints is not entirely the same. Francis is more transcendent and trinitarian in his approach to God whereas Bonaventure places a firm emphasis on the Incarnate Word as center. Not only his spirituality but his entire thought is centered on Christ. Christ is the center of everything: the middle one of the divine persons, the exemplary cause of the whole creation, the mediator of salvation and life, the light who brings understanding and truth. He is the goal toward whom all efforts of ascesis tend and the desire of the soul in its quest for God through contemplation. Through a continued deepening of his understanding of the Crucified in light of the stigmatized Francis, Bonaventure ultimately develops a world view that is decisively Christocentric. It is a world view that is distinctly Franciscan and, at the same time, distinctly Bonaventurian. Francis provides the foundation but Bonaventure contructs the vision, and it is one that is uniquely his own. Let us turn now to see this vision.

Bonaventure's God

Bonaventure's theology, as Etienne Gilson once observed, is marked by unity and harmony. The late, great medievalist stated that, "Bonaventure's theology is so comprehensive that the totality of the system is so much that the mere notion of fragments has no meaning at all. You can either see the general economy of his doctrine in its totality or see none of it."[18] The various parts are not only integrally connected with one another but form together such a unity and totality that they cannot be understood in their real meaning when considered separately. Ewert Cousins has described his theology as a Gothic cathedral with the two great spires of Trinity and Christology forming the frame of the structure. Bonaventure's doctrine of Trinity contains a strong Christocentric or Logos-centered dimension whereby the Son is center of the Trinity.[19] To understand Bonaventure's mysticism of the Crucified Christ and the centrality of this mystery, it is first necessary to understand who God is for Bonaventure and this means to understand the Trinity.

God as Father

The Seraphic Doctor, in his *De Mysterio Trinitatis*, maintains that God is a primary mystery of loving, self-communicative goodness, a mystery of eternal productivity from all eternity. This idea follows the Greek model of the Trinity as a self-diffusive fountain of goodness (*pēge*) whereby the distinction of persons in the Trinity is based on origin and primacy. Bonaventure describes the Father or first person of the Trinity as first or primal since the Father is without origin (*innascibilis*) compared to the Son and Spirit.[20] Bonaventure employs the Neoplatonist maxim: "The more a being is prior, the more it is the fontal cause of production."[21] The Father is the fountain fullness (*fontalis plenitudo*) because he is *innascibilis* (unbegotten). As *innascibilis*, the Father is unborn, unbegotten; he has no origin or source. However, it is precisely because of this that the Father is the cause of the other two divine persons.[22] He is the source of all production, first of the Word and Spirit, then of creation. Because primacy begins with the Father, it is in the first person of the Trinity that one finds the ultimate basis of Bonaventure's metaphysical system, the notion of *egressus* and *regressus*, whereby all comes forth from the Father and returns to the Father.

Bonaventure follows the Dionysian concept of the self-diffusive good (*bonum est diffusivum sui*). Good is the name of God given to us in the New Testament (see *Itin.* 5, 2). As primal and *innascibilis*, the Father is the fecund primordiality of goodness, overflowing by his very nature to the Son and Spirit. The divine fecundity and self-diffusive good that characterize the Father unite as opposites two personal properties of the Father: innascibility and paternity.[23] As the source of absolute fecundity, the Father is fountain fullness from which flows the self-diffusive good. Since innascibility and fecundity are mutually complementary opposites which cannot be formally reduced to one or the other, there is an irreducible dialectical structure of opposites grounded in the mystery of the Father.

As the fountain fullness of the self-diffusive good, the Father is personal, self-communicative and thus relational. By his very nature the Father gives everything he has and everything he is to the Son and Spirit. It is in the very "self-giving" of divine goodness that the Father finds the fullness of his personal reality. The Father is Father in the fullest sense in the act of generation. Because the Father is *innascibilis*, he is absolutely first, and because he is absolutely first, is the fecund source of others. The Father, therefore, is a dynamic source whose fecundity finds its expression in the two inner-divine emanations.

God as Son

The center of Bonaventure's thought is the Son or Word of the Father. The Son is the total and complete expression of the Father. He is the *persona media* in the very inner life of God and his personal mystery is situated at the very center of the Trinitarian dynamic. Just as there are three modes of love within the Trinity; one that is totally free (the Father), another that is totally due (the Spirit), and one that is a "mixture of both," (the Son), so there follows the same type of structure in the mystery of origin.[24] There is one who is origin alone (the Father), there is one who comes forth but is in no way origin of another (the Spirit), and there is one who comes from another and is principle of another (the Son). The uniqueness of the second person as that person who is *medium* or center is explained by Bonaventure: "This, by necessity, must be the central one of persons: for if there is one who produces and is not produced and another who is produced and does not produce, there must necessarily be a central one who is produced and produces."[25]

The eternal generation of the Son is ultimately rooted in the Dionysian metaphysics of the good. This implies a certain type of necessity expressed by the term—emanation *per modum naturae*—since God is conceived in terms of a necessary self-communication which arises by reason of his very nature as the good.[26] The primal self-diffusion of the Father consists of his self-knowledge, a knowledge which *is* the Son. The Son is the total and complete expression of the Father because the Son is everything the Father is in one other than the Father. In the Son the Father expresses the totality of his being and the totality of what he can produce. In the *Hexaëmeron* (1, 13) Bonaventure states: "From all eternity the Father begets a Son similar to himself and expresses himself and a likeness similar to himself, and in so doing he expresses the sum total of his potency."[27] As the full and total expression of God's primal fullness, the Son is simultaneously the expression of all that God can be in relation to the finite. Everything other than the Father is grounded in the Son so that the relationship between Son and Father is the ontological basis of all other relationships.[28]

The title "image" designates the Son as the perfect likeness of the Father. While the term Son (*filius*) refers to the hypostatic equality of the second person with the Father in full possession of divinity, the term Image (*imago*) points to how he reveals the Father's hidden reality as the one unique and absolutely pure expression of the person of the Father. The term Image is applied to the Son alone and means the total expressive likeness to the Father.[29]

While all three titles—Son, Image, and Word—apply to the second person of the Trinity, the pre-eminent title is that of Word. The Word is the *ars patris*, the divine exemplar, the cause of all expression and manifestation of the Father.[30] Here the second person is related not only to the Father but to the entire mystery of creation, revelation and incarnation. He is the one through whom the Father's self-communications take place. The title Word presupposes knowledge and gives expression to God's self-knowledge as loving source of all. As the *similitudo expressiva* of the Father, the Word encompasses four types of relationships: 1) relationship to the Father as speaker; 2) relationship to the world understood as what the Word forms in his role as exemplary cause; 3) relationship to human nature which is put on in the incarnation; 4) relationship to the teaching enshrined in the words of Scripture. In his *Commentary on John*, Bonaventure describes the various relations of the Word:

> . . . the term "Word" expresses not only a relation to the one speaking, but to that which is expressed through the Word, to the sound with which it clothes itself, and to the knowledge effected in others through the mediation of the Word. And since here the Son of God is to be described not only in terms of his relation to the Father from whom he proceeds, but also in terms of his relation to the creatures which he has made, as well as to the flesh with which he was clothed and to the truth which he has given us, he is most nobly and fittingly described as the Word; for that name includes all these relations, and a more fitting name could not be found anywhere in the world.[31]

The significance of the Word is its capacity to express. Because only one substance can exist in God, the image which expresses him must be the highest expression, that is, a unique expression. The Son, as the pure imitation and likeness of the Father, is the unique expression of God. The Son transmits the image as copy and archetype laying the foundation for every creaturely attitude before God. The Son is not only the archetype of which images are made in the world, but he is God as expression, that is, as truth, and therefore is the principle of all expressed things in creation. The generation of the Son means that the Father expresses himself uniquely and definitely and in expressing himself, he expresses his whole power and his whole capacity. If the Father has really given expression in the Son to his whole being and capacity, then in the Son everything that is possible through God takes on reality.[32]

God as Holy Spirit

The Spirit is the third divine person arising from the Father and the Son. The Son as center of Trinity means that he is both receptive and communicative, mediating between the Father and the Spirit. The Son with the Father spirates the Spirit. Just as emanation of the Son proceeds from the inner divine fecundity of the Father, so too, the full perfection of God requires that there also be a voluntary emanation proceeding from pure liberality since God is not an impersonal God but one who is the supreme personal good. The perfect actuality of being is to exist as love, and love is an act of the will from which flows all liberality. The procession of the Spirit, therefore, proceeds *per modum voluntatis*.[33] The Spirit is personal love that proceeds from the intimate mutual love between the Father and Son who, as one principle, breathe forth the Spirit. The Spirit is referred to as the *nexus* or bond between Father and Son represented by the circumference or intelligibility of the sphere, intelligibility being the basis of order.

While the emanation of the Spirit is from the most perfect act of will, the liberality from which the Spirit proceeds is distinguished from the freedom by which God creates the world. The liberality by which the Spirit emanates is a necessary quality of the mystery of divine love while the freedom by which God creates is an emanation that is a completely free act. Bonaventure elucidates this concept by distinguishing the emanations of the Son and Spirit from the created order. The Son proceeds from God as the exemplar of all reality and is therefore the *ratio exemplandi*. Similarly, the Spirit proceeds as the *ratio volendi* which differs from created reality as an actual object of the divine will.[34] By considering the two emanations together, Bonaventure concludes that the created world is known by God in the knowledge whereby he generates the Son and is loved by him in that love by which the Spirit flows. While the inner emanations of the Son and Spirit are intrinsic to God's nature as supreme goodness and love, the creation of the world, as a free act expressing God's knowledge and love, is radically contingent on the divine order.

Creation

As the Word is the self-expression of the Father within the Godhead, the world is the external objectification of that self-utterance in that which is not God. It is the Son who is the medium between the Father and the world through whom the Father himself is operative. As the incarnate Word, the Son mediates between the Trinity and creation and is the center of creation. The Son, therefore, is the metaphysical center between God and creation. Bonaventure sees creation of the world united to the generation of the Son from Father. Just as the Word is the inner expression of God, the created order is the external expression of inner Word. The act of creation *ad extra* arises from the eternal fecundity of the Father and is an overflow of that fecundity.[35] The fountain fullness of the Father is recapitulated in creation. One might say that the cosmic order is a vast symbol in which God speaks his own mystery into that which is not himself. The creative Trinity not only provides a basis for creation but imparts its dynamism to creation. Because the universe shares in the mystery of the Trinity, it is caught up in this dynamic process of self-transcendence and self-communication of interpenetrating relationships and creative love. Creation, therefore, possesses in its inner constitution a congruous relation to the uncreated Word—the *ars patris*. This means that it is directed in its inner core to a fulfillment and completion in God.

As the expression of all divine ideas, the Word is the ground of exemplarity. Exemplarity is defined as the doctrine of relations of expression between God and creatures.[36] As we have already stated, God is dynamic and expressive—the Father expresses himself in generating his Son who is the perfect Image and Word. In generating the Son, the Father produces in the Son the divine ideas or *rationes aeternae* of all that he can create. These *rationes aeternae* within the Son are the ontological foundation of creation *ad extra* and of exemplarism.[37] The *rationes aeternae* are expressive and give rise to the created world. Since the uncreated Word is the expression of the inner Trinitarian structure of God, the Word also expresses and represents the ideas of all created things; ideas which act as exemplary causes of these things. Things are fully and ultimately known when known in relation to the Word, the eternal exemplar.

Bonaventure sees the universal structure of created reality root-ed in Trinitarian exemplarism. In the *Breviloquium* he indicates that all creatures have their origin in God from whom they proceed; hav-ing been created they reflect God, their divine model or exemplar, according to which they were made; they finally return to God from whom they were created and who is their end.[38] God has made the visible world in order to express and manifest himself. Following the symbolic theology of the Victorines, he describes the world as a book which reflects its trinitarian author at three levels: vestige, image, similitude. The vestige bears a distant resemblance to the Creator; the image a closer resemblance; and the similitude means being conformed to God through grace. The purpose of the sensible world is to serve as a mirror through which the human person is led back to loving God and praising him. It is interesting that Bonaventure does not advocate a *fuga mundi* as if the world imposed an obstacle to seeking God. Conversely, the world is a mirror just as the human soul is a mirror, although both mirrors are clouded by sin. Originally we were meant to be able to read the book of nature to know God (experientially), but this ability was lost because of sin. Revelation is to enable humanity to read the book. We recover this ability to "ready properly" through Christ, the Word uncreated and incarnate. Christ is the book written within and without, wisdom and its works.[39] He is the divine and temporal exemplar. As image and exemplar, Christ sums up in himself the world as a sign of God and reveals in himself the Trinity to the world. Because Christ embodies the mystery of God and the world, it is precisely in and through the Word that God is in the world and the world is in God. Contemplation of the world, therefore, should lead us back to the exemplar of all things—the Word. This is the reason why Francis, in becoming more like Christ, could perceive the presence of God in creation. Union with Christ enabled him to open his eyes to the truth of created reality because Christ is the center of all reality.

The Incarnate Word

Bonaventure's Christ mysticism is essentially a mystical theology of the Word—the Word who is the complete and absolute expression of the Father, eternally loving the Father in the Spirit. He elucidates the mystery of the Word in his *Reductione artium ad theologiam*:

> Likewise, we see the eternal Word, whom the Father him-
> self begets eternally by means of generation. . . . But in order to
> become perceptible to the human sense, he put on the form of
> flesh, *and the Word was made flesh, and dwelt among us,* and yet he
> remained in the *bosom of the Father.*[40]

Bonaventure elucidates the relationship between the eternal Word and the incarnate Word through the analogy of language whereby all speech signifies a mental concept (*mentis conceptum*). The inner concept is the word of the mind and the mind's offspring which is known to the person who conceives it. This mental word is then expression in sensible form, namely, a word which can be heard by a listener. The same type of expressiveness can be found in the eternal Word, who is conceived by the Father and who then takes on flesh to be known in sensible form. Commenting on the mystery of the Word in the incarnation, Zachary Hayes writes: "As the Word is the self-expression of the Father within the Godhead, the humanity of Jesus is the fullest objectification of the self-utterance within the created world."[41] The principal ideas, therefore, are that the Word is in ontological union with the Father and is the total expression of the Father, and the incarnate Word is the complete expression of the Father in the created world.

The divine nature of expression and love which mark the relationship of the divine persons are crucial for understanding Bonaventure's mysticism of the Crucified Christ. Expressiveness is found in the eternal Word who is conceived by the Father and who takes on flesh in the incarnation to be known in sensible form. Bonaventure marvels at the wonder of the mystery of the incarnation, that God who is Most High humbled himself and emptied himself to become intimately related to us by taking on our humanity. In one of his Christmas sermons he states: "See therefore, the Father loves the Son and has given all things into his hands keeping nothing to himself. When he gives us the Son he gives us all that he has to give in him and in this way he wonderfully enriches us."[42]

The significance of the Word for Bonaventure is its capacity to express. The Word is the Father's total and perfect self-expression, the "archetypal word" or divine exemplar—the one through whom the Father's self-communications take place. Because only one substance can exist in God, the image which expresses him must be of the highest expression, that is, total expression.[43] The generation of the Son *per modum naturae* means that the Father expresses himself uniquely and definitely and in expressing himself, expresses his whole power and his whole capacity. If the Father has really given expression in the Son to his whole being and capacity, then in the Son everything that is possible through God has taken on reality: "The divine truth expresses itself and everything else through the one unique highest expression."[44] According to von Balthasar, the Son is archetype because as Son he wishes to be nothing else than the image of the Father. He transmits this image, therefore, as copy and archetype, laying the foundation for every creaturely attitude before God.[45] The Son is not only the archetype of which images are made in the world, he is God as expression, that is, as truth, and therefore the principle of all expressed things in creation: "All things are true and are created to express themselves through the expression of that highest light."[46] Creatures are true when they find expression in the Son.

Bonaventure's theology of expression is made lucid by von Balthasar in his treatise on Bonaventure's theology. Balthasar draws upon the Seraphic Doctor among others to elucidate the meaning of image. In his *Theologik*, von Balthasar indicates that the etymology of the word "image" means a pressing outward of an inward content in all forms of "expression." Peter Casarella clarifies this idea when he states that the outward form is not a detached product or mere medium of the expression. Rather, form poured into appearances constitutes as well as conveys meaning. Form is the emergence of a concrete expression which co-determines the expressed content.[47] It has the same being and is grasped by the same act of knowing as its expression. As Casarella points out, to say that Jesus is the theophany of God means that in the invisible form of the revelation of Jesus Christ, God has been revealed as fully not-other. Christ, the complete and perfected human, constitutes the entirety of the experience of who God is.[48] Commenting on the theology of image and expression in the writings of von Balthasar, Casarella highlights the meaning of the expressed Word in a way that illuminates Bonaventure's theology of the Word. He writes:

> Christ is the self-interpretation or exegesis of the Father because he alone is the perfect image of the invisible God (Col 1:15) . . . the true logic of Christ's form is self-involving. . . . The expressed content of what is revealed in the Word is the Father's free decision to make himself visible to all. "No one knows the Son but the Father, and no one knows the Father but the Son— and anyone to whom the Son wishes to reveal him" (Matt 11:27). The form of this disclosure is the life and words of Jesus. In taking on human flesh, God's Word is expressed in human form. The mysterious truth revealed in the incarnate man Jesus Christ is not (pace Arius) a second god. Nor is it a Nestorian truth whereby the inner content does not enter into full union with the incarnate form of human expression. The Chalcedonian confession of faith gives us a language to express the dogmatic truth of the incarnate Word's unique mode of verbal presence.[49]

For Bonaventure, the humanity of Jesus is the fullest and most perfect external Word that gives expression to the inner eternal Word as its proper content. He describes the mystery of the Word uncreated and incarnate when he writes: "He who is the image of the invisible God . . . is united by the grace of union to an individual of rational nature . . . through this union he leads us back to the Father as to the fountain source and object."[50] The Word who is the image of the Father, the *ars patris* and divine exemplar, takes on our humanity expressing that divine image and, as exemplar, leads us back to the Father. In the *Itinerarium* he writes: "If an image is an expressed likeness, when our mind contemplates in Christ, the Son of God . . . our humanity reaches something perfect."[51] Since the Word, who is image, is an *expressed* likeness of God, when the Word becomes incarnate, God is expressed in both spirit and flesh.

The reason for the incarnation is not a simple one for the Seraphic Doctor. Rather, there are multiple reasons for the Word becoming flesh, the first of which is to manifest the power, wisdom, and goodness of God.[52] Redemption and completion of the world are also reasons for this event although they are not primary reasons. Bonaventure states that through the Word-made-flesh the true light and knowledge of God is revealed, and fallen humanity is restored to its true image in God. The prayerful desire to be united to Christ, Bonaventure states, is rooted in humanity's fallen nature.[53] Because of the fall humans lost the ability to contemplate God properly. Bent over and blinded by the decision to turn away from the divine light, humans lacked the gift of grace necessary for contemplation.[54] That grace was restored when the Word was made flesh. Because sin affected both body and spirit, the whole had to be assumed that the whole might be healed.[55] For the total restoration of body and soul to occur, Bonaventure states, God had to undergo a greater condescension and humiliation, not by "in-animation" but by "in-carnation."[56]

It was most fitting that the Word assume flesh, since the Word is the perfect image and splendor of the Father.[57] As the eternal art of the Father,[58] he is the perfect expression of all things. Being the eternal Word, he is coequal and consubstantial with the Father.[59] As the incarnate Word, he manifests the supreme power, wisdom and goodness of the Trinity because he is the work of the Trinity.[60] In discussing the incarnate Word in Bonaventure's theology Hayes writes:

> When theology says that Jesus is the Word incarnate, it is saying that the created humanity of Jesus of Nazareth exists in such an intimate relation with the divine Word that the subsistent act of divine self-awareness and all contained within it impinges in some mysterious way on the human soul of Jesus. This relation between the divine Word and human nature is described by theology as a "hypostatic union." The union is understood to be so intimate that there is, in fact, only one subject to whom are attributed both the human and the divine qualities and acts, when such predications are made in the concrete and not in the abstract. And the subject of all such predications is the eternal Word of God.[61]

The Word, Bonaventure states, became incarnate, offering himself to all, to reveal truth and to impart the grace of healing.[62] The disease is original sin which infects the mind through ignorance and the flesh through concupiscence.[63] Christ restores us by sustaining the penalty of sin and by infusing into us reforming grace which, because it links us with its source, makes us members of Christ and of the Trinity. Through the grace of the Holy Spirit, the soul is reformed in the likeness of the Trinity and Christ.[64] Bonaventure is not indicating that humans are formed to two images, the Trinity and Christ; rather, the triune powers of the soul—memory, understanding and will—are restored to their true image by being conformed to the one perfect image which is Christ.[65] Thus, he exhorts us to contemplate the Trinity itself and the humanity of Christ, indicating that the humanity of Christ will lead to the fullness of contemplation because Christ is truly God.[66]

The incarnation is a profound mystery for Bonaventure, an event that is at once so sublime and mysterious and yet so intimately close to us. In the *Breviloquium* he maintains that God is to be perceived *altissime* and *piissime*[67] and in his sermon on the nativity he states:

> *The Word was made flesh*, John one. These words give expression to that heavenly mystery and that admirable sacrament, that magnificent work of infinite kindness, namely, that the eternal God has humbly bent down and lifted the lowliness of our nature into unity with his own person.[68]

As humanity was created through the Word, so now, was it recreated through the Word-made-flesh and restored to its true image in God through a mysterious union of divinity and humanity.[69] This union of the divine Word with human flesh is an inexhaustible mystery which he describes in a sermon given on the third Sunday of Advent based on the text, "I am not worthy to untie the strap of his sandal" (Jn 1:27):

> Just as the sandal touches the foot so the human nature touches the divine nature. Yet, the human nature is external to the divine nature just as the sandal is external to the foot. The strap is of so great sublimeness that *I am not worthy to undo it*, that is, to explain this mystery. Do you see why he does not wish to undo it? Because the union of divinity with humanity is a union of the first with the last, the highest with the lowest, that is, God with earth, the most simple with the most composite, because the eternal Word is most simple and the human

nature is most composite. How is it possible that human nature and divine nature can be so united with one another?[70]

The incarnation is the loving condescension of God who took flesh and made himself visible for sinners because they could no longer grasp his divinity and contemplate him.[71] Bonaventure states that before his birth the Word was incomprehensible but after his birth he was like a word expressed by the voice, clothed in flesh and perceptible to the senses. In the incarnation, the Word became not only audible but visible, for in itself a word is more readily heard than seen; but the Word of the Father could be neither seen nor heard, until through his birth he became visible and audible.[72] In the incarnation, therefore, God is both manifest and hidden in Christ.[73] That Word which was with the Father from all eternity and through whom all things are made becomes flesh and Bonaventure exclaims, "It is a wonder in our eyes."[74]

The coming of Christ as the light of the world is paradoxical in that the Son of God illuminates humanity shrouding the brilliance of his eternal light in the mantle of temporal flesh. As Bonaventure states: "And therefore it was necessary that [the true light] be cloaked in flesh so that the people might be able to see and imitate it."[75] Although the Son was from all eternity true light, he was inaccessible to humanity before the incarnation because they could not comprehend him. In the incarnation, Bonaventure writes, the flesh serves as a filtering material like a cloud covering the sun, thereby allowing humanity to gaze upon the splendor of the Son.[76] As a result, men and women can look upon the Son and, illuminated by his witness to the truth, they can imitate his example of virtue.[77] Once illuminated by the divine light, the faithful can perceive and offer assent to the truth of Christ's incarnation, as well as grow in their understanding of this salvific advent by imitating his example.[78] Through the Word-made-flesh, humankind once again has the opportunity to contemplate God.

The historical life of Jesus is in time the eternal mystery in which all created reality is grounded. The possibility of incarnation is grounded in the possibility of God as Creator which is further grounded in the mystery of God as triune mystery of self-communicative love. In Christ the created order finds its highest fulfillment. Christ is the purest actualization of a potential that lies at the heart of the created order. As Hayes states, it is from Jesus that humans learn to read the meaning of the book of creation both in nature and in human reality. As they come to shape their lives after the historical life of Jesus, they enter more deeply into personal union with the Word that lies at the center both of created and uncreated reality. Therefore, the humanity of Christ is essential, it unlocks to us the meaning of all reality—created and uncreated.[79] Spirituality, as the journey of the human soul "into God," is made possible by conforming one's personal life to the mystery of the eternal Word enfleshed in the history of Jesus.

3

The Journey into God

K nowing who God is for Bonaventure, we can begin to understand his Christ mysticism by understanding the relation of the human person to God. The dynamic life of the Trinity, as an eternal diffusion of love with the Word as center, indicates that the human journey to God must also be dynamic and centered in the Word. In this chapter we will explore the journey into God through Christ as a journey into the depths of divine love. Although the journey to God is fundamental to Bonaventure's theology, I do not maintain that it is the synthesizing principle of this theology. Rather, Bonaventure indicates that Christ is the center of his theology since it is through Christ, the Word, that everything comes into being and returns to God. In the first *collatio* of the *Hexaëmeron* he proclaims: "This is our entire metaphysics; emanation, exemplarity, consummation, that you may be illumined by spiritual rays and return to the Most High."[1] For Bonaventure, Christ is the center who holds all things together. Since all things emanate through the Word and must return to God through the Word, all reality is grounded in Christ the center. The Word, therefore, is essential to the contemplation of God. As the absolute center of God, the Word, particularly the Crucified Word, is the synthesizing principle of Bonaventure's theology.

The *Itinerarium Mentis in Deum* (*The Soul's Journey Into God*) is Bonaventure's profound insight to the mystery of the Word incarnate and Crucified as the absolute way to God. It begins and ends with

Francis, the exemplary Christ mystic, and incorporates Francis' vision of the fiery seraph with its three pair of wings in the form of a crucified man as the organizing principle of the journey. The image of the fiery seraph provides the structure of the *Itinerarium*:

> The six wings of the Seraph can rightly be taken to symbolize the six levels of illumination by which, as if by steps or stages, the soul can pass over to peace through ecstatic elevations of Christian wisdom. There is no other path but through the burning love of the Crucified, a love which so transformed Paul into Christ when he was carried up to the third heaven that he could say: *With Christ I am nailed to the cross. I live, now not I, but Christ lives in me* (Gal 2:20). This love also so absorbed the soul of Francis that his spirit shone through his flesh when for two years before his death he carried in his body the sacred stigmata of the passion. The six wings of the Seraph, therefore, symbolize the six steps of illumination that begin from creatures and lead up to God, whom no one rightly enters except through the Crucified.[2]

The six wings of the seraph symbolize God, the soul, and creation which comprise the stages of the journey. It is a "fiery" seraph because, as Hugh of St. Victor indicates, this image symbolizes burning love.[3] Bonaventure associates "burning love" with the passion of Christ when he states: "His unquenchable fire of love for the good Jesus had been fanned into such a blaze of flames that many waters could not quench so powerful a love."[4] Bonaventure, therefore, uses the image of the fiery seraph to describe the journey into God, the journey that led Francis to a union of love with the burning love of the Crucified.

Bonaventure begins the journey to God by considering the role of creation. Francis had a love of creation and was captivated by God's goodness, rejoicing in the world around him. In light of Francis, Bonaventure sees that creation is good and sacred flowing like a river from God. The sacred purpose of creation is to awaken the human spirit to God who is Creator. It is an expression of the divine or a theophany—a world of signs whose purpose is to lead us back to the Source of all life.

When we rationally reflect on our experience of the world

around us we can gain "created knowledge." All created realities originate from God and are reflections of the essential goodness of God. Through a prayerful approach to creation we perceive the presence of God; creation is a sign of God's presence. In order to know reality, it is necessary to understand the sacred transcendent aspect of creation and to know that everything comes from God. We can know this insofar as God regulates and motivates us to appreciate and understand the world; God cooperates in our search for knowledge through the divine light within.[5] When we begin to perceive God, we desire to know God more because we are made in the image of God; thus, we have a "built-in" capacity for God. Creation is symbolic, pointing to a deeper reality. Through the transcendental mystery of creation we learn that life has more than a material dimension as Francis shows us in his sacred approach to nature. Created knowledge is gained through experience of the world and finds its ultimate signficance when it leads us closer to God. However, knowledge from creation is limited and thus we must begin to search for God within.

Once we have recognized the divine power, wisdom and glory in the wonder of creation, we are impelled to enter within since our desire for God, awakened in creation, cannot be here fully satisfied. Bonaventure states that we must enter within the depth of our soul. He follows the Plotinian scheme of introversion and ascension,[6] using the mirror of creation with its trinitarian stamp as the basis for entering within. He writes: "Enter into yourself, then, and see that your soul loves itself most fervently; that it could not love itself unless it knew itself, nor know itself unless it remembered itself, because our intellect grasps only what is present to our memory."[7] The soul is that mysterious and unique center of the individual which reflects God since it is made in his image according to its three powers of memory, intellect and will. Following Augustine, Bonaventure claims that these powers of the soul render it an image of the Trinity. He indicates that in the depths of the soul's faculties, in the memory, intellect and will, one finds a reflection of God: "See, therefore, how close the soul is to God, and how, through their activity, the memory leads us to eternity, the intelligence to truth and the power of choice to the highest good."[8] In this way creation reflects God as triune at a deeper level, namely, in the human person who is created in the image of God. Using the two Augustinian triads: memory - intelligence - will; and mind - knowedge - love to describe the image in the human person he states:

> The intellectual creature has memory, intelligence, and will; or mind knowledge, and love; mind, like a parent, knowledge like an offspring, and love like a bond proceeding from both and joining them together. For the mind cannot fail to love the word which it generates. Therefore, these not only indicate origin and emanation which leads to distinction among them; but they indicate also quality, consubstantiality, and inseparability, from which an express testimony is given to the fact that God is a trinity.[9]

Although Bonaventure holds that the human person is created as an image of God, "a unity of essence and a trinity of powers,"[10] he qualifies this by saying that the "image" is the inner ordering of human nature to the mystery of the second divine person, the Son or Word of God.[11] The human person is in the image of God, the Seraphic Doctor states, not in the general sense of being like God but in the specific sense of being like the Son. The status of the human person as an image of God is grounded in the Word as image of the Father. Bonaventure describes this inner ordering of the human person to the Word as *convenientia ordinis*; it is the ontological and epistemological basis of the human person as image. In the mystery of the incarnation, the created image is filled with the eternal, exemplary Image so that humanity reaches its fullest participation in the divine archetype and the deepest fulfillment of its potential.[12] Bonaventure views the depths of the soul as the mystery of the Trinity and Christ. He states that when the soul considers itself, it rises through itself as through a mirror to behold the blessed Trinity of the Father, Word and Love; three persons, coeternal, coequal and consubstantial.[13] Ultimately, as the soul approaches the center more closely, it sees that the mystery of the Trinity is contained in Christ. The triune powers of the soul are summed up in Christ, who is the center of the soul, indicating that the "image" is the inner ordering of human nature to the mystery of the second divine person, the Word of God.[14]

Bonaventure states that God made the human person right (*rec-*

tus) by making the human person an image of the Son and turning him or her to God through grace.[15] In the second part of the *Breviloquium* he states that the whole person, created by God, was placed in paradise and given a two-fold perception, interior and exterior, consisting of the mind and of the flesh,[16] and a double range of senses, inner and outer, one in reason and one in the flesh. Through the eye of the flesh, the human could see things outside in creation, with the eye of reason, the things within, with the eye of contemplation, the things above. The human person, however, freely turned away from God. Sin means a corruption of the created will, a turning away from God and toward other creatures, investing in them the truth and goodness that rightly belongs to God.[17] Instead of the human person standing "upright" (*rectus*) turned toward God, the person is "bent over," turned away from God, blinded in intellect, and suffering from one's own endless desires. With sin humans presumed themselves equal to God which was an affront against the Son who alone is the perfect image of the Father, possessing all that is of God and equal to him.[18] Because of sin humanity lay fallen on the ground immersed in the things of sense and in need of help in being lifted up.

The outstanding feature of Bonaventure's doctrine is that sin affects both the soul and body.[19] He sees the body as actively involved in sin since Adam was initially given a two-fold perception: of the mind and of the flesh. Sin, he states, took place through spiritual pride and physical gluttony.[20] Because the body was initially completely obedient to the soul, it was free from all hostility and rebellion. However, being also parallel to the soul, the body was liable to fall into sin and suffering. As he states in the *Breviloquium*, the body had the potency to die or not to die, to obey the soul or rise up against it. Abandoning the soul's true good for the sake of material satisfaction, the soul became separated against its will from the body through the body's death. The body is not simply the victim of the soul's corruption but a responsible partner in sin.[21] Because sin affects both soul and body, the whole had to be assumed in order to heal. As a result of the fall the line of *egressus* was carried out in a destructive way away from God; humanity lay fallen on the ground immersed in the things of sense and in need of help in being lifted upright so that one could see his or her true self as image of God, with the eternal Truth shining within the self.[22] Although humanity fell from uprightness, losing uprightness itself, it lost the habit of it, not the inclination or aptitude for it.[23]

To explain the restoration of the image, Bonaventure uses the symbol of the ladder. The sin of humankind had broken the first ladder but Christ restored the broken ladder linking humankind with God in his crucifixion.[24] It is through the obedience of Jesus Christ that the movement of *egressus* bends into *regressus* and the circle closes once again.[25] As *persona media* of the Trinity and the medium in whom God and world coincide, Christ takes upon himself in the incarnation the depths of finitude and the burden of sin. By entering into death he brings forth life and restores to its primitive rectitude the fallen image of humankind.

The restoration that Christ brought about in the incarnation fulfills humanity's greatest potential which is its ability to be united to the divine.[26] Bonaventure follows the Augustinian idea that the memory is able to contain or bear a spiritual substance thus rendering the soul able to receive God (*capax Dei*). He discusses the notion of the soul as *capax Dei* in the first book of the *Sentences*:

> The soul is in the image of God by which it is capable of God and able to participate in him. To be capable does not mean that God is present in his substance or essence because he is thus present in every creature, but to be capable of God means that he is present through knowledge and love. Therefore, God is able to be known by creatures.[27]

The soul therefore contains God as that object known and loved; it possesses God in the depths of memory.[28] As such, the capacity of the soul for God is so great, Bonaventure states, that no creature lower than God suffices to satisfy its longing.[29] A person is capable of transformation through a grace-filled encounter with God because we are ordered to God immediately.

Divine Illumination

Our potency for union with God corresponds to communication with God through Christ. As image, the human person is like a mirror turned to the radiating light of the divine essence. We can know God with a certain amount of certitude because we have within us the divine light. Our knowledge of God does not come entirely from the created world but is supported by a knowledge of God that is already present within the soul. Bonaventure holds that within the soul there is a changeless light which enables the soul to recall changeless truth.[30] This changeless light is the eternal exemplar, and it is by means of this that we judge all things including our soul and its reflections. This changeless light is necessary for the soul to arrive at immutable and eternal truth and it does so by exercizing an influence on the human intellect. Although the eternal truth is not the soul's ground of human knowledge nor is God seen by the intellect in his naked reality, the intellect "contuits" the eternal reasons.[31] Bonaventure clarifies this by saying that the term "principle of knowledge" does not mean that God is the only, or bare, or total means of knowledge. If this were true, there would be no difference between knowledge in the Word and knowledge of a thing in its own right. Moreover, if he were the bare and open ground of knowledge, there would be no difference between our knowledge in this life and our knowledge in heaven.[32] Rather, knowledge is generated in us by way of sense, memory and experience, from which the universal is formed in us.[33]

As the center of the soul, Christ is the inner teacher of truth and the source of divine illumination because he is the eternal sun, the image of the Father and the splendor of his glory.[34] As the archetype and expression of the three divine Persons, he is the highest reality that can present itself to the intellect, not as an idea or conceptually, but in a profoundly personal relationship realized by the created spirit. Since the archetype freely discloses itself in the copy,[35] it is recognized and acknowledged there as the "inner teacher" when the spiritual impulse toward absoluteness in all intellectual knowing and striving is correctly understood and accepted as the goal.[36]

The Incarnate Word is the true source of knowledge because he is the Word who is the font of wisdom (Sir. 1:5).[37] This is an essential aspect of the mystery of Christ. Because of sin, humans were unable to ascend to God; thus, the Word became flesh in order that humans could be lifted up to the inaccessible light (1 Tim. 6:16).[38] Christ is the

true light of knowledge who teaches both interiorly and exteriorly.
He is teacher, Bonaventure states, because he took on flesh and stood
in our midst.[39] As the interior teacher, it is only through him that
truth is known through divine illumination:

> Christ teaches interiorly, so that no truth is known except
> through him, not through speech as it is with us, but through
> inner enlightenment. Wherefore he must necessarily have
> within himself the most clear species, which he cannot possibly
> have received from another. He himself, then, is intimate to
> every soul and he shines forth by means of his most clear
> species upon the obscure species of our understanding. And in
> this manner, these obscure species, mixed with the darkness of
> images, are lit up in such a way that the intellect understands.
> If, indeed, to know a thing is to understand that it cannot be
> otherwise than it is, by necessity he alone will make it known
> who knows the truth and possesses the truth within himself.[40]

The divine illumination that comes from Christ leads one along
the path from faith through reason to contemplation.[41] In his sermon
"Christ, the One Teacher of All," Bonaventure shows how Christ
sums up in himself both the gift of wisdom and the gift of knowledge thus revealing the deficiencies of both Plato and Aristotle. He
claims that Aristotle was right to understand human knowledge as
arising on the road of the senses, the memory and experience, and
therefore he holds that Plato was justly criticized by Aristotle
because he "derives all certain knowledge from the ideal world," however, Plato correctly posits the existence of these ideals or eternal reasons of being.[42] The successful marriage of the ideal and the real,
according to Bonaventure, was achieved by Moses in the Old
Covenant and Paul in the New Covenant and above all in Christ himself since he is both pilgrim and possessor[43] and thereby possesses
full knowledge of God.[44]

Christ also teaches exteriorly because as the perfect Image and
Exemplar, he is the foundation for every creaturely attitude before
God. Bonaventure states that true knowledge is not only by way of
intellect but also by way of example. Christ is teacher, Bonaventure
states, because he took on flesh and stood in our midst.[45] Since Christ
is the divine-temporal exemplar, it is both by word and example, that

is, imitation of the exemplar, that one arrives at true wisdom.[46] The imitation of Christ is grounded in the metaphysical principle of exemplarity.

> Jesus stood in the midst of the Jews as a model of holiness because men stood in need both of teaching and of example, since example moves more than words. He who is beyond reproach has created man in his own image, and has made himself capable of being imitated. For our generation, formation, and creation take place after the image of the Word. . . . The Word himself came down to our humanity so that we might follow his example and be reformed through imitation of him.[47]

The mystery of Christ, according to Bonaventure, is that the humanity of Christ enables us to attain true knowledge of God, a knowledge that is not only conceptual and abstract but one that is experiential, since knowledge is gained not only by word but by example of Christ which underscores bodily imitation. Knowledge through imitation of Christ leads to the true contemplation of God; for knowledge is a necessary step in the path to contemplation.[48]

Christ-Centered Hierarchy

The significance of Christ as teacher corresponds to his role as true hierarch. Bonaventure uses the term "hierarchy" to describe the illumination of the soul in conformity to Christ through grace.[49] He adopts the term from the Pseudo-Dionysius to describe God-likeness[50] and defines it as follows: "Hierarchy is a divine order, a knowledge and action assimilated as much as possible to the deiform, and rising proportionately in the likeness of God toward the lights conferred upon it from on high."[51] Hierarchy means a conformity of the soul to God through grace or divine influence. The purpose of this influence is to lead the soul back to God. Bonaventure identifies Christ, the Word uncreated and incarnate, as the true hierarch,[52] since he who restored heaven and earth had to have touched both heaven and earth.[53] "This hierarch," he states, "had to be preeminent, endowed with awareness, acceptable to God, victorious, most generous and just."[54] As the uncreated Word and *ars patris* and the medium in the emanation of creation, Christ is the archetype of all God-likeness.[55] As incarnate, he is the *medium reducens* who leads fallen creation back to the Father.[56] As hierarch, he is also the *praelatus* who exercises the threefold hierarchic act in human persons to purify, enlighten and perfect them.[57] Since Christ is center of the soul, he divinely illuminates it through grace, enabling the soul to become hierarchical.

Bonaventure describes the hierarchization of the soul as the grace of divine illumination and compares it to the radiations of the Sun. Through the eternal Sun, that is, eternal wisdom, God lifts up the contemplative soul to the perception of eternal truth and eternal reason.[58] The hierarchized soul has a radiation that is constant, beautiful and joyful.[59] The constant radiation means that the soul has order and strength; its beauty is the splendor of wisdom; and it joyfully radiates because it is conformed to the divine Spirit and has desire.[60] Bonaventure compares the hierarchization of the soul to the angelic hierarchies and the ecclesiastical hierarchies. Concerning the angelic hierarchy, he identifies three hierarchies corresponding to the three persons of the Trinity: thrones, cherubim and seraphim correspond to the Father; dominations, virtues and powers correspond to the Son; and principalities, archangels and angels correspond to the Holy Spirit.[61] Similarly, he states that a triple hierarchization, analogous to the nine choirs of angels, must take place in the soul. These interior hierarchies dispose the soul according to ascension, descension and return to God, thus permitting the soul to be elevated to God, receive divine illuminations, and return to God in passing through the sensible world. When the soul is made hierarchical, Bonaventure states, it enters the heavenly Jerusalem where God is seen as all in all (1 Cor 15:28).[62] Although it seems *prima facie* that he is referring to a mystical ascent transcending Christ, he is speaking of conformity to Christ and the entrance of the soul into the mystery of Christ.

We can relate the hierarchical soul to the soul that "sees" the heavenly Jerusalem which is a symbolic reference to Jesus Christ. In the *Hexaëmeron* Bonaventure states that the soul lifted up (hierarchized) sees Jerusalem in a threefold manner: standing in heaven, coming down from heaven and going up to heaven. All three movements refer to Christ and in no other way, Bonaventure states, can the soul be contemplative.[63] He describes the descent of the city of Jerusalem in the incarnation.[64] The soul that is lifted up by divine strength, light and warmth, comprehends the humanity of Christ in his nativity, crucifixion, ascension and final judgment.[65] The hierarchized soul sees the city going up to heaven when it comprehends divine charity and when it possesses the fire and consolation of divine charity, that is, when it is sealed by the fire of the Holy Spirit and loves with the same breadth, length, height and depth as Christ (Eph 3:17, 18). Then the soul itself dwells in the heavenly Jerusalem, that is, in Christ.[66] Dwelling in Christ, the soul, conformed to God through grace, becomes like Christ, the heavenly Jerusalem, and the dwelling place of God who is Trinity. In the *Itinerarium* he writes:

> Finally, we are led through the hierarchies and hierarchical orders which are to be arranged in our soul as in the heavenly Jerusalem. Filled with all these intellectual illuminations, our mind like the house of God is inhabited by divine wisdom; it is made a daughter of God, his spouse and friend; it is made a member of Christ the head, his sister and coheir; it is made a temple of the Holy Spirit . . . all of this is accomplished by a most sincere love of Christ without . . . whom we cannot know the secret things of God.[67]

As the soul is made hierarchical in accordance with Christ the center, it is made a daughter of the Father, a spouse of Christ, and a temple of the Holy Spirit.[68] The "spirit enters the heavenly Jerusalem," through purgation which is the expulsion of sin, illumination which consists in the imitation of Christ, and perfection which consists in union with the Spouse.[69] By this threefold path, the soul is lifted up to God as the goal. In being "lifted up" the soul receives divine illuminations, through revelation it knows the secrets of God, and in union it is elevated to ecstasy. Bonaventure describes the hierarchical soul as the soul sealed by the Holy Spirit, the fire of love.[70]

In light of the hierarchization of the soul, Bonaventure does not conceive of contemplation as an ascent of the soul to uncreated divinity in a purely intellectual manner; rather, contemplation takes place in imitation of Christ. The higher the soul ascends to God through divine illumination and the power of grace, the lower it descends in humility in imitation of Christ. The journey to God is not simply a Neoplatonic flight upwards (ascent) nor is it entirely intellectual (characteristic of the Neoplatonic ascent). Rather, it is also a descent in the flesh meaning imitation of Christ in his poverty and humility. The soul turned to Christ is reformed in him through the ordering of its knowledge and power. At the same time, there is imitation of Christ both in word and example which is manifested in the body, so that soul and body both ascend and descend in conformity to Christ. As the soul becomes hierarchical, illumined and perfected in Christ, the body becomes shaped to poverty, humility, and suffering in imitation of Christ. Both the soul and body, therefore, ascend and descend in conformity to Christ.

Christ Crucified: The Mystical Center

As the soul enters more deeply into the mystery of the Word it approaches the center and sees that the mystery of the Trinity is manifested in Christ. The soul enters into the tabernacle where the two cherubim (symbols of knowledge) face each other over the Mercy Seat, the symbol of Christ Crucified (and place of atonement).[71] The cherubim represent the highest form of knowing, one concerned with the essential attributes of God, the other with those proper to the Persons of the Trinity. Bonaventure first contemplates God in the unity of his essence by engaging in a dialectic of being and non-being, identifying Anselm's ontological proof of God: God is that than which no greater can be thought.[72] He then unites this Anselmian principle with the Platonic axiom that the good is self-diffusive.[73] Bonaventure uses this axiom to describe the mystery of the Trinity, thus providing an explanation of the archetype of created things, making it possible to trace them back to their origin without absorbing them monistically into the rays of the light that is their source.[74] Based on the concept of the self-diffusive good, he shows how the supreme self-diffusiveness of the divinity requires the procession of the Son and the Holy Spirit. His logic is linear beginning with the primacy of the Father, the *fontalis plenitudo*. From this supreme fecundity comes a trinity of persons, from which follows supreme sharing and intimacy. As he states:

From supreme goodness, it is necessary that there be in the persons supreme communicability; from supreme communicability, supreme consubstantiality; from supreme consubstantiality, supreme configurability; and from these supreme coequality and hence supreme coeternity; finally, from all of the above, supreme mutual intimacy, by which one is necessarily in the other by supreme interpenetration and one acts with the other in absolute lack of division of the substance, power and operation of the most blessed Trinity itself.[75]

He goes on to say, "When you contemplate these things do not think that you have comprehended the incomprehensible." The most startling feature of this divine unity is that it is simultaneously a coincidence of opposites through the six properties of the self-diffusive good: "For here is supreme communicability with individuality of persons, supreme consubstantiality with plurality of hypostases, supreme configurability with distinct personality, supreme coequality with degree, supreme coeternity with emanation, supreme mutual intimacy with mission."[76] The coincidence of opposites is the "archetypal structure" of God insofar as the self-diffusive good of the Father gives rise to the Son and Spirit. Whereas the Father is the fountain and source of the good and thus total productivity, the Spirit is generated by the Father and Son and thus total receptivity; the Son is both generated by nature of the Father's good and together with the Father generates the Spirit as from one principle. Within the very nature of God, therefore, there is a coincidence of opposites: productivity and receptivity. The Word who is *medium* of the Trinity is the center of the coincidence of opposites since the Word both receives from the Father and together with the Father spirates the Spirit.

Bonaventure sets up a parallel between the coincidence of opposites in the divine nature and the more striking expression in Christ by focusing on the Cherubim who contemplate the mystery of opposites in the Word Incarnate: "For we should wonder not only at the essential and personal properties of God in themselves but also in comparison with the superwonderful union of God and man in the unity of the person of Christ."[77] Here he reveals the relationship between the Trinity and Christ in light of the coincidence of oppo-

sites, the structure of opposites that characterizes the very nature of
God. He states that if we wondered that in the Trinity there is a
coincidence of unity and plurality, we will be amazed at Christ. After
describing the opposites of unity and plurality in the Trinity, he bids
us to look at this mystery in Christ:

> If you are the other cherub contemplating the properties of the
> persons and you are amazed . . . look at the Mercy Seat and
> wonder that in Christ personal union exists with a trinity of
> substances and a duality of natures; that complete agreement
> exists with a plurality of wills; that mutual predication of God
> and man exists with a plurality of properties; that coadoration
> exists with a plurality of excellence, that coexaltation above all
> things exists with a plurality of dignity; that codomination
> exists with a plurality of powers.[78]

Bonaventure's insight is that the mystery of the triune God of
love is embodied in the mystery of Christ. The Crucified Christ is
the mystery hidden from all eternity (Eph 3:9). He asks the reader to
become each cherub and to contemplate the opposites in Christ, not
only in the divine nature but in the realization that they are one in
Christ along with all the attributes of his humanity. By identifying
the mystery of Christ as the union of all opposites in the universe—
the union of immensity with smallness, strength with weakness,
clarity with obscurity, immortality with mortality, divinity with
humanity, the first with the last, the highest with the lowest, circumference and center, Alpha and Omega, caused and cause, Creator
and creature—Bonaventure indicates that in Christ we arrive at perfect reality. Christ is the central point of all creation in whom perfect
order is seen. Christ is the most perfect realization of the potential of
humanity as well as the perfection of the universe. Christ Crucified
is the perfect communication of God's love. Thus it is *only in union
with Christ*, and moreover, Christ Crucified, that our humanity can
contemplate perfection—and return to God.

4

Ecstatic Union

Although Bonaventure places divine illumination and knowledge of God as a necessary stage in divine contemplation, he does not maintain that contemplation is ultimately knowledge but love, a love that knows God not with the intellect but with the heart, a love that is wisdom. The emphasis on God as the highest good means that God is not only being, but, moreover, God is love. Indeed, what Bonaventure illuminates at the highest stage of the mystical journey is that God *is* love and this love is not only embodied but manifested in the Crucified Christ. The human response, therefore, cannot simply be one of intellectual contemplation but must lead the person into a union of love with the primordial mystery of love. My intention here is to show how Bonaventure illuminates love as the metaphysical foundation of the journey to God. Since Christ is the temporal expression of the eternal mystery of sonship, union with him leads one into relationship with the Father. The mystery of Christ dwelling in the center of the soul means that the soul transformed in Christ by grace is brought into the central mystery of the Crucified. Christ Crucified is the one who dies and rises to draw us beyond sin, beyond the limits of the world, beyond ourselves into mystical union with God. In order to make the passage into God, Bonaventure states that all intellectual activity must be abandoned and one must go beyond opposites, beyond being and non-being, to divine darkness. Our instrument for making the passage is the cross.

In the last chapter of the *Itinerarium*, Bonaventure indicates that as the soul approaches the highest stage of contemplation, the intellect is in darkness.[1] This means that intellectual concepts no longer participate in the experience of God; God cannot be known by anything in the created world. Bonaventure uses this negative or apophatic theology of the Pseudo-Dionysius to say that all intellectual activity must be abandoned and one must pass beyond opposites to the shining ray of divine darkness. He uses the Pseudo-Dionysian terms superluminous and superessential to highlight the fact that the mystery of God is so much greater than we can describe or know. Ultimately, the journey to God is an apophatic ascent which means it is completely ineffable, transcending the intellect. The perfection of the soul in union with Christ leads to a blinding illumination rendering the intellect dark. As Bonaventure states: "In this passing beyond, if it is perfect, it is necessary that all intellectual operations be left behind and that the apex affections be totally transferred and transformed into God. This is mystical and secret."[2] The striking aspect of Bonaventure's doctrine of ecstasy is that it is not an exclusive privilege but is possible for all Christians, and he considers it a normal and ordinary way in the spiritual life[3] since, as the highest degree of love, ecstasy is the way to peace.[4]

The journey to ecstatic union, as Bonaventure conceives it, is a return to the interior of the soul and ascent to its highest point, the *apex mentis*, which as the highest level of affectivity means leaving behind all intellectual activity. Ecstasy is an intimate experience of God in which the soul touches God in an embrace of love and is distinguished from rapture.[5] While contemplation in its various levels involves the intellect and will, ecstasy, according to Bonaventure, surpasses the intellect since it is realized in the *apex affectus*. It is an affectivity which is higher and more interior than the intellect, indicating that the innermost part of the human lies beyond the intellect.[6] In the *Hexaëmeron* he states:

> In order to reach this summit, it is good for us to be carried above every sense, every rational operation related to the imagination, even to dismiss the angelical intelligences . . . this is what Dionysius teaches, to dismiss sensible and intellectual things, beings and non-beings; and by non-beings he means

temporal things because they are in a constant state of flux, thus to enter the radiance of darkness. It is called darkness because it does not bear upon the intelligence,and yet the soul is supremely flooded with light. . . . And understand that it is said, not in regard to God, but in regard to our intellect, for the Trinity is substance to a greater degree than our intelligence can perceive. . . . For Christ goes away when the mind attempts to behold this wisdom through intellectual eyes; since it is not the intellect that can go in there, but the heart . . for the heart reaches down into the depths of Christ.[7]

Although Bonaventure describes ecstasy as an affective experience of the will that goes beyond the intellect, scholars have debated whether or not it affords a type of knowledge of God mediated by grace. Bonaventure distinguishes two kinds of higher knowledge of God, one deriving from the workings of God's grace in the soul, the other residing in a certain immediacy.[8] Ephrem Longpré states that, for Bonaventure, ecstasy means that God is known not in his substance, that is, in himself, but in his operation, that is, in his interior effects.[9] The experiential object of contemplation, therefore, is not God himself but his proper interior effects by divine grace.[10] Dunstan Dobbins, too, holds that the higher knowledge of God obtained in ecstasy is not by direct intuition but by grace which floods the soul with a deeper knowledge of God; it is an act of love in the will inflamed by grace.[11] Balthasar states that ecstasy imparts a genuine knowledge of God and the highest manner of knowledge; it is an *anagogicus excessus*.[12] According to Karl Rahner, however, Bonaventure draws a distinction between knowledge through grace (*cognoscere in effectu gratiae*) and knowledge through intimate union (*cognitio per intimam unionem*). He states that the higher of the two, intimate union, is not achieved through the medium of the operations of grace:[13]

Ecstasy, on the contrary, is to be sharply distinguished from intellectual experience of the created effects of grace, even of a mystical kind, since it is the direct experience of God, direct in the proper ontological sense, and not only in the sense that the experience of the created effects of grace (which are, therefore, recognized) allows a practically direct knowledge of

God as their underlying cause (in the form of a "medium in quo").[14]

In the third book of the *Sentences* Bonaventure distinguishes between knowledge through grace and knowledge through union:

> Knowledge of [God] has many levels; God is known in a vestige, he is known in an image, and he is known through the effects of grace. He is also known through the intimate union of God and the soul according to that which the Apostle states: Who adheres to God is one spirit [with him] And this knowledge is most excellent, as Dionysius teaches, in ecstatic love and rises above the knowlege of faith according to the common state.[15]

Although Rahner does not discount the effects of created grace altogether, he distinguishes between knowledge of God in his interior effects under the influence of grace, and ecstasy as a direct experience of God without any intermediate perception. In the *Sentences*, Bonaventure speaks of an "unknowing ascent" (*ignote ascendere*)[16] and of a "learned ignorance" (*docta ignorantia*)[17] and in his *Commentary on John* he speaks of a knowledge of God in "darkness" (*caligine*) which is more "feeling" (*sentire*) than knowledge (*cognoscere*).[18] In the *Hexaëmeron* he indicates that ecstasy is to be distinguished from intellectual experience even of a mystical kind, since it is an experience of God through the union of love; it is an experience one obtains by grace:

> In its burning desire, the soul becomes not only an agile flame swift to rise: it even transcends itself, entering mystical darkness and ecstasy through a certain wise unknowing. . . . Experience alone can tell the wonder of this obscure, delightful light; divine grace alone can procure such experience; and those alone who strive for it may receive such grace.[19]

In view of Bonaventure's writings, ecstasy can be described as an experience of God that transcends the intellect but is procured under the influence of grace. It is not knowledge in the proper sense but it is an experiential knowledge of God[20] in which the soul enters into a union of love: *Haec est suprema unitio per amorem.*[21] Bonaventure, like the Pseudo-Dionysius, maintains that ecstasy is a *docta ignorantia*, a learned ignorance in which love surpasses knowledge,[22] underscoring the aspect of mystical darkness in which love alone ascends to the divine.[23]

Spiritual Senses

Bonaventure states that this union of love leads one in the state of ecstasy to a mystical sleep whereby the physical senses are at rest and the mind is joined to God:

> In this union the mind is joined to God, wherefore in a certain sense it sleeps, while in another it keeps vigil . . . only the affective power keeps vigil and imposes silence upon all the other powers; then man becomes foreign to his senses: he is in ecstasy and hears secret words that man may not repeat, because they are only in the heart. Hence, because nothing can be expressed unless it is conceived, or conceived unless it is understood, and here the intelligence does not speak; it follows that a man can hardly speak or explain anything.[24]

The sleep of the physical senses is paradoxically the height of the spiritual senses: hearing and sight belong to the uncreated Word; smell to the inspired Word; taste and touch to the incarnate Word (see *Itin* 4, 3). Bonaventure's doctrine of the spiritual senses is a hallmark of his mystical theology and relates to the experience of ecstasy.[25] Whereas Gregory of Nyssa held that the spiritual senses develop with the extinction of the carnal senses,[26] Bonaventure states that these senses share a common root with the physical senses in the single intellectual-material nature of the human person.[27] At the foot of the ascent to union with God, the spiritual senses touch the bodily senses and they endure through all the stages of the intellect's perception until ecstasy. Whereas the physical senses are endowed by nature, the spiritual senses are bestowed with grace and the gifts of the Holy Spirit.[28]

Bonaventure's tree of spiritual senses is related to the full height of the form of God in his revelation. The spiritual senses are the means of apprehending the mystical presence of God in Christ. Unlike the Pseudo-Dionysius for whom the mystical ascent progresses toward divine transcendence,[29] Bonaventure entertains the highest contemplation of God precisely in the three dimensions of the Word as eternal, incarnate and inspired.[30] The highest blessing, that of peace, is to be found in spiritual touch which takes place with the incarnate Word. In the *Breviloquium* Bonaventure writes: "He is the incarnate Word dwelling bodily in our midst, offering himself to our touch, our kiss, our embrace, through ardent love which makes our soul pass, by ecstatic rapture, from this world to the Father."[31]

The spiritual senses, therefore, are the means of apprehending the mystical presence of God in Christ. They remain ordered to the form of appearence of God in the Word which reaches from his form as human into his very form as divine expression and can be perceived only in the unity of this one inseparable form of revelation in faith, hope and love.[32] Balthasar captures the meaning of the spiritual senses as they relate to Bonaventure's Christ mysticism:

> The Word as the eternal expression of the Father, ray of light, word, wisdom, is spiritually seen and heard and tasted; as inspired prophetic word-fragrance, he is breathed into the heart; in his incarnated states he is touched fully, and embraced. From this contact with the incarnated Word, the whole tree grows from earth to heaven just as Francis was caught up into nuptial ecstasy precisely in the direct palpable contact with the wounds of Christ.[33]

At the level of ecstasy, the humanity of Christ is not lost or transcended. Rather, the incarnate Word is in continuity with both the uncreated Word and the inspired Word, so that union with Christ by means of the spiritual senses leads one into union with God.

Passover in the Crucified

By entering into the paschal mystery through the spiritual senses and contemplating Christ as the coincidence of opposites, one reaches a point where all opposites disappear because one ceases to think in concepts or engage in intellectual contemplation. The Word, which is the *ratio experimendi* of the Father's power, wisdom and goodness in creation, now becomes the *ratio manifestandi* of his overflowing love on the cross.[34] The incarnate and crucified Word who holds a middle place between the Father and the world now brings the human person united to him into affective union with the Father:

> Let us, then, die and enter into the darkness; let us impose silence upon our cares, our desires and our imaginings. With Christ crucified let us pass *out of this world to the Father* so that when the Father is shown to us, we may say with Philip: *It is enough for us.*[35]

In the final chapter of the *Soul's Journey* Bonaventure writes: "Whoever loves this death can see God."[36] The heart of fire that yearns for God discovers in the dark mystery of the Crucified the Spouse who is God. This transcendent passing beyond, or *transitus*, can only be attained in and through Christ in his death on the cross. Bonaventure's great insight to the journey into God is presented in the final chapter where he indicates that knowledge which leads to God leads us to the heart of God as love. The great mystery is that love, as the highest good, is expressed in the Crucified Christ. Christ Crucified manifests the Trinity of love. Bonaventure's understanding of the Word as the expressive likeness of the Father is crucial here. The Crucified Word is both image of the Father and Son; thus, the Crucified expresses the self-communicating goodness or outpouring love of the Father. Yet, the Crucified is the Son of the Father and is united to the Father in the one Spirit of self-communicating love: "The Word expresses the Father as the principle producing from itself and thus explains and represents the production of the Holy Spirit and his own generation."[37] In the Crucified Christ, the entire Trinity, Father, Son and Spirit, is manifested as the self-diffusive love of God. Bonaventure writes in the *Soliloquium*: "On the cross the whole Trinity cries out to you."[38] The great mystery that Bonaventure unfolds is that the mystery of love in the Crucified *is* the self-diffusive love of the Trinity.

The knowledge of God which draws us beyond ourselves ultimately impels us to leave behind the intellect and understanding and to rely only on desire, the fire of the Spirit within; here the mind gives way to the heart and we are drawn to the One whom we can never fully understand but whom we desire from the depth of our being. In this ecstatic union, God gifts us with an overwhelming experience of divine love, an experience which no words are adequate to express. This mystery was revealed to Francis in the vision of the Seraph and reception of the Stigmata; the mystery of "mystical death" brought about through grace, not instruction or knowledge; the fire of the Spirit, not understanding; the groaning of prayer, not diligent reading; the spouse, not the teacher; God, not humans; darkness, not clarity. It is "not light but fire that totally inflames and carries us into God"—the fire that is Christ burning with love in the heat of his passion.[39] It is a "mystical death" because we are drawn beyond ourselves into the hidden silent mystery of the God of love embracing us in the cross of the Crucified. Through the mystery of the Crucified we enter into the hiddenness of the Father.

Bonaventure views ecstatic union as the summit of love between the soul and the crucified Word, drawing one into the glory of the Trinity in union with the Father and the Spirit; this is the mystical passover in Christ. It is love which joins the lover to the beloved and unites them to one another and brings them closer, and which alone can make a soul rise above itself and turn more deeply toward another. Wayne Hellmann states that the ecstatic contemplation of the transcendent glory of God in the cross transforms one into the compassionate Crucified Christ:

> This "burning love" is the "passion of Christ" in which the soul is transformed into the depths of compassionate love. Seraphic love is compassionate love. It is indeed compassionate love that Bonaventure develops to the fullest. For Bonaventure, Francis' mystical experience of ecstatic contemplation of the transcendent glory of God transforms him into the compassionate crucified Christ. Seraphic glory and the divine intimacy of mystical contemplation not only places one in the seraphic order of angels. It places one on the cross, crucified with Christ.[40]

Although Bonaventure affirms union as an ascent to God, ecstatic union with the burning love of the Crucified also draws one out to one's neighbor.[41] It is a love that impels one in the direction of ascent and descent, upward to God and outward to neighbor and world.[42] Richard of St. Victor states that in the fourth degree of love, the soul is transformed into a servant. The contemplative who ascends to the glory of God is conformed to the humility of Christ. Whereas in the third degree of love, the soul is conformed to the likeness of God, in the fourth degree "she begins to empty herself, taking the form of a servant," following Christ in his passion.[43] In the highest degree of love he states, "the soul goes forth on God's behalf and descends below herself. . . because of her neighbor."[44]

Bonaventure indicates that union with Christ brings about a more perfect relationship with God than the first Adam enjoyed. As the new Adam who repairs the damage wrought by sin, Christ functions not only as mediator and restorer but also as the model of the contemplation of God. Whereas the first Adam had a proper love of God and enjoyed the contemplation of God through the book of creation, the second Adam shows that true love of God is in tension with sin[45] and thus it is only by way of the cross that contemplation of God is restored because the cross is the mystery of divine love and the heart of wisdom. The Seraphic Doctor, therefore, does not perceive the soul's return to God merely as a return to the original state of the first Adam; rather, in Christ the center, the soul and body are reformed in the true image of the Son and, in union with the Son, are brought into union with the Father. In Christ, Bonaventure states, all things are not only restored but are advanced and completed through the Word united to the flesh. Jesus Christ is the desired end.[46]

Theological Metaphysics

The journey that Bonaventure describes in the *Itinerarium* is rooted in the summons to imitate Christ and to be transformed in him. As we have already noted, Francis functions as the model in the *Itinerarium* and, according to E. R. Daniel, Bonaventure's *Legenda Major* seeks to clarify this mystical quest.[47] The question of significant import underlying the *Itinerarium* is whether or not the journey is a true Neoplatonic ascent or whether Bonaventure offers a new metaphysical construct with Christ as center. One can make the claim that Bonaventure's Christocentricity, whereby Christ functions as beginning, middle and end of the journey to God, distinguishes him from the classical Neoplatonic ascent which is an intellectual ascent rooted in philosophy and theology. Daniel points out that nei-

ther the Pseudo-Dionysius nor Augustine, both of whom influenced
Bonaventure, focused their quest on the Crucified Christ but on the
idea that truth is found only by going beyond vestiges of the sensible
world to the intelligible one.[48]

It is clear that Bonaventure distinguished his epistemology from
Greek metaphysics. In his sermon, "Christ, the One Teacher of All,"
he illuminates Christ as the center of knowledge; indeed, a center of
perfect truth and knowledge that overcomes the deficiencies in the
doctrines of Plato and Aristotle. In his lectures on the *Hexaëmeron*
he attacks the tenets of Aritotelianism that divorce the created world
from the Creator and undermine the capacity of the human soul created in the image of God. The Seraphic Doctor maintains that a
Christian theologian cannot accept Greek metaphysics (or the Old
Testament) in an uncritical way for every form of philosophical metaphysics must stand open to correction and completion in the New
Testament.[49] However, he upholds the work of philosophy which is to
know the one divine essence as the exemplary cause of finite reality.
Only in light of exemplarity will the deepest nature of created reality be unlocked.

Zachary Hayes, in an insightful study on Christology and metaphysics in Bonaventure,[50] provides a basis for arguing that
Bonaventure forms a distinct Franciscan world view because he formulates a new metaphysics, a theological metaphysics, grounded in
Christ the center. Metaphysics is the branch of philosophy that
examines the structure of created reality. The word itself is a combination of the prefix, *meta*, meaning going beyond or transcending,
and the Greek, *physis*, or nature. Metaphysics, therefore, is concerned
with understanding the structure or foundation of universal reality
based on principles that govern particulars. Because this reality
forms our view of the world, that is, our relation to God, creation
and neighbor, metaphysics is essential to shaping our world view.
Bonaventure establishes a theological metaphysics in the *Hexaëmeron*
when he states:

> A beginning should be made from the center, that is, from
> Christ. . . . Although the metaphysician is able to rise from the
> consideration of created and particular susbstances to that of
> the universal and uncreated and to the very notion of being, so

that he reaches the ideas of beginning, center and final end, yet he does not attain the notions of Father, Son, and Holy Spirit. For the metaphysican rises to the notion of this being by seeing it in the light of the original principle of all things and in this he meets physical science that studies the origin of things. He also rises to the notion of this being in the light of the final end, and in this he meets moral philosophy or ethics, which leads all things back to the one Supreme Good as to the final end by considering either practical or speculative happiness. But when he considers this being in the light of that principle which is the exemplary principle of all things, he meets no other science, but is a true metaphysician. For from all eternity the Father begets a Son similar to himself and expresses himself and a likeness similar to himself, and in doing so he expresses the sum total of his potency; he expresses what he can do, and what he wills to do, and he expresses everything in him, that is, in the Son or in that very center.[51]

Here the metaphysical question, that is, the basis of created reality, coincides with the Christological question in that the problem of exemplarity which is focused in metaphysics at the philosophical level is related to the exemplarity of the Word incarnate in Jesus Christ at the theological level. Whereas in Neoplatonism there is no link between the absolute realm of expression (ideas) and the created world, Bonaventure maintains that Christ, the Word uncreated and incarnate, is the total expression of God, and thus, the archetype in whom all the ideals are expressed. As the divine art of the Father, the Word expresses the Father and the things made through him, and he is foremost in leading us to the unity of the Father who brings all things together. "For this reason he is the tree of life, because through this center we return and are given life in the fountain of life . . . this is the metaphysical center that leads back and this is the sum total of our metaphysics: emanation, exemplarity, and consummation, to be illumined by spiritual rays and to return to the Most High."[52]

Since the uncreated Word is the ontological condition, the source and origin for the existence of finite reality, and since the same Word as incarnate brings the world to its redemptive completion, it is in the incarnate Word that the truth of reason and faith are unified and

lead back to God. Thus, Bonaventure begins with the center of reality which is Christ. With this center we come to know how all things
come forth into being and how they are brought to completion. The
Word that lies at the center of the divine life is the ontological basis
for all that is other than the Father. The relation between the Word
and Father is the first and primal relation and the basis of all other
relations. If it is true that the triune God creates after his image, the
Word, then it follows that whatever created reality exists possesses in
its inner constitution a relation to this uncreated Word. Moreover,
since the Word is the expression of the inner trinitarian structure of
God, that which is created is an expression of the Word and bears an
imprint of the Trinity itself.

Whereas the philosopher seeks the exemplary cause in the one
divine essence, Bonaventure maintains that the theologian comes to
know this cause as the person of the Word, the center of the divine
life and the exemplar in whom the whole trintarian structure of
divine nature expresses itself as exemplar of all finite reality.
Through the mystery of the Word and its capacity to express God,
Bonaventure transforms the Neoplatonic ideal into a Christocentric
ideal, achieving a synthesis of Francis' Christ-centered visionary
mysticism and Christian Neoplatonism. As Ewert Cousins states,
Bonaventure "Franciscanizes Neoplatonism."[53] Denys Turner, in his
book, *The Darkness of God*, remarks that "the Neoplatonism of the
Itinerarium is resolved into the historically concrete fact of the cross
so that the significance of that uniquely individual fact can be
opened up into its universal dimensions by the Neoplatonism."[54]
Unlike the Neoplatonic ascent, Bonaventure's *Itinerarium* is not
strictly intellectual but a progressive dialectic of intellect and love.
As Turner states, "the intellect is engaged in perfect unity with love
through every stage of the ascent into God, except when it passes
into the final *excessus* into which only love can proceed."[55] Turner distinguishes Bonaventure's ascent from that of the Pseudo-Dionysius
by saying: "When Denys says that in the apophatic ecstasy, 'all intellectual activities must be relinquished' he means that intellect is
transported *as intellect* beyond what it can do by itself into its own
dazzling darkness; whereas Bonaventure can quote this same passage
and mean: love *takes over from intellect*, leaving it behind."[56]

Turner's insight further enables us to distinguish Bonaventure's metaphysics from Neoplatonism. Whereas Neoplatonism is based on the pursuit of truth, Bonaventure sees that truth and knowledge are grounded in Christ in whom the ground of being is the ground of knowing. In Christ, the Word is historicized with such explicitness that from that point on light is shed on all reality. Christ is the Alpha and Omega, the one through whom all things are made and the means by which all things return to God. Hayes states that in the final analysis there is but one metaphysics and that is the one for which the Christ mystery becomes paradigmatic for our understanding of all reality. The search for intelligibility of the created order coincides with the christological mystery.[57]

To say that Bonaventure transforms Neoplatonism into an incarnational metaphysics, however, is only the beginning of what lies at the heart of his theological enterprise, that is, a metaphysics of the good or a metaphysics of love. While knowledge holds its place in Bonaventure's doctrine, the metaphysical level of consummation by which all things return to God is not based on knowledge but on love. A full scale philosophical treatment of Bonaventure's metaphysics of the good is certainly merited but not within the context of the present work. Here I will simply touch upon his metaphysics of the good as I see it related to his mysticism of the Crucified Christ.

As we have already mentioned, Bonaventure's theology of the Word enabled him to formulate a metaphysics in which God, the absolute One, is intimately united to the created world through the Word incarnate, Jesus Christ. Indeed, his metaphysics is Christocentric because all reality is based on the same source, namely, the Word of God. For Bonaventure, the ontological basis of all relationships is the relationship of the Word and the Father which is grounded in the self-diffusive goodness of the Father by which the Word is eternally generated. It is in this respect that his last three chapters of the *Itinerarium* become crucial in the unfolding of his metaphysics of the good which culminates in the absolute center of the Crucified Christ. In chapter five, Bonaventure contemplates the divine unity through its primary name which is being (*ens/esse*). His argument is essentially the Anselmian argument of being: "God is that than which no greater can be thought." God "exists" because it

is more perfect to be than not to be. Although God is "called primary being," Bonaventure views this not as the ultimate of that which
God is but the beginning of the mystery of God. As he states, "you
have something here to *lift you up*,"[58] that is, to take you beyond God
as primary being. Through a series of coincidence of opposites that
characterize God (first/last; eternal/present; simple/greatest;
actual/unchangeable; perfect/immense; one/all-inclusive; last/first;
beginning/consummation; Alpha/Omega; present/eternal)[59] Bonaventure leads us into the mystery of God, the mystery that God is
"all-inclusive not as the essence of all things but as the supremely
excellent and most universal and most sufficient cause of all
essences."[60] Bonaventure perceives that the mark of God's greatness
is that God is "supremely one and all-inclusive and therefore all in
all."[61] He, therefore, lifts God out of any limitations of "being" by
identifying God as the "one and all-inclusive" which, in essence,
includes being itself. In a similar manner, the Pseudo-Dionysius
writes:

> Given that the Good transcends everything, as indeed it
> does, its nature, unconfined by form, is the creator of all form.
> In it is nonbeing really an excess of being. It is not *a* life, but is,
> rather, superabundant life. It is not *a* mind, but is superabun-
> dant Wisdom. Whatever partakes of the Good partakes of
> what preeminently gives form to the formless. And one might
> even say that nonbeing itself longs for the Good which is above
> being.[62]

Bonaventure was undoubtedly influenced by the Pseudo-
Dionysius for whom Good is the primary name of God (*Itin.* 5, 2).
The Pseudo-Dionysius posits that God is the principle of beings
from whom all beings including all being itself issue. As the Pseudo-
Dionysius indicates: "The first gift therefore of the absolutely transcendent Goodness is the gift of being, and that Goodness is praised
from those that first and principally have a share of being. From it
and in it are Being itself, the source of beings, all beings and whatever else has a portion of existence."[63] God gives being to beings only
because he precedes not only all beings, but also the gift that allows
them to be. In this way the preeminence of Being over beings itself

refers to the precedence of gift over Being, hence finally of the one who delivers the gift over Being.[64]

The idea that goodness precedes being may be a difficult concept to understand but it is a powerful one, and one that can significantly influence our understanding of God as Trinity. Because God is often conceptualized as Being, we envision the persons of the Trinity in "human" form. But to speak of the good as the preeminence of being is to preclude any anthropomorphic image of God. The Father, therefore, is not a patriarchical figure of any sort but *absolute transcendent goodness.* The divine person who is without origin is the infinite source of the self-diffusive good. While this may impart an impersonal perception of the first person of the Trinity, it renders, paradoxically, the first person, the Father, as most personal because the good that is infinite, transcendent and self-diffusive, shares itself completely with an Other which, in the eternal life of the Trinity, is the Son. Thus, within the Trinity, the absolute good, the Father, as the origin of the Son and Spirit, precedes eternal being so that the nature of God's being is God's goodness. Using more technical language, the Postmodernist philosopher, Jean Luc Marion, states:

> Being is only uncovered in being dispensed by a gift; the gift, which Being itself thus requires, is accomplished only in allowing the disclosures in it of the gesture of a giving as much imprescriptable as indescribable, which receives the name, in praise, of goodness. The ultimate nomination recedes from Being to goodness, whose denomination opens a properly unconditional field to the Requisite, over all and even over nothing: 'for the divine denomination of the good manifests all the procession of the Requisite of all things, and extends as much to beings as to nonbeings.'[65]

According to Marion, being is the gift of God's goodness and since all of created reality flows out of the divine good, that which gives rise to all reality and sustains it is divine goodness; thus, creation is truly gift. This idea illuminates Bonaventure's metaphysics of the good in relation to the Crucified Christ.

Clearly, Bonaventure not only adapts the Pseudo-Dionysian con-

cept of the absolute Good but he explicates the good as the very
dynamic of the Trinity. He goes beyond the Pseudo-Dionysius by
grounding the good not simply in the incomprehensible One
(Pseudo-Dionysius' God) but in the triune God who is communicative and self-expressive. The good, as he indicates in the sixth chapter of the *Itinerarium*, is self-diffusive and, therefore, by nature gives
itself away. For Bonaventure, the self-diffusive good underscores the
all-inclusiveness and oneness of God and, thus, all reality since, by its
very nature, the good cannot be self-contained but overflows into
one other than the source of the good itself. In the eternal life of the
Trinity, this dynamic of the good gives rise to the three-divine persons, indicating that the good necessitates the highest communicability by its very nature. Bonaventure states that the nature of God as
good means that the "one diffusing communicates to the other his
entire substance and nature."⁶⁶ This nature of the good underscores a
Trinity of eternal love whose immensity of divine goodness is such
that no greater good can be thought. The Seraphic Doctor writes,
"the purity of goodness is the pure act of a principle loving in charity with a love that is both free and due and a mixture of both."⁶⁷ If
the highest form of the good is love, then God ultimately loves
before being. God loves "by way of the Word in which all things are
said, and by way of the Gift, in which other gifts are given."⁶⁸ God,
therefore, *is* love and expresses himself in Word and gives himself as
Gift. As Marion states, "God gives himself to be known insofar as he
gives himself-according to the horizon of the gift itself. The gift constitutes at once the mode and the body of his revelation. In the end
the gift gives only itself, but in this way it gives absolutely everything."⁶⁹

Bonaventure elucidates the preeminence of goodness over being
by linking the self-diffusive good of the Trinity to the mystery of
Christ Crucified. In chapter six of the *Itinerarium* he states that if
you contemplate the highest communicability of the good as a
Trinity of Father, Son and Holy Spirit, "do not think you have comprehended the incomprehensible."⁷⁰ The divine persons are distinguished by their properties and plurality of hypostases but are one in
substance and in "essence, form, dignity, eternity, existence and
unlimitedness."⁷¹ If you are amazed, he states, at this self-diffusing

good which gives rise to the Trinity of persons distinguished by their personal properties yet one in susbtance, you will be further amazed to discover that the highest good which gives itself totally is the mystery of Jesus Christ, the Crucified Christ, symbolized by the Mercy Seat.[72] For in him is joined "the first principle with the last; God with man; eternal with temporal; most simple with the most composite; most perfect and immense with the most lowly."[73] Bonaventure, therefore, links the self-diffusive good to the coincidence of opposites in the mystery of Christ Crucified. He indicates that it is precisely because God *is* good (love) that Christ Crucified expresses the mystery of God who is love in the created world. The Father, therefore, is hidden in Christ not as the unmoved Mover or absolute being but as absolute goodness or the highest personal love. It is the Spirit who is Gift who leads us into this mystery of love.

In light of the Crucified, we can say that God's *being* is the embodiment of the self-diffusive good. Being is embodied love—an agapic love which possesses nothing for itself but rather gives itself entirely and completely to the other just as the Father eternally diffuses his entire good to the Son and Spirit. Anders Nygren describes agapic love as God's love unveiled at its deepest in the cross of Jesus Christ.[74] Bonaventure seems to make no distinction between *agape* and *eros* since God's desire for us is his compassionate love revealed in the cross. As the good longs to give itself to another, so God longs to give himself to us as beloved. Bonaventure, therefore, indicates that there is no greater good than the God who gives himself completely as love in the person of Jesus Crucified. Agapic love is the foundation of all created reality. If we understand Bonaventure in light of Marion, we can say that creation is truly loved into being. By linking the good to the coincidence of opposites in the mystery of Jesus Crucified, Bonaventure illuminates an authentic Christian metaphysics of love with the Crucified Christ as center.

In light of this we can say that the consummation of the human person and of all created reality is not participation in absolute being but in absolute good or love. This idea underscores Bonaventure's Christ mysticism with the Crucified Christ as center. Since God's life is his love, then to attain the fullness of life is to participate in the love that is God which, according to Bonaventure, is manifested

in the Crucified Christ. To be united to Christ Crucified is to participate in the good; it means to be dynamic and self-expressive as God
is expressed in the overflowing love of the Crucified. It refers to the
way the human person can share in or possess the life of God. In
union with Christ Crucified, God inter-penetrates one's being and
imparts a dynamic and creative presence that opens one to infinite
possibilities, to be creative and to transcend onself. It is goodness
itself that provides the metaphysical basis for participating in the
dynamic life of the Trinity. The human person must be diffusive in
goodness as his or her creation is diffusive, for this is what it is to be
and no real *telos* is achieved in its absence. To be God-like is to join in
the intense generosity of goodness itself, a generosity that paradoxically grounds intimacy in diversity.

The view that emanation of the good takes place principally for
the sake of a deep and personal relationship of love lies at the heart
of Bonaventure's Christ mysticism. In union with Christ Crucified,
one is brought into union with the Father and the Spirit and, at the
same time, into union with one's neighbor and the created world.
The spirit of compassionate love that draws one upward into God
also draws one outward to humanity and creation. Francis is the
exemplary Christ mystic who arrived at the perfect contemplation of
God in union with Christ. In the life of Francis, the self-diffusing
goodness of God became perfectly and clearly manifested not only
in his conformity to Christ but in his relation to his neighbor and to
creation. In the *Legenda Major* Bonaventure writes that Francis was
drawn "up to God through devotion, transformed into Christ
through compassion, attracted to his neighbor through condenscen-
sion and returned to the state of original innocence through universal reconciliation with everything."[75] By joining himself to Christ
Crucified through the spirit of burning love, Francis became united
to the one who is the center of all creation. In light of Francis,
Bonaventure signifies that conformity to Christ Crucified leads one
into God and into the world created by God. This two-fold movement toward God and creation is an ever-deepening of divine love in
union with Christ. It is a growth in love by which the human person
attains the fullest realization of creative goodness, becoming diffusive in love as God's love diffuses in the suffering of the cross. Only

when each person is conformed to the Crucified Christ, Bonaventure affirms, will the entire created order, permeated with divine love, attain its fullness of life in God.

5

Conformity to Christ

Having briefly explored Bonaventure's metaphysics of the good, we can now try to clarify the meaning of the divine good in regard to his Christ mysticism. Since, as we have seen, the metaphysics of the good underscores the involvement of God in the created world as personal love, we can begin to understand Bonaventure's Christ mysticism as a mysticism of love. The Seraphic Doctor elucidates his Christ mysticism on two levels: the level of the individual journey to God, and the level of cosmic Christocentricity. In this chapter we will examine the journey to God as a development of love in relationship to Christ. In the following chapter, the mystery of Christ as cosmic center will be elucidated, and the synthesis of these discussions will culminate in the final chapter on Bonaventure's world view.

To begin to probe into Bonaventure's doctrine of Christ mysticism, it is necessary to bring to light the model of Francis who, as the exemplary Christ mystic, leads us into Bonaventure's world view. E. R. Daniel claims that the *Legenda Major*, Bonaventure's major life of Francis, should be read as a commentary on Bonaventure's *Itinerarium* since it was composed shortly after the *Itinerarium* in 1261. This means that the journey into God as described in the *Itinerarium* is not entirely an inward spiritual process but one that encompasses the whole person. As Daniel writes:

> The later work shows that in composing it, Bonaventure
> kept the earlier one in mind. The *Legenda* portrays Francis as a

mystic whose spiritual quest was focused totally on Christ, especially but not exclusively on the passion. In this work Bonaventure drew a clear portrait of Francis as the exemplar, as the model of the quest for God. . . . In the *Legenda* Francis functions clearly as an exemplar of Christ mysticism. If the *Legenda* is the key to understanding the *Itinerarium*, then the earlier treatise must be understood as fundamentally expounding Christ mysticism also.[1]

The Christ mysticism that predominates in both the *Itinerarium* and the *Legenda Major* allows us to explore an important area for the Seraphic Doctor, namely, the created image of the human person. In the *Itinerarium*, Bonaventure highlights the image as the interior powers of the soul which culminate in Christ the center. In the *Legenda Major* he explores the image in light of Francis, the Christ mystic, and his journey to union with God. In the latter, he writes that Francis was restored as true image in Christ through his conformity to Christ Crucified. Bonaventure views union with Christ as the power of the Spirit that both impresses and expresses. The burning love of the Spirit, the love of *excessus*, is expressed in the Crucified Christ and impressed in the soul purified, illumined and perfected according to Christ. In describing the Stigmata, he states that Francis was both "inwardly inflamed and outwardly marked," indicating that Francis was both impressed by the burning love of the Spirit and expressed this love in his own flesh. The notion of impression-expression links the concept of image with that of union. We are images of God, according to Bonaventure, in that we are images of the Son. To be in union with Christ means to be inflamed with the burning love of the Spirit and this love is both impressive and expressive, rendering one a true image of Christ. This is how Bonaventure describes Francis after the Stigmata:

> When the true love of Christ had transformed his lover into his image. . . the angelic man Francis came down from the mountain bearing with him the image of the Crucified . . . engraved in the members of his body by the finger of the living God.[2]

In light of Francis, Bonaventure indicates that to be a true image of Christ is to be conformed to him in body and spirit; it is to be empowered by the Spirit. We are not only ordered to the Son who is the perfect image of the Father but we are ordered to the Son as the incarnate Word who remains the perfect image of the Father and exemplar. Thus, we are ordered to him in body and spirit. The model of Francis shows that in the soul's journey to God, the body is not divorced from the soul's ascent even at the height of mystical union. Since it is the *stigmatized* Francis who is conformed to *Christ Crucified*, the role of the body in union with God is essential. Bonaventure's doctrine of image as that which involves bodily expression corresponds to his theology of the Word as image and exemplar.

I would like to clarify what I mean by saying that mystical union involves body and soul. In the state of innocence, when the image was not distant but conformed to God through grace, the book of creation sufficed to enable the human person to perceive the light of divine wisdom.[3] In the *Breviloquium* Bonaventure states that the whole person, created by God, was placed in paradise,[4] an idea reiterated in the first chapter of the *Itinerarium*: "In the initial state of creation, the human person was made fit for the quiet of contemplation."[5] Bonaventure's doctrine of creation before the fall holds up two principal ideas: the first human was made fit for the contemplation of God, and contemplation involved the whole person, body and soul. Like Hugh of St. Victor, he speaks of a threefold vision: the eye of the flesh, of reason and of contemplation.[6] Through the eye of the flesh, the human could see things outside in creation; with the eye of reason, the things within; with the eye of contemplation, the things above.[7] The first Adam did not perceive the essence of God but enjoyed an intellectual type of contemplation in that the book of creation was read as the book of wisdom and her works.[8]

The true nature of human existence, according to the Seraphic Doctor, is not an isolated spirit-soul, but a body-soul relationship. As a union of matter and spirit, the human person is the perfection of the created order because s/he reveals God's power, wisdom and goodness.[9] He indicates that creation, in order to possess perfection and manifest the Creator, must have three characteristics: greatness of extension, a sufficient order and the influence of goodness.[10] For the Seraphic Doctor, this threefold perfection is found in the human person in whom is united the threefold structure of matter, spirit and the union of these.[11] God's power is revealed because the material nature of the human person which is close to nothingness and the spiritual nature which is close to God are united in a single nature and person. His wisdom is revealed because God governs in an orderly fashion. The highest part of the human person, the soul, he rules directly by illumination while the lowest part, the body, he rules through the human's free will. He assigns a certain superiority to the soul in that it is not subject to any physical power.[12] However, he insists that the soul is given its nobility by the body and that the human body is fitted to receive the noble form of the soul.[13] Thus the body and all its functions are subject to the spirit, while the spirit is subject to God.[14] God's goodness is manifested because goodness requires a giver, a receiver and the act of communication which takes place in the union of body and soul.[15] The Trinity, therefore, manifested by the principles of power, wisdom and goodness, is revealed in the human person who unites in a single person the spiritual and material worlds.

Creation by God, according to Bonaventure, establishes the rational spirit in the proximity of God and makes it capable of receiving God. From the outset, there is a "proportion" between body and soul. This proportion unites in the human person "natures which are the furthest distance from each other."[16] When God created the body, he joined it to the soul; he united the two in a natural and mutual relationship, but assigned the government of the body to the soul, so that the soul should incline to the body and govern it for the sake of acquiring merit.[17] Because a spiritual soul must demand the highest from its instrument the body, the human body possesses the "greatest variety of organs endowed with the greatest beauty and skill and manageableness."[18] Thus the human body possesses the noblest constitution and organization that exists in nature, and therefore it finds its complementary fulfillment only in the noblest form or nature which is the soul.[19] The joy of beatitude, he states, will be the perfect reunion of soul and body; this will be the mark of peace.[20] Bonaventure maintains that the soul cannot be fully happy unless the body is returned to it, for the two have a natural ordination to each other: "Just as the soul, by reason of the body and to gain merit, now lives on earth, so will the body, by reason of the soul and to gain reward, some day live in heaven."[21] The body of eternal life, according to Bonaventure, will be "perfectly obedient and spiritual; a body of such quality that it shall be for you a help in contemplation and a cause of greater bliss."[22] The mark of eternal life, therefore, is the contemplation of God which is made possible and perfect by the union of soul and body. Indeed, the purpose of the body is to aid contemplation. Describing the state of eternal beatitude, he states: "Certainly, the soul would never desire to be united to a new body, if this body, glorious as it may be, were to hinder divine contemplation."[23]

The notion of contemplation, as one involving soul and body, is fundamental to Bonaventure's Christ mysticism. In his sermons, the Seraphic Doctor highlights the fact that the Word of God entered into union with the flesh to ennoble our nature[24] by creating the object of contemplation necessary for the beatification of our nature.[25] The object of contemplation is Christ, God and man, who assumed human nature for the salvation of both spirit and flesh: "And in my flesh I shall see God" (Jb 19:26). For Bonaventure, the humanity of Christ is essential to the contemplation of God, not simply at the lower stages of contemplation but even at the highest stage of mystical union.[26] True contemplation, he suggests, can take place only when the body and spirit are brought into proper relationship. In his second "Sermon on the Nativity," he claims that divine wisdom, which orders all things, came in the flesh when he saw that order in the world had been corrupted. In Christ, wisdom subjected the flesh to the spirit.[27] The ordering of the flesh to the spirit does not render the flesh a negative principle, one that imprisons the soul as Plato held.[28] Conversely, the assumption of the flesh by the Word is precisely for the salvation of both spirit and flesh: "All flesh shall see the salvation of God" (Lk 3:6).

The Seraphic Doctor describes Christ as master of contemplative knowledge because he teaches by word and example. Christ teaches both interiorly and exteriorly, so that one may go in to his divinity and find pasture and go out to his humanity and find pasture. This twofold movement of "going-in" and "going-out" means that contemplation is both interior and exterior, in the spirit and in the flesh. In his sermon on "Christ the One Teacher" Bonaventure states:

> The human person has two senses; the one interior and the other exterior. Each of these has its own good in which it delights; the interior sense in the contemplation of the divinity, and the exterior sense in the contemplation of the humanity. He will go in to the Word and find pasture in the contemplation of his divinity; and he will go out to the flesh and find pasture in the contemplation of his humanity. For this reason, God became man in order to beatify the whole person in himself.[29]

That Christ became human to beatify the whole human person signifies that in the ascent to God the whole person must enter into union with the whole Christ. As the interior teacher, Christ is the true light of knowledge. He teaches exteriorly as the perfect image and archetype because he is the foundation for every creaturely attitude before God. True knowledge, therefore, is not only by way of intellect but also by way of example. This twofold movement of contemplation, interior and exterior, both restores and completes created reality.[30]

The notion of Christ as the divine-temporal exemplar who teaches by word and example corresponds to the renewal of the human image. What gives form to the image is the content or inner spirit whereas the image itself is an expressed likeness, that is, the spirit expressed in the flesh. When considered in light of the stigmatized Francis we see that the expression and impression of God's Word are inseparable—the intratrinitarian outpouring of love appears simultaneously with its concrete imprint on the life of the saint.[31] The life of Francis shows that the soul's journey to God is made by being conformed to Christ interiorly and exteriorly. In union with Christ, the soul and body are brought into harmonious union and this is the basis of contemplation in earthly life and in eternity.

The *Lignum Vitae* (Tree of Life)

Understanding the role of soul and body with regard to image and expression helps us appreciate Bonaventure's spiritual classic the *Lignum vitae* composed shortly after the *Itinerarium*. The work belongs to the genre of the *vitae Christi* tradition characterized by the gospel harmony, a type of meditation that was popular in the thirteenth century in which, through use of the senses and imagination, one could envision the course of Christ's earthly life and achieve a type of imitation of Christ that would lead to penance and conversion. The *Lignum vitae* has been interpreted as a pious work that underscores moral conversion; yet, we can appreciate it as a companion to the *Itinerarium* when we consider mystical union not simply as a flight of the soul to God but one that has bodily expression.

Denise Depres has identified the *Lignum vitae* as part of a visionary trend in late-medieval piety, emphasizing fellowship with Christ and individual participation in the events of Christ's life.[32] The new meditative and literary style of the gospel harmony encouraged the believer not only to envision the course of Christ's life but also to consider simultaneously one's own spiritual role in the historical scheme of salvation.[33] The purpose of such literature, according to Depres, was to transform the ideal of spiritual perfection, through penance and a heightening of religious sensibilities, from a vocation possible only for contemplatives to a life of charity possible for all Christians in differing degrees.

Bonaventure's *Lignum vitae* is a gospel harmony whereby he amalgamates the four Gospels without losing the flow of the life of Christ.[34] George Marcil states that the *Lignum vitae* represents a new departure in the trend in spirituality stressing the imitation of Christ.[35] John Fleming states that the poetical and lyrical style which is characteristic of the *Lignum vitae* stimulated an artistic movement that eventually spread Franciscan devotional elements throughout Europe.[36] Similarly, Sandro Sticca claims that Bonaventure's devotional writings constituted a homiletic trend toward pietism and human realism[37] with an emphasis on Christ's earthly life and sufferings. Bonaventure, he writes, is typical of the new *zeitgeist* of late medieval piety that looked less at Christ in his complete work and more at Christ incarnate, in his earthly suffering.[38]

The structure of the *Lignum vitae* as a whole underscores Bonaventure's metaphysics of emanation, exemplarity and return.[39] The purpose of the work is to lead one back to God because Jesus is "the end of all happiness" and no one reaches this state except by union with him.[40] In the first chapter of the *Lignum vitae* he writes: "When you hear that Jesus is begotten of God, beware lest some inadequate thought of the flesh appear before your mind's eye. . . . From that Eternal Light which is at the same time measureless and most simple, most brilliant and most hidden, there emerges a coeternal, coequal and consubstantial splendor, who is the power and wisdom of the Father."[41] The Seraphic Doctor clearly warns against any type of carnal love of Christ that excludes his divinity but rather maintains that Christ is truly God; the purpose of the meditations on the tree of life is to return to God.

The *Lignum vitae* is, in a sense, the practical guidebook on how to make the journey to God whereby one becomes, like the stigmatized Francis, conformed to Christ in body and spirit. As he writes in the prologue of the *Lignum vitae*:

> The true worshipper of God and disciple of Christ, who desires to conform perfectly to the Savior of all people crucified for him, should, above all, strive with an earnest endeavor of soul to carry about continuously, both in the body and soul and in the flesh, the cross of Christ.[42]

The concept of image as conformity to Christ in body and spirit underlines the meditations of the *Lignum vitae*. By kindling the affections and shaping the intellect, memory and will to Christ, one is to become an image of Christ. Conformity to Christ leads to union with God.

In the *Lignum vitae* Bonaventure fashions brief but vivid iconographic representations of Christ's life as the focal points of meditation. The narrative sections in the text, analogous to "compositions" in meditative lyrics, precede emotional responses to the scenes that are transformed into a series of prayers ending with a petition. The structure of the meditations is significant for each is composed of two parts: one part describes the earthly life of Christ and the other part points to the nature of Christ as true God. In describing the crucifixion, for example, he writes: "See now, my soul, how he who is God blessed above all things is totally submerged in the waters of suffering."[43] Although his purpose in combining meditation with sequential narrative is affective, the affections are directed toward God and not toward a carnal love of Christ. By emphasizing the common fabric of Christ's life, through concrete detailed description, he establishes a bond between the believer and God. Describing the child in the manger, for example, he writes: "Now then, my soul, embrace that divine manger; press your lips upon and kiss the boy's feet."[44]

Through highly descriptive compositions, Bonaventure urges the meditator to participate in the devotions like an actor or actress assuming a role in the drama. Most of the compositions conclude with a direct invocation to the reader to enter imaginatively into the narrative, actively responding to each scene. He asks us, for example, to accompany the three kings and become a first witness of the Epiphany: "Do not now turn away from the brilliance of that star in the east which guides you. Become a companion of the holy kings."[45] In the chapters following, he bids us to hold the infant Jesus and rejoice with Anna when Mary comes to meet her. We are to flee into Egypt with them and later help Mary seek her son, teaching in the temple. The meditations therefore mimetically reinforce the Gospel stories in their proper sequence.

The meditations of the *Lignum vitae* underscore what Ewert Cousins has termed a mysticism of the historical event. In this type of mysticism, one enters into the drama of the event as an actress or actor and, through the spiritual power of the event, attains union with God. The question that has been raised is whether or not this type of mysticism anticipates the transcendent act of mystical union or whether itself is the act of union. The question leads us back to Christ who is image, exemplar and expression. Christ the Word is the full and perfect image and expression of the Father. To be conformed to Christ in word and deed is to be shaped in the likeness of the Son and thus in union with the Father. The *act* of mystical union insofar as it is an ecstatic experience is a transcendence of the mind; yet, in no way is it separated from the flesh which, at this stage of the journey, is in such harmony with the spirit that it allows the spirit to be fully one with God. Thus, one can say that the mysticism of the historical event underscores union with God without moving beyond the humanity of Christ. As Hayes states, "The historical life of Jesus is the way for Bonaventure by which one enters more deeply into personal union with the Word that lies at the center of both created and uncreated reality."[46] Denys Turner, too, affirms that the Christ of the *Itinerarium* is not the mystical Christ.

> Bonaventure locates the *transitus*. . . not abstractly in the incarnate Christ as some generalized symbol; rather, Bonaventure locates the *transitus* in the broken, crucified Christ. . . . It is in this, the most radical conclusion of his *Itinerarium* that we find the unity of Bonaventure's Neoplatonic "exemplarism" with the almost brutal concreteness and historical specificness of his meditations on the life of Christ in the *Lignum vitae*.[47]

Thus, it is not sheer coincidence that Bonaventure concludes the *Itinerarium* with the pass over of the Crucified and begins the *Lignum vitae* by stating, "With Christ I am nailed to the cross" (Gal 2:19). It is precisely the poor humble Christ on the cross that inspires the new direction of Bonaventure's theological enterprise—the way to peace through the burning love of the Crucified.[48]

Imagination and Imitation

Bonaventure's *Lignum vitae* is similar to another medieval work, the *Meditationes vitae Christi*, the most widely disseminated Franciscan work in the Middle Ages, originally attributed to Bonaventure, but later ascribed to the Tuscan author, Johannes a Caulibus.[49] This work was translated into middle English at least seven times in the first hundred years after Bonaventure's death in 1274.[50] Although the *Meditationes* were probably written for a Poor Clare Franciscan, the work does not direct itself solely to cloistered nuns. Rather, its purpose is to transform the believer into a true image of Christ; thus it describes imitation of Christ as the path of righteous living in keeping with Franciscan spirituality. The author consistently stresses the importance of experiencing Gospel events and encourages an individual approach in visualizing Gospel scenes, invoking a type of "imaginative freedom," a freedom criticized for feeding the faithful on "glosses and pious embroideries."[51] The reader is urged to recognize that the meditations are replete with liturgical and sacramental significance.[52]

Like the *Meditationes*, the *Lignum vitae* draws on the imagination of the reader to enter into the life of Christ as true God and man. Each meditation is replete with the mystery of Christ because the flesh of Christ, Bonaventure states, is like a filtering material that hides the brilliant light of his divinity.[53] In the *Breviloquium*, he describes the role of the senses and imagination in preparing for contemplation "which starts from the senses, reaches the imagination, proceeds from the imagination to reason, from reason to the intellect, from the intellect to understanding, and from understanding to wisdom, that ecstatical knowledge which begins in this life to reach fulfillment in eternal glory."[54] Imagination is the aid to understanding which in turn informs the memory and will and helps them turn toward God.[55] The significant aspect of Bonaventure's scheme from imagination to contemplation is that the whole ladder of successive steps is contained in Christ. The imagination is directed to the humanity of Christ to enable one to enter the mystery of Christ as true God. Through his humanity, Bonaventure indicates, the Son of God is set up on earth. Although Christ is ascended and glorified, his flesh, though transformed, remains in union with us. Thus, it is only by descending with Christ that one can ascend to God.[56]

For Bonaventure, Francis is the perfect imitator of Christ who, because of his conformity to Christ, reached the heights of contemplation. Francis, he claims, "was totally obedient to the Lord's command: Go up after me by following me literally."[57] Through imitation "he was made utterly Christlike and configured to the Crucified."[58] He "ascended in Christ" by descending in poverty and humility through imitation of the suffering humanity of Christ, and his imitation of Christ led him to the heights of contemplation and glory:

> The Lord said to him: Go up because of me whom you shall contemplate at last and in that you will be glorified. We read in the Song of Solomon: *I will climb the palm tree and lay hold of its branches.* The palm tree has a trunk whose lower part is very narrow. The section nearest the ground is thinner than the higher section of the trunk which is not the case with any

other tree. The palm tree is a figure of Jesus Christ, who in his
humanity was made a little less than the angels, and was small
and weak in this world, and in his divinity is Lord and Creator
of the angels and of all things.[59]

Bonaventure affirms that the humanity of Christ is our "link" to
God because he hides within himself the splendor of the divinity.[60]
Christ is the tree of life and the one who, like Francis, is configured
to him in his earthly life, partakes of the fruit of the tree which consists in "the vision, possession, and enjoyment of God."[61] Since this
fruit is the height of contemplation, the example of Francis and his
imitation of Christ show that the humanity of Christ is essential for
the one who desires to attain to God.

The Exemplarity of Poverty and Humility

For Bonaventure, the imitation of Christ is grounded in his
teaching on divine exemplarism.[62] This teaching focuses on the Son
of God who, as the Word, proceeds from the Father by reason of
exemplarity.[63] Since the Son, the Word, is the perfect expression of
the Father, he is the similitude, or exemplar, of the Father.[64] He is also
the exemplar of creation for all things were created through him and
are called to return to the Father with him.[65] As the uncreated Word,
the Son is the eternal exemplar of the Father.[66] All creatures derive
their perfection from the eternal exemplar according to their participation in the goodness of God and shine forth in the mirror of the
uncreated Word.

As the incarnate Word, the Son is the temporal exemplar and
mirror of all graces, virtues and merits. While every action of Christ
offers an insight into the way of salvation, not every one is meant to
be imitated.[67] Bonaventure clearly distinguishes between those
actions of Christ that are to be imitated and those that are not.[68] He
states that imperfect acts directed toward the weak do not always
have to be imitated and in some circumstances it is better not to imitate them.[69] On the other hand, no restrictions are placed on the imitation of those actions of Christ which directly concern the perfection of life. Christ demonstrated these actions by: ". . . observing
poverty, maintaining virginity, subjecting himself to God and

human beings, spending watchful nights in prayer, interceding for those crucifying him and offering himself to death out of the highest love even for his enemies."[70] Prayer clearly holds a prominent place among the actions of Christ pertaining directly to the perfection of life. All are called to reflect on the perfection of Christ by conforming themselves to this essential aspect of his life.[71]

Bonaventure exhorts all Christians to imitate Christ, for only by imitating Christ does one enter into the mystery of the one who is both divine and human. The two characteristics of Christ's life that Bonaventure consistently emphasizes are those of poverty and humility. The imitation of Christ must essentially be a conformity to Christ who was poor and humble. For Bonaventure, poverty and humility are not simply accidental qualities of the earthly life of Jesus; rather, they express the very nature of God hidden in the earthly life of Christ. Poverty is the foundation of the imitation of Christ since the very manner of Christ's entry into this world reveals, in a concrete way, the self-emptying of God and calls us to imitate him. Bonaventure sees in poverty the renewal of the innocence and freedom of paradise. The mystery of poverty is the *re-creatio* where one can stand before God without demands. He states that the poor, naked, crucified Christ penetrated the heart of Francis because he grasped the meaning of poverty as the means of uniting himself with Christ on the cross. In light of Francis, Bonaventure claims that poverty returns one to original innocence because it is fulfillment of the new law which does not promise temporal goods but love. Just as the Stigmata of Francis became the perfect sign and symbol of union with God, those who imitate his example through absolute poverty share in the life of God. In his *Legenda Major* Bonaventure states, "In all things he wished to be conformed to Christ crucified who hung on the cross poor, suffering and naked."[72] By turning to God through the Crucified, Francis came to appreciate his absolute dependence on God.

It is interesting that Bonaventure begins the *Itinerarium* by stating, "Here begins the speculation of the poor man in the desert." As Wayne Hellman notes, when one asks the question, "Who am I?" one begins the life of poverty because one articulates dependency on another for the very fact of existence.[73] To be in the desert means that we are created *ex nihilo*. Human poverty is rooted in existence as creature; it means radical dependency. In this way, poverty means receptivity—God fills one's emptiness. Humanity is ontologically rooted in poverty, Bonaventure claims, because it is created by God and thus is essentially dependent on God.[74] Yet, the first sin of humankind was to possess rather than accept the poverty of created-ness. The sin of humanity was a sin directed against the Son.[75] By presuming itself equal to God, humanity presumed itself equal to the Son who alone is the perfect image of the Father, possessing all that is of God and therefore equal to him. It is this same Son, then, who accepts the poverty of the human condition to show that equali-ty with God is not something to be grasped at. On the cross, God himself becomes poor. Poverty becomes manifest in the historical career of Jesus and is expressed in the naked figure on the Cross who invites us to follow him, placing our absolute trust in God alone. Poverty is grounded metaphysically in our total dependence in being.

For the Seraphic Doctor, the life of Jesus in its concrete form of poverty is a manifestation of the humility of God. The dereliction of the cross is the intense revelation of divine humility and the piercing of the human heart of Christ is the opening to humanity of the depth of divine love embodied in the love of the incarnate Son. He views the humility of Christ as a fundamental divine mystery: "The depth of God-made-man, that is, in his humility, is such that reason fails."[76] Alexander Gerken, in his study on Bonaventure's Christology, states that the humility of God is expressed concretely in the incar-nation in the humility and poverty of Christ.[77] Since Christ in his human existence externalizes the eternal mystery of sonship, the humanity of Christ is not a second word related to the inner Word, but it is precisely the form the inner Word of God takes when it is expressed externally.[78] The life of Christ in its unexpected poverty is a manifestation of the humility of God's love.[79] It is part of the essen-tial humility of the Son, precisely because he is and desires nothing else than to be the expression of the Father, that he possesses no other role than one that mediates: and therefore he continually hum-bles himself by referring all things back to the Father.[80]

In the *Lignum viate* Bonaventure refers to humility as the "root and guardian of all virtues" and the true path to salvation. Humility is part of the very nature of God and is expressed in the descent of the Word, the incarnation, whereby God "humbly bends down and lifts the lowliness of our nature into unity with his own person."[81] The mystery of God revealed in Christ is that he is at once the Most High (*altissime*) and, yet, at the same time, most intimately related to us (*piissime*). For Bonaventure, it is in the humbling of self that the height of imitation lies and this self-humbling leads to truth and the experiential knowledge of one's own reality.[82] Only the poor and humble can enter into the humble love of God.

From Meditation to Contemplation

Because Bonaventure apprehends the deep mystery of eternal sonship made visible in the poor and humble birth of Jesus, he implores us to turn our spiritual eyes and ears to contemplate Jesus as God. Imitation of Christ is closely linked with the senses. The physical senses according to Bonaventure are developed together with the spiritual senses by which the Word as God is apprehended.[83] He weaves together the physical senses and imagination as a means of enkindling the spiritual senses, inspiring faith and leading one in mature faith to the realization of God. In all things, he says, we must see and hear what God has done for us.[84] By meditating on the earthly life of Christ, our desire for God is to be kindled. In a meditation on the birth of Jesus, he asks us to actually touch the child using our imagination and senses:

> Now, then, my soul, embrace that divine manger; press your lips upon and kiss the boy's feet. Then in your mind keep the shepherd's watch, marvel at the assembling host of angels, join in the heavenly melody, singing with your voice and heart: *Glory to God in the highest and on earth peace to men of good will* (Lk 2:14).[85]

In this meditation Bonaventure draws the reader into the Christmas scene through use of the senses and imagination. Yet, at the same time, he underscores the mystery of the incarnate Word in his twofold nature as human and divine. The kiss is offered by the reader to "the boy's feet," that is, to the humanity of Christ. As God has united himself to us in the holy kiss of the incarnation, so too, we are to be united to Christ. The coming of Christ in the flesh, however, cannot be perceived unless there is a corresponding advent in the mind.[86] While Christ comes into the world as a poor and humble child, he also comes to the faithful in prayer as a penetrating light enlightening the mind. This coming of divine light illuminates the mind to spiritual truths hidden in the shadow of sin. Like a fire, it illuminates the faithful with the splendor of truth.[87] The truth that Bonaventure makes known in this meditation is that Christ is truly God. He signifies the divinity of Christ by the angels who glorify God. In the incarnation, he states, God is glorified because "in this work is shown the greatest goodness, wisdom, power and justice of God."[88] Since the goodness of God refers to the Father, the wisdom of God to the Son, and the power of God to the Holy Spirit, the incarnation manifests the entire Trinity.[89] To be united to Christ in his humanity is to be drawn into the marvel of the incarnation which reveals to us the mystery of the triune God.[90]

Although there is an advent of light in the mind with the coming of the Word in the flesh, Bonaventure claims, there is, at the same time, a coming of Christ in the spirit since it is not possible to reach a clear revelation of faith except by the coming of Christ into the rational spirit.[91] The Spirit bears witness to the truth and through the Spirit one comes to a greater likeness in Christ. Bonaventure states that in order for the spirit of a person to attain to the knowledge of faith, it is necessary that a due proportionality with respect to God be established in the spirit. This is produced through the light of faith, which is a presence of God in the soul transmitting a type of knowledge which is not abstracted but imprinted on the soul.[92] By turning oneself to Christ and entering the mystery of God in Christ through imitation and use of the senses and imagination, the glory of the Lord becomes ever the more "visible." Through the inspired Word, there is a vision of faith, and more essentially, a configuration to the image in a process that stamps an impression so that unity forms between the expression and impression through the Spirit. In this way, the person "regenerated" through imitation of Christ enters into the mystery of Christ to behold the presence of God. This is the primary purpose of the

Lignum vitae as Bonaventure indicates in his meditation on the transfiguration:

> You also, accompany him faithfully, and once regenerated in him, explore his secrets so that on the banks of the Jordan you may discern the Father in the voice, the Son in the flesh and the Holy Spirit in the dove, and when the heaven of the Trinity is opened to you, you will be taken up into God.[93]

The power of the Spirit in forming one to the likeness of Christ underscores the mysticism of the historical event. Devotion to Christ in his humanity and the nurturing of the life of the Spirit through imitation of his historical life leads one to the contemplation of God in Christ. By use of the imagination and senses and the imitation of the poor and humble Christ, the desire of the kindled heart enables the soul to ascend to the object of its love which is God. Bonaventure describes the goal of contemplation in his meditation on the transfiguration:

> So the soul devoted to Christ, strengthened in the truth and borne to the summit of virtue can faithfully say with Peter: Lord it is good for us to be here, in the serene enjoyment of contemplating you. When heavenly repose and ecstasy are given to the soul, it will hear the secret words which man is not permitted to speak.[94]

The purpose of meditation, therefore, as described in the *Lignum vitae*, is not limited to penance but is directed to the goal of contemplation. The partaking of the fruits of the tree of life is to lead one to "the joys of eternal sweetness and everlasting glory," the "vision, possession and enjoyment of God."[95] The historical life of Jesus is the way which one enters more deeply into personal union with the Word who lies at the center of both created and uncreated reality. Through conformity to Christ in body and spirit, we are restored in the image of God and, being restored, we are transformed in the love of God.

6

The Mystery of Crucified Love

Bonaventure's mysticism is intellectual but ultimately it is a love mysticism, a mysticism of relationship in union with Christ, the Word of God. It is not surprising that the new direction initiated by the *Itinerarium* focuses on relationship with the Crucified Christ, for the Crucified is the manifest love of God. The path to God revealed to Bonaventure on the mountain of La Verna is through the burning love of the Crucified. In the beginning of the *Lignum vitae* he states that the principal purpose of the work is to "enkindle in us affection"; for it is love alone that draws us into the silent mystery of God. This chapter will examine the manifestation of divine love in the mystery of Christ Crucified both in relation to the human person and to the completion of the cosmic order.

Bonaventure's doctrine of love is influenced by the medieval writer Richard of St. Victor. According to Richard, God is the highest good. Since nothing can be said to be a higher good than love, God must be the fullness of love since it is the nature of God to be the highest good.[1] Consequently, Richard argues, there must be a number of persons within the Trinity, since love involves the relation of one to another. There must be more than one person within God, otherwise the communication of love would not be possible. Moreover, the fullness of love is to be found when the love which exists between two persons is shared with a third person. The life of God, then, as the fullness of love, is the life of the unending communication of that love between three persons, Father, Son and Spirit.

Following Richard, Bonaventure is able to speak of God not only in terms of expressive goodness but also in terms of a communication of love. According to the Seraphic Doctor, love is the supreme form of good, and goodness is the preeminent attribute of God; it is the very definition of the superessential Godhead and the deepest basis for God's creative activity. Since God is good and since the good is by nature self-diffusive, it follows that God is necessarily self-communicative.[2] God is the one who communicates, who reaches out and embraces the human soul in the fullness of love. Therefore, love belongs to the very nature of God as the self-diffusive good. Bonaventure describes love as *affectus adhaesionem respectu amati*.[3] Love is a union that results from the soul's going out of itself to unite itself with another object. The Seraphic Doctor is convinced that a transformation takes place in every love and he sees the fundamental reason for this transformation in the fact of union. Following Hugh of St. Victor he states: "Love transforms because love unites."[4] By the very fact that one is united with an object, one is impelled to conform in action with the object while the union exists. It does not mean complete transformation into the beloved or that the lover loses his or her own personality, for in the metaphysical order the union of love is a purely accidental one.[5] It means rather that the lover is transformed into the likeness of the beloved and not into the beloved himself, to the extent that while one is united to the beloved she or he will be like the beloved in action, for her or his actions will be of such a kind that they will be in accord with the nature of the beloved.[6]

Recognizing love as the core of Bonaventure's doctrine enables us to understand more clearly the mystery of divine love manifested in the Crucified Christ. The journey into God, described in the *Itinerarium*, is the journey into the mystery of divine love. At the highest stage of the journey, language breaks down in the brokenness of the cross, and through a transcendence of the mind, the soul enters into the darkness, the hiddenness of the Father who is the fountain fullness of divine love. The final chapters of the *Itinerarium* constitute the originality of Bonaventure's thought, namely, the mystical presence of the triune God of love in the passion of the Crucified Christ. He illuminates the Trinity of love in the mystery of the Crucified when he writes:

> For good is said to be self-diffusive; therefore the highest
> good must be most self-diffusive . . . Therefore, unless there
> were eternally in the highest good a production which is actual
> and consubstantial . . . the Father and the Son and the Holy
> Spirit—unless these were present, it would by no means be the
> highest good because it would not diffuse itself in the highest
> degree. . . If, therefore, you can behold with your mind's eye
> the purity of goodness, which is the pure act of a principle lov-
> ing in charity with a love that is both free and due and a mix-
> ture of both, which is the fullest diffusion by way of nature and
> will, which is a diffusion by way of the Word, in which all
> things are said, and by way of the Gift, in which other gifts are
> given, then you can see that through the highest communcabili-
> ty of the good, there must be a Trinity of the Father and the
> Son and the Holy Spirit. . . . and if you are amazed because the
> divine Being is both first and last, eternal and most present. . .
> look at the Mercy Seat and wonder that in him there is joined
> the first principle with the last. . . the supreme and all-inclusive
> one with a composite individual distinct from others, that is,
> the man Jesus Christ.[7]

For Bonaventure, Christ Crucified *is* the mystery of God's
love in the world that leads us into the very heart of the mystery of
God. He links the divine outpouring of love to the poverty of the
cross. The Pseudo-Dionysian apophasis, the stripping away of all
intellectual knowledge of God, becomes the Franciscan ideal of
poverty. Mystical union with the Crucified is the highest poverty
both on the part of God who, on the cross, empties himself of divine
power and, on the part of the human person, who is purified, illumined and perfected through conformity to Christ. The poverty of
the cross is one with and identical to the mystery of ecstatic divine
love; it is *mysterium*, an overflowing of love.[8] The passion is the revelation of the heart of God in the heart of Jesus disclosing the mystery of the cross as the overflowing fountain of God's love.[9] In his
De perfectione vitae Bonaventure writes:

> No sorrow was ever comparable to Yours, O Lord Jesus
> Christ! Your blood was shed so abundantly that Your whole

body was soaked with it. Not just a drop, O good Jesus, most sweet Lord, but a welling stream of blood sprang from five parts of Your body: the hands and feet in the crucifixion, the head in the crowning of thorns, the whole body in the flagellation and the heart in the opening of Your side. Not an ounce of blood could have possible remained in Your veins.[10]

In this short meditation, Bonaventure views the passion extending beyond redemption to the completion of the world in the form of love.[11] The idea that love is the principal reason of the passion rather than redemption makes the doctrine of the absolute primacy of Christ seem original to Bonaventure. While it is in some way implicit in his doctrine of the incarnation, Bonaventure does not deny the historical circumstance of sin and, thus, maintains that satisfaction is an important reason for the incarnation, although it is not the primary reason.[12] Rather, the primary reason for the incarnation is to manifest the power, wisdom, and glory of God. Nowhere are these manifested more powerfully than in the passion, death, and resurrection of Jesus Christ.

The mystery of the cross is the mystery of poverty because here God is not possessing but fully communicating the mystery of his love in radical openness to and acceptance of humanity. The poverty of the cross corresponds to the very nature of God as love. To join with God in the poverty and suffering of the cross is to be filled with the fullness of God's love in the world. The mystery of divine love in the world is grounded in the Trinity where the Father gratuitously loves the Son who in turn loves the Father and loves with the Father in the Spirit.[13] In the passion the Son loves the Father by surrendering his entire life to the Father, and manifests the Father's love through his total self-giving. The poverty of the cross, therefore, is relational;[14] it is the bond between the giver and receiver which gives rise to the dialectic of emptiness and fullness. Bonaventure claims that love is a union that results from the soul going out of itself to unite itself with another object, and he calls us to this union through compassionate love.[15]

Bonaventure's emphasis on the highest love of God manifested in the Crucified Christ suggests that it is by way of compassionate love that God draws the soul into union. This is different from some of the monastic Fathers such as the Pseudo-Dionysius for whom union underscores ecstatic love that is essentially *eros*. *Eros* is the passionate desire to love God who is love. Rather, Bonaventure's doctrine of union highlights compassionate love that is essentially *agape*. Bernard McGinn defines *eros* (in its Platonic meaning) as "love for the good that seeks to beget the good";[16] it is the desire of union with the ineffable God. Agapic love is God's love unveiled at its deepest in the cross of Christ. It is in union with this love, in the poverty of the Crucified, that one is transformed into the depths of compassionate love.

For Bonaventure, the piercing of the human heart of Christ is the opening to humankind of the depth of divine love embodied in the love of the Son of God. It is love which joins the lover to the beloved, which unites them to one another and brings them closer, and which alone can make a soul rise above itself and turn more deeply toward another. In the *Lignum vitae* he highlights compassionate love as the transforming love between the lover and the beloved. In the *De triplici via* he defines compassion as "sharing the pains of the utterly blameless, meek, noble and loving Christ."[17] The emphasis on compassion gives rise to transformation by which the old self is destroyed and the new self recreated in Christ. Compassion draws us into the mystery of God as love through the poverty and humility of the Crucified. Through the use of the senses and imagination, Bonaventure impels us to imitate the Crucified in our own lives by exhibiting compassionate cruciform love. In this way we are drawn into the mystery of filiation through the grace of the Crucified.[18]

In the *Lignum vitae* the Seraphic Doctor arouses the sluggishness of the human heart to the compassionate love of God by vividly describing the sufferings Jesus endured. Although as mediator Christ brought about the reconciliation of divinity and humanity through suffering, Bonaventure asserts his divine nature did not suffer.[19] His human nature, however, underwent the most tortuous suffering and the Seraphic Doctor spares no words in vividly describing the agony of the crucifixion:

> Thrown roughly upon the wood of the cross, spread out, pulled forward and stretched back and forth like a hide, he was pierced by pointed nails, fixed to the cross by his sacred hands

and feet and most roughly torn with wounds. . . . he was
stripped of his garments, so that he seemed to be a leper from
the bruises and cuts in his flesh . . . from the blows of the
scourges.[20]

Bonaventure brings the historical event of the passion to an immediate awareness so that one is impelled to participate in the agony and
suffering of Christ. Meditation on the passion, he indicates, is an
effective way to foster prayer because it draws one closer to God
whose measureless love is revealed in the cross. As he writes to a
Poor Clare nun on the perfection of the spiritual life: "Your heart is
to be an altar of God. It is here that the fire of intense love must
burn always. You are to feed it every day with the wood of the cross
of Christ and the commemoration of his passion."[21] Similarly, he
advises the novices that meditation on Christ's suffering humanity is
to be the foundation of prayer. "Picture the bloody sweat, the outra-
geous blows, the stinging lashes, the thorny crown, the blasphemous
spit, the mocking words, the weighty cross. Picture him hanging
from the cross, the bloodshot eyes, the pallid lips, the gall and vine-
gar, the bowed head, the agony of death. No need for more! Life
itself has died for us!"[22]

The model of compassion that Bonaventure presents as a para-
digm of Christian discipleship is Mary, the mother of Jesus, and he
describes her presence at the scene of the crucifixion as a vicarious
martyrdom:

What tongue can tell what intellect grasp the heavy weight
of your desolation, blessed Virgin? You were present at all these
events, standing close by and participating in them in every
way. This blessed and most holy flesh—which you so chastely
conceived . . . now torn by the blows of the scourges, now
pierced by the points of the thorns, now struck by the reed,
now beaten by hands and fists, now pierced by nails and fixed to
the wood of the cross . . . he looked upon you standing before
him and spoke to you these loving words: "Woman, behold
your son," in order to console in its trials your soul, which he
knew had been more deeply pierced by a sword of compassion
than if you had suffered in your own body.[23]

The significance of Mary at Calvary lies precisely in her role as sharer in the passion of her Son. Physically seeing the external sufferings of Jesus, which are now recapitulated, and experiencing his interior anguish by means of "seeing within," she is a model for all those who desire to participate in mystical death with Christ.[24] We are to be as united to Jesus as Mary was by spiritually giving birth to the Word of God within our soul. Bonaventure illuminates the theme of spiritual motherhood by describing the power of the Holy Spirit within the soul. Giving birth to Jesus in the same way as Mary did, the soul conceives mystically by a gift of grace. Spiritual motherhood is the work of the Spirit in the soul perfected through grace, enabling the soul to become both mother and spouse of the Crucified.[25]

Bonaventure views the compassionate love of the Crucified as the love of *excessus* or overflowing love, shown in the torments that Christ suffered[26] and the streams of blood that he shed in the passion: "Lord Jesus Christ . . . Your blood was shed so abundantly that your whole body was soaked with it."[27] Since the poverty of the cross is the mystery of God's overflowing love, Bonaventure interprets the passion and cross as a wedding in which God betrothes himself to humanity. Devotion to the humanity of Christ is to lead one to the marriage of the cross where the Crucified is Spouse. This is the highest level of contemplation where the sorrow of the passion is woven into joy and contrition into compassionate love. Bonaventure describes the "wedding of the cross" in the *Soliloquium*:

> Christ on the cross bows his head, waiting for you, that he may kiss you; he stretches out his arms, that he may embrace you; his hands are open, that he may enrich you; his body is spread out, that he may give himself totally; his feet are nailed, that he may stay there; his side is open for you, that he may let you enter there.[28]

Incorporating the nuptial language of Cistercian theology, Bonaventure advocates union with God through the poor and humble crucified humanity of Christ, since it is here that the love of the Trinity is most completely expressed. In the *Lignum vitae* he writes that the Crucified Christ "transfixed with nails . . . appeared to you as your beloved."[29] Bonaventure draws upon the senses and imagina-

tion to penetrate the depths of God's love poured out in the
Crucified by calling to mind the ingratitude of the hardened heart:
"Behold how much I bear for you! I call to you who die for you:
behold the torments I endure, see the nails that pierce Me, hear the
abuse that disgraces Me. And yet, great as the external pain may be,
I suffer a greater internal torture at the sight of your ingratitude."[30]
Our desire for God, therefore, is to be directed to the Crucified, to
be united with him in the cross.[31] Each Christian, Bonaventure
states, should always "see before him/her, with the eyes of one's
heart, Christ dying on the cross,"[32] longing to become fully like the
Crucified, just as the genuine love of Christ transformed the loving
Francis into the same image when the sword of compassionate pain
pierced his soul.[33]

The Seraphic Doctor develops the theme of compassionate love
most fully in describing Francis' encounter with the fiery seraph.
The seraph is a Dionysian symbol used to signify divine illumination,[34] but Bonaventure develops it into a symbol of burning love
similar to that described by Hugh of St. Victor. On La Verna,
Bonaventure writes, Francis experienced Christ Crucified "not by
martyrdom of his flesh but by the fire of his love consuming his
soul."[35] Bonaventure adds another element by associating "burning
love" with the passion of Christ: "His unquenchable fire of love for
the good Jesus had been fanned into such a blaze of flames that
many waters could not quench so powerful a love."[36] Richard of St.
Victor, in his "Four Degrees of Passionate Charity," makes the connection between love and woundedness stating that the highest
degree of love "penetrates the inmost mind of man, piercing his
affections."[37] Bonaventure develops this idea by stating that Francis'
encounter with the crucified seraph was a mixture of joy and sorrow:
"He rejoiced because of the gracious way Christ looked upon him
under the appearance of the Seraph, but the fact that he was fastened
to a cross pierced his soul with a sword of compassionate sorrow."[38]
He describes Francis as one who was transformed in Christ through
compassionate love and views this as the key to his life:

> Just as iron when heated to the point where it becomes
> molten can take the imprint of any mark or sign, so a heart
> burning fervently with love of Christ crucified can receive the

imprint of the crucified Lord himself or his cross. Such a loving heart is carried over to the crucified Lord or transformed in him. That is what happened with St. Francis.[39]

The life of Francis shows that mystical union with the Crucified is the highest poverty both on the part of God who, on the cross, emptied himself of divine power and glory, and on the part of the person who, like Francis, has been purified, illumined and perfected through imitation of and conformity to Christ. It is precisely in the poverty of the cross that the nuptial union with the Crucified takes place. Poverty, as the dynamic outpouring of God's love in the created world, is the ground of ecstatic union with God.

Since we are made in the image of the Son, according to Bonaventure, we have by nature a propensity to love.[40] Sin, however, has distorted our divine image, tempting us to be equal to the Son, so that our love for God has become distorted. The Son takes up the cross to show us that equality with God is not something to be grasped at. In his passion and death on the cross, Christ reveals to us in our human nature what God is in his divine nature, a continuous and dynamic outpouring of love. Bonaventure clearly indicates that the path to God is through the burning love of the Crucified; for it is in the brokenness of the cross that God pours himself out in the world in the form of compassionate love. To ascend to God is to become one with Christ on the cross, and this union comes about thought the Spirit of compassionate love. At the end of the *Lignum vitae* Bonaventure prays "to the most kind Father through you, his only-begotten Son, who for us became man, was *crucified and glorified*, that he send us the Spirit of sevenfold grace."[41]

Cruciform Love

To be intimately united to Christ, according to Bonaventure, is to be conformed to him as Crucified since it is in the cross that the fire of love burns ardently. This "burning love" is the power of the Holy Spirit;[42] it is the power of love that transforms us into the likeness of Christ, leading us to union with God by leading us in Christ to the heart of the Trinity. As he states in the last chapter of the *Itinerarium*:

If you wish to know how these things come about, ask grace not instruction, desire not understanding, the groaning of prayer not diligent reading, the Spouse not the teacher, God not man, darkness not clarity, not light but the fire that totally inflames and carries us into God by ecstatic unctions and burning affections. This fire is God, and his furnace is in Jerusalem; and Christ enkindles it in the heat of his burning passion.[43]

Imitation of and conformity to the Crucified is the true path to mystical union made possible through the power of the Spirit and the work of grace.[44] We have a predisposition toward perfect form, but to become the likeness of that form means to be open to sanctifying grace. Grace is a gift bestowed and infused directly by God. Together with grace and by means of grace, we receive the Holy Spirit, the "uncreated gift, the good and perfect gift coming down from the Father of lights through the Word made flesh."[45] Whereas grace perfects the soul, love is the power of the spirit which impels the soul to union with God. In describing the highest level of mystical union, Bonaventure states: the soul becomes "an agile flame swift to rise, transcending itself and entering mystical darkness; it is an experience of "burning love."[46] In the *Breviloquium* he writes:

In its burning desire, the soul becomes not only an agile flame swift to rise: it even transcends itself, entering mystical darkness and ecstasy through a certain wise unknowing. . . . Experience alone can tell the wonder of this obscure, delightful light; divine grace alone can procure such experience; and those alone who strive for it may receive such grace.[47]

The power of the Spirit that transforms one into the likeness of the crucified Christ transforms through grace and the power of love. In the *Legenda Major* Bonaventure describes the stigmatized Francis as "transformed into him who chose to be crucified because of the excess of his love."[48] In a sermon on Francis, he states: "Some people are surprised that a seraph was sent as the instrument of the Stigmata since none of the seraphim are crucified. But the seraphim are the angels whose name comes from 'burning flame' indicating that Francis was aflame with love when the seraph was sent to him."[49] Similarly, in the *De perfectione vitae*, Bonaventure advises the nun to attain union with God by desiring to be fixed with him to the cross:

> Transformed into Christ by your burning love for the Crucified, pierced by the nails of the fear of God, wounded by the spear of superabounding love, transfixed by the sword of intimate compassion, seek nothing, desire nothing, wish for no consolation, other than to be able to die with Christ on the cross. Then you may cry out with the apostle Paul: "With Christ I am nailed to the cross."[50]

The burning love of the Spirit is the love of God expressed in the Crucified Christ and impressed in the soul purified, illumined and perfected according to Christ.[51] We have a predisposition toward perfect form, Bonaventure states, but to become the likeness of that form means to be open to sanctifying grace.[52] The Crucified is the perfect form of God's image, the form of kenotic love, which expresses itself both actively and passively. The expression of God's ecstatic love on the cross seeks to impress itself in the other who is wholly worthy to receive this love in poverty and to express this love like the Son. What is unique to Bonaventure is the *expression* of the form. Form refers to the visible manifestation of the very concreteness of things and participates in the image—it is the expression of image so that what constitutes the image is precisely that which gives rise to form. Christ Crucified is the form of God (cf. Phil 2:6) who expresses God in the dynamic outpouring of compassionate love. Symbolic form is the beauty of Christ's humiliation on the cross and demands not only vision but an active involvement with the true beauty of form, a "transformation into expressed form" which means a participation or self-involvement.[53] The type of form that Bonaventure describes is that which demands a kenosis of one's self, not as an emptying of self but as a total self-giving.

Bonaventure views union with Christ Crucified as the power of the Spirit that both impresses and expresses. As we noted earlier, impression and expression are inseparable so that what is impressed in the image is expressed in the form. What does this mean with regard to Bonaventure's doctrine of union? It means that union with the Crucified interiorly is to be expressed exteriorly. Through the burning love of the Crucified interiorly, one acquires the form of crucified love exteriorly. We become what we love. Through a loving union with the Crucified we become "cruciform" in love. Bonaventure viewed Francis, the perfect lover of Christ, as one who expressed cruciform love: "The passion of Christ," he writes, "was renewed in Francis." In a sermon on the feast of St. Francis he states: "Love of the Crucified Lord was supremely and gloriously aflame in his heart, and so the Crucified himself, in the *form of the Seraph*—an angelic spirit—burning with the fire of love, appeared before his saintly eyes and imprinted the sacred stigmata on his body."[54] Through reception of the mystical wounds, Francis was both "inwardly inflamed and outwardly marked,"[55] meaning that Francis was both impressed by the burning love of the Spirit and expressed this love in his own flesh. "Ardent love," Bonaventure states, "is a quality of the heart and the stronger this love burns in a person's heart, the more heroic and virtuous are his deeds."[56] The burning love in the heart of Francis, according to Bonaventure, was expressed in his desire for martyrdom, a desire fulfilled "not by the martyrdom of his flesh, but by the fire of his love consuming his soul."[57]

The notion of impression-expression links the concept of image with that of union. We are images of God, according to Bonaventure, in that we are images of the Son.[58] To be in union with Christ means to be inflamed with the burning love of the Spirit, and this love is both impressive and expressive, rendering one a true image of Christ. This is how Bonaventure describes Francis after the Stigmata: "When the true love of Christ had transformed his lover into his image . . . the angelic man Francis came down from the mountain bearing with him the image of the Crucified . . . engraved in the members of his body by the finger of the living God."[59] In light of Francis, Bonaventure indicates that to be a true image of Christ is to be conformed to him in body and spirit; it is to be empowered by the Spirit. We are not only ordered to the Son who is the perfect image of the Father but we are ordered to the Son as the incarnate Word who, in his suffering humanity, remains the perfect image and exemplar of the Father. The notion of conformity to Christ in body and spirit corresponds to the significance of Christ as the incarnate Word who expresses not only his relation to the Father but also to the created world and, moreover, to the human person who is shaped to be an instrument for mediating the divine Word in history. Zachary Hayes states that, with the incarnate Word, there is an inner ordering between the outer word (= the flesh) and the inner Word (= the divine person) whereby the history of Jesus is the historicization of the eternal Word in which all is created.[60] Through the inspired Word there is, in an analogous fashion, an ordering between the spirit expressed in the flesh and the spirit impressed in the soul. In this way union with Christ, although not a hypostatic union, is an intimate union made possible by the Spirit in such a way that conformity to Christ renders one like Christ in body and spirit; one becomes a "re-incarnation" of the crucified Word of God.

In describing Francis' conformity to the Crucified, Bonaventure indicates that to become a true image of Christ means to be in union with Christ which is not something apart from but rather constitutes the very object of devotion to the humanity of Christ. It is the goal of the *Lignum vitae* as he writes in the prologue: "The true worshipper of God and disciple of Christ who desires to conform perfectly to the Savior of all men crucified for him, should, above all, strive with an earnest endeavor of soul to carry about continuously both in his soul and in his flesh, the cross of Christ."[61] Imitation of and devotion to the humanity of Christ leads one to the summit of divine love by which the soul inflamed with the Spirit passes over in Christ to the Father. Even at the highest stage of union the humanity of Christ is present: it is the soul which transcends itself passing over in Christ to the Father.[62]

The Crucified, the Treasury of Wisdom

The synthesizing principle of Bonaventure's theology, that which unifies God, humanity and creation, is the Crucified Christ who is the center of God's diffusive love in the world. The cross is the most powerful and convincing statement of the quality and extent of God's love. It is a symbol of God's total openness to the world. When we "take up the cross" we open ourselves totally to God who is love. Since the cross stands in a world broken through with sin, we must experience the cross deep within ourselves which means to be at odds with the dynamism of human structures—polit-

ical, social and economic. The passion is, indeed, the manifestation of
the mystery of God; a mystery not so much of the divine eternal
kenosis but of the divine eternal self-diffusive goodness.[63] Bonaventure places the emphasis on self-giving not self-emptying. Jesus'
love in the poverty and humility of the cross is a self-giving of God's
love to the world, reflecting the eternal self-diffusiveness of the triune God.[64] It is this love, as Dante so eloquently expressed, that
"moves the sun and the other stars."[65]

Throughout his writings, Bonaventure refers to the cross as the
hidden wisdom of God or the treasury of wisdom and knowledge.[66]
This is an idea not original to Bonaventure but one that can be
found, for example, in St. Paul's letter to the Corinthians (1 Cor. 1:23-
24). Wisdom is the principle of knowing; it is light, mirror, exemplar,
book of life.[67] As the knowledge and right ordering of all things, wisdom is "utterly simple and perfect" and therefore can arise from no
other than God.[68] Wisdom belongs specifically and uniquely to the
Word; as the *medium* in the Trinity the Word, precisely as middle
between two extremes, the Father and Spirit, enables the Trinity to
be perfectly ordered as unity and trinity.[69] In the incarnation,
Bonaventure describes the cross of the Crucified as the place where
God's wisdom is truly manifested. In his "Sermon on the Feast of St.
Andrew" he states that the cross is the fountain of wisdom because it
contains Christ, the Word uncreated and incarnate, who is the treasury of wisdom and knowledge.[70] The cross is the mystery of God's
love and humility, whereby he reaches down to the depths of the
world and draws all things back to himself. Yearning or strong desire
is the door to wisdom, and holiness is its immediate disposition.

In his commentary on the *Sentences*, Bonaventure states that wisdom is linked with experiential knowledge of God. Wisdom is the
most excellent knowledge because of the role played by charity in
the contemplative ascent.[71] Wisdom is the expression of affective
union in love deepened by charity. Bonaventure describes the
passover in the Crucified as a passover in ecstatic wisdom. As the
fullness of love, wisdom is an interior affective "tasting" or "delight-
ing" in the divine.[72] The gift of wisdom delights in God as good
revealed in the interior of the soul.

In the *Lignum vitae* Bonaventure describes Christ the Word

uncreated and incarnate as the manifold wisdom of God—the book written within and without.[73] He describes Francis' encounter with the Crucified as an encounter with the beauty of divine wisdom. The beauty of wisdom, he states, appeared to Francis in the form of the crucified seraph—outwardly it appeared disfigured and distorted, inwardly it was illuminating.[74] The Stigmata were proof that Christian wisdom was "ploughed into his flesh" by the "finger of God,"[75] the power of the living Spirit of God.[76] For Bonaventure, the cross is the sign of wisdom and the Crucified is the wisdom of God revealed. He is the true source of wisdom, the illuminating light, the fountain of the Spirit's gifts, and the true path to peace. Bonaventure concludes the *Lignum vitae* by praying for the seven gifts of the Holy Spirit, beginning with the gift of wisdom:

> We, therefore, pray to the most kind Father through you, his only-begotten Son, who for us became man, was crucified and glorified, that he send us out of his treasures the Spirit of sevenfold grace who rested upon you in all fulness: the Spirit, I say, of wisdom, that we may taste the life-giving flavors of the fruit of the tree of life, which you truly are; the gift also of understanding, by which the intentions of our mind are illumined; the gift of counsel, by which we may follow in your footsteps on the right paths; the gift of fortitude, by which we may be able to weaken the violence of our enemies attacks; the gift of knowledge, by which we may be filled with the brilliant light of your sacred teaching to distinguish good and evil; the gift of piety, by which we may acquire a merciful heart; the gift of fear, by which we may draw away from all evil and be set at peace by submitting in awe to your eternal majesty. For you have wished that we ask for these things in that sacred prayer which you have taught us; and now we ask to obtain them, through your cross, for the praise of your most holy name.[77]

Once we have the gift of wisdom, Bonaventure states, we are united to the supremely true and good who is Christ so that through the wealth of spiritual gifts obtained from the fruits of the tree of life one is ready for contemplation and the embrace of the spouse through the spiritual senses. Through the fire of the Spirit's love we become a spouse of Christ, daughter of the Father, and temple of the

Holy Spirit. In union with Christ, the wisdom of God, one passes over from this world to the Father.

The Cosmic Crucified Christ

Bonaventure's theology of the Crucified Word becomes the foundation of a cosmic vision in the *Hexaëmeron* where in the first *collatio* he presents the seven mysteries of the Word from his eternal generation to his ascension and function as eschatological judge.[78] He indicates that by virtue of his humanity, Christ is the center of all reality since in the unity of his person he combines corporeal, spiritual and eternal natures. Christ, the incarnate Word, is the highest and noblest perfection in the universe:

> The noblest perfection in the universe is not attained until such time as the nature that contains germs that make for the spirit (*rationes seminales*) and the nature that contains the concepts of reason (*rationes intellectuales*) and the nature that contains the archetypal designs of the world (*rationes ideales*) are united to form one single person: and this happened at the incarnation of the Son of God.[79]

As Christ is center of the soul, so too, he is center of the world and the midpoint to which the entire universe is oriented. Christ is center because he is medium; as the uncreated Word he is the medium of the Trinity who both produces and is produced; as the incarnate Word he is the center of creation because he is the center of emanation and return. Joseph Ratzinger states that the figure of Jesus Christ, the middle person of the Trinity and the mediator between God and humanity becomes the synthesis of everything that is expressed for Bonaventure in the concept of center.[80] Christ the center, the mystery in which are united all the polarities of divine and created reality, provides the point around which Bonaventure organizes his entire vision of the world. He writes: "Our intent, then, is to show that in Christ *are hidden all the treasures of wisdom and knowledge*, and that he himself is the central point of all understanding."[81] Bonaventure summarizes the notion of Christ as center by stating:

He is the central point in a sevenfold sense, in terms of essence, nature, distance, doctrine, moderation, justice and concord. The first is in the metaphysical order, the second in the physical, the third in the mathematical, the fourth in the logical, the fifth in the ethical, the sixth in the political or juridical, and the seventh in the theological. The first center is first by eternal origin, the second is most strong through the diffusion of power, the third is most deep because of the centrality of position, the fourth is most clear by rational proof, the fifth is most important because of choice of moral good, the sixth is outstanding because of the retribution of justice, the seventh is at peace through universal reconciliation.[82]

Bonaventure devotes the first *collatio* to the explanation of these seven mysteries of Christ because it provides the foundation of his global vision encompassing Christ, humanity, the church, creation and eschatology.

The first consideration relates to Christ the center in his essence. This corresponds to the uncreated Word and his dynamic role in exemplarism, emanation and return, and is related to the metaphysical order. Bonaventure compares this center to the Tree of Life, since the Son leads us back to the Father by giving life from his own fullness of life.[83] The eternally generated Word is the indissoluble bond between the Father and created reality, confounding those who see no relation whatsoever between the divinity and the cosmos.[84] In the dynamic movement of creation, the opposites of emanation and return coincide in the Word, the Alpha and Omega; for he is the *persona media trinitatis*, the means of the Father's outgoing self-expression and the return in the unity of the Spirit.[85]

By identifying the second center in the order of nature, Bonaventure explains how Christ is the *medium physicum* in his incarnation. This is most strong, he says, because of the diffusion of power which affects all aspects of the universe and created life.[86] The physical world has a two-fold center, that of the macrocosm and of the microcosm. The Sun is center of the macrocosm and the human heart is center of the microcosm.[87] Christ is the unique medium who diffuses light and life since in his incarnation he is the sun and the heart.[88] Like the sun in the macrocosm and the human heart in the microcosm, he is an energizing center, the head of the mystical body, diffusing the energies of the Spirit throughout the members who are united to him. Thus as *medium physicum*, Christ brings the cosmos to its fullness by uniting the maximum and the minimum, the highest and the lowest, the divine and matter, united through the microcosm of human nature in the hypostatic union.[89]

The mystery of Christ as the coincidence of opposites (*coincidentia oppositorum*) is manifested in the notion of Christ as *medium physicum* since the *maximum* is joined with the *minimum*, that is, the hypostatic union joins the person of the Word with human nature, which includes within itself material nature. The maximum in the realm of being, that is, the divinity, is joined in an intimate union with the least substance. This union of the divinity and matter in Christ then becomes a microcosm reflecting the macrocosm of the entire universe, for God's presence pervades the entire universe, even the least particle of matter.[90] Although Christ is the microcosm in comparison with the entire universe, by reason of intensification he is the macrocosm, the greatest of all realities, the maximum manifestation of divinity. By this reversal of opposites through the concept of intensity, Christ becomes the Alpha and Omega. By uniting the maximum and the minimum and the microcosm and the macrocosm in the intensity of the hypostatic union, Christ is seen as the model in which the universe has been made, the goal of divinization to which it is going and the vehicle by which it will make the passover. Since Christ is the Alpha and Omega, all of material creation points to Christ and tends to Christ.[91]

The mystery of Christ, the Alpha and Omega to whom the whole universe tends, takes on profound significance when considered in relation to the Crucified Christ. The extreme depth of the Christ mystery, according to the Seraphic Doctor, considers Christ as the *medium mathematicum* in his crucifixion. Bonaventure relates this to the notion of Christ as center in the order of distance. As the mathematician measures the earth, which for the medievalist stood at the lowest level of the universe, so Christ plumbed the depths of earthly existence in his crucifixion and "wrought salvation in the midst of the earth."[92] Bonaventure expresses here the kenotic aspect of the incarnation in which the divine Word humbled himself and assumed the form of a slave. The Son of God not only became part of humankind but he wanted to experience the most profound feeling of material reality by accepting death on a cross and descent into the underworld. Thus Bonaventure speaks of the poverty and humility of the Son of God and the humility of the cross in which the humble God manifested his divine wisdom.[93] Because the Crucified One unites heaven, earth and the underworld he can be referred to as the *axis mundi* which Mircea Eliade describes as follows:

> This communication [between levels] is sometimes expressed through the image of a universal pillar, *axis mundi*, which at once connects and supports heaven and earth and whose base is fixed in the world below (the infernal regions) . . . around this cosmic axis lies the world (our world), hence the axis is located "in the middle, at the navel of the earth," it is the center of the world.[94]

Although Christ as the *axis mundi* restores the cosmic harmony and provides a center for the integration of the universe, each soul must go through the cosmic process on its return to the Father.[95]

Bonaventure also affirms that Christ is center with regard to the order of doctrine. He begins by stating that "it is most clear by rational proof," (*Hex.*1, 25) using the science of logic to show that Christ is center in his resurrection. Logic is built upon the syllogism, which is essentially composed of two extremes and a middle term. The middle term is connected with both the argument and conclusion, therefore it functions as a medium drawing together two extreme propositions.[96] Bonaventure constructs a syllogism to prove the logic of the divinity. The major premise is: the Son of God enjoyed conformity of nature with the Father, equality of power and immortality of life. The minor premise is: the suffering of Christ. Bonaventure then concludes: Christ is center in his resurrection. Christ confronts Satan in a type of cosmic *quaestio disputata*. Because God and humankind were separated by sin, Christ had to be both divine and human, and had to assume human nature in all of its suffering, poverty and death. Christ's major proposition was from all eternity. As uncreated Word, Christ had conformity in nature, equality in power and immortality of life with God. The minor premise consisted in his union with humankind as an incarnate Word, by

accepting suffering, misery and death. The conclusion was in the resurrection where suffering was won over by impassibility, misery by
power and death by life.[97] Bonaventure states that Christ tricked the
devil and overcame the logic of sin by submitting to the destructive
force of sin and death:

> For Christ did not say: "Allow me to live," but "allow me to
> take on death, to be joined with the opposite extreme, to suffer
> and to die." The conclusion follows from that and so he himself
> made a fool of the devil.[98]

Because of Christ's victory Bonaventure exhorts us to use the logic
of Christ: "This is our logic, this is our reasoning which must be
used against the devil who constantly argues with us."[99] The "theo-
logic" of the fourth center shows that Christian existence is a life
conformed to the model of Christ's humiliation.

Bonaventure continues by saying that, having shattered the hold
of evil, Christ can lead not only the human person but the entire
cosmos back to the Father. On the return, Christ is first the *medium
ethicum* in his ascension. Bonaventure uses the symbol of Moses'
ascent of the mountain to illustrate the progress one should make in
the life of virtue, the foundation of which is faith.[100] After one has
climbed from the foot of the mountain to its summit, one must
stand before Christ as judge.[101] The mountain symbolizes the meet-
ing place between the divine and human.[102] Bonaventure refers to
Christ as *medium iudiciale* or *politicum* since he renders judgment
and determines reward and punishment.[103] He then refers to Ezekiel's
vision of the fiery chariot, symbolizing the holiness of God. Christ is
depicted in his two-fold nature and Bonaventure indicates that the
eschatological judge is the crucified Word, risen and glorified.[104] Finally, he
is the *medium theologicum* in eternal happiness, not as the uncreated
Logos but as the incarnate Word, crucified and glorified.[105] The
Lamb of God from whom flows the fountain of life is the crucified
Christ, the Tree of Life, who reconciles all with the Father. Thus
having begun from the Word as *persona media* in the Trinity, we
return through this *medium* or center to the goal which is the Tree
of Life, the crucified Christ, who unites heaven and earth in whom
true peace and wisdom is found.

The first *collatio* of Bonaventure's *Hexaëmeron* is the pinnacle of his deep insight to the mystery of the Crucified Christ as center. As the final synthesis of his life's work, the *Hexaëmeron* is a cosmic blueprint of the *Itinerarium*, the soul's journey into God. Just as the Crucified Christ is the mystical center of the soul, so too, he is the mystical center of the world, the universe, all history and time. He is the center of all knowledge because he himself is the treasury of wisdom and knowledge, the wisdom of God that both sustains and contradicts the world in the "brokenness" of the cross. As Turner indicates, the Crucified Christ is a similarity so dissimilar as to dramatize with paradoxical intensity the "brokenness" and failure of all our language and knowledge of God.[106] Through the cross, God "humbly bends down" to the very depths of the world, the "cinders of humility," and draws all things back to himself. True knowledge is the knowledge of divine love that leads to the restoration of all things in God.

Bonaventure's Divine Milieu

The identification of Christ as the center of all sciences signifies that he is the center of all knowledge. However, Bonaventure does not limit the mystery of Christ to the realm of knowledge since the nature of God as good transcends knowledge in the order of love. The revelation of divine love in the cross leads Bonaventure to proclaim a new and eternal science, the science of *sapientia* revealed in the crucified Christ.[107] With Christ as the center and wisdom of God, we can return to the idea that Bonaventure sees redemptive love in the form of cosmic completion. The significance of the cross as the principle of restoration corresponds to the role of Christ as mediator who reconciles in the unity of his persons the two extremes: matter and spirit. As the most noble perfection, he unites these with the divine nature. Alexander Gerken refers to Christ as the first and ultimate because in Christ all of creation is brought to completion and perfection.[108] Bonaventure himself describes Christ as the principle of perfection in his second "Sermon on the Nativity." He describes perfection not only in reference to the human person but to the entire created order:

It is in the Word that we discover the perfection of that
greatness of heart which brings all reality to its consummation
and completion, since the figure of the circle attests to the perfection of bodies both in the macrocosm and in the microcosm.
. . . But this figure is not complete in the universe. Now, if this
figure is to be as perfect as possible, the line of the universe
must be curved into a circle. Indeed, God is simply the first.
And the last among the works of the world is man. Therefore,
when God became man, the works of God were brought to perfection. This is why Christ, the God- man, is called the alpha
and the omega, the beginning and the end. For this reason, as
you have heard, the last of all things, namely man, is said to be
first and last. The ability of human nature to be united in a
unity of person with the divine . . . is reduced to act so that it
would not be a mere empty potency. And since it is reduced to
act, the perfection of the entire created order is realized, for in
that one being the unity of all reality is brought to consummation.[109]

Bonaventure's cosmic vision with Christ as center, which he summarizes here, can be identified in six points: 1) The cycle of emanation
and return which characterizes the circle of perfection is realized in
Christ; 2) Completion and consummation of creation are predicated
on the incarnate Word because God became human thus taking on
material reality; 3) The humanity of Christ brings not only the
human person to perfection but the entire created order; 4) The ability of human nature to be united to the divine is reduced to act;
thus humanity realizes its consummation in union with Christ; 5)
The perfection of humanity in Christ through union realizes the
perfection of the entire created order; 6) Christ has perfected all
things in himself, but the perfection of the circle is not complete in
the universe.

It is interesting that in this sermon which concerns incarnation
and redemption, there is no mention of satisfaction or debt. Rather,
the incarnation is described with a view toward order. Bonaventure's
theology, on the whole, is a theology of order because the Trinity is
the perfection of order with the Word as center. In the Trinity, the
Father who is total productivity is in union with the Spirit who is

total receptivity through the Word who is both productive and receptive.[110] Within the Godhead, therefore, emanation and return take place through the Word who is *medium.* Bonaventure envisions the same process in creation symbolized by the circle, which signifies order in its perfect configuration.[111] Creation, which comes from God, is destined to return to God through the incarnate Word. It is "programmed" to order but sin has created disorder. The notion of Christ Crucified as center means that he is restores restores order in the world and reconciles it to the Father through the power of the Spirit.

The dilemma that presents itself in Bonaventure's doctrine is the twofold emphasis on satisfaction and completion, both of which are fruits of the incarnation. According to Rufinus Silic, Christ's mediatorship in Bonaventure's doctrine is accomplished in his passion and death, thus supporting Anselm's satisfaction theory.[112] Conversely, Romano Guardini interprets redemption not as satisfaction but as reconciliation between two distinct natures: divine and human. Guardini's physico-mystical theory does not maintain Christ's mediatorship as a juridical satisfaction but rather as reconciliation, giving rise to a new creation in Christ.[113] Gerken describes Bonaventure's soteriology as a completion theory, emphasizing the consummation of creation as completion but with a minimal role of the cross.[114] Since Bonaventure does not view satisfaction and completion as opposing theories, an alternate interpretation which more fully addresses this twofold nature of redemption can be found in the concept of mystical union. The ground of mystical union is the Crucified Christ who, as center, is both the principle of restoration and completion. Christ, the Word uncreated and incarnate, restores order in the world precisely as incarnate and crucified. The created order could not be restored unless the Word took on flesh, indeed, all material reality; and the circle of life disrupted by sin, could not be completed, because of sin, without the cross. It is Christ in his crucified humanity who perfects the world and completes it because he unites in his person corporeal, spiritual and divine natures.

The concept of union, in light of the cross, is of paramount importance for the consummation of the created order when considered as mystical union. Since Christ is center of the soul and center of the world, this applies to the human person and to all of creation below humanity. All things in the created world must pass through Christ, the crucified center, in order to transcend to the Father. The created world, however, cannot attain to God without the human person. Although Christ has achieved the perfection of the entire created order in the incarnation, the figure of the circle in the universe is incomplete until humanity itself realizes its perfection in Christ through union with the Crucified.

Bonaventure draws an analogy between the perfection of the human person and the perfection of the universe. Just as God in creating the world created in the human a potential for beatitude so that the human might freely choose and merit it, so too, he created matter lacking its final perfection of form so that it might "cry out" (*clamaret*) for perfection.[115] In Bonaventure's terms, the material world is incapable in itself of experiencing this destiny; for it is, by its very nature, incapable of any personal relation with God. It is, however, involved in this destiny in and through the destiny of the spiritual creation. As a whole, in its existence, it is ordered toward the human person who stands in the center of creation as the most noble of forms, uniting matter and spirit in a single entity.[116] Because the soul is united to the body, it is united to the corporeal world.[117]

Bonaventure indicates that the relationship of creation to God is contingent on the human person since creation (material reality) has nothing in common with God (spiritual reality) unless through the human person in whom matter and spirit are united. In the order of creation, the human person is created last but in consummation the human person is first because the capacity for God is realized in the incarnation.[118] Because the human is first in the order of consummation, the consummation of creation depends on the human person. As Hayes states, the destiny of the material cosmos is intertwined with that of humanity.[119] In light of this concept Bonaventure writes: "The ability of human nature to be united in a unity of person with the divine . . . is reduced to act. . . . And since it is reduced to act, the perfection of the entire created order is realized."[120]

The key to perfection, as Bonaventure describes it, is union— union of matter and spirit, body and soul, and union of these with Christ. In Christ, human nature is united to divine nature in a perfect hypostatic union. The humanity of Christ enables humanity to be united to God and, indeed, unites humanity to God. However, humans can freely accept or reject God; the element of distinction is faith. To accept God in Christ is the beginning of the perfection that Bonaventure envisions. True perfection takes place in mystical union. With Christ, the center of the soul and center of the world, mystical union is the perfection of humanity, and with humanity, the whole created order. Since the form of existence of the human person as body and soul is more full and perfect than the form which the soul is by itself, the whole person—that is the perfection of nature— must be transfigured. As the human person is to bring his/her body into blessedness, so too, through the body the whole physical world below, which is ordered toward transfiguration through the human person, is brought to perfection.

Bonaventure and Teilhard

Bonaventure's doctrine of Christocentricity has been compared to the cosmic scheme of Pierre Teilhard de Chardin.[121] For Bonaventure, Christ is the perfection of the universe since in his person all "seminal, intellectual, and ideal causes are combined."[122] Similarly, Teilhard de Chardin claims that the universe is an evolving Christogenesis since all things in the universe tend toward Christ who is the Alpha and Omega.[123] Both Bonaventure and Teilhard present a dynamic view of the universe which is oriented toward Christ the center. Their spiritualities are cosmic, incarnational and Christocentric. Both have a strong sense of relation to the cosmos and an experience of God's presence in the world. For Teilhard, the divine involvement in the creative process of the world is linked to Christ. The world is a divine milieu with Christ as the personal center. Teilhard's cosmic Christ is similar to Bonaventure's doctrine of the Son as the center of the divine presence and of the return of creatures to the unity of the Father.[124] Christ is the Omega point of the evolutionary process, drawing all things to their fulfillment. Teilhard emphasizes finality or completion whereby the love of Christ is the energy or drawing force into which the elements of creation are fused without losing their identity. The human person is co-creator with God in the transformation of the universe.

Teilhard's religious sensiblity is closely related to that of Francis and Bonaventure. As Ewert Cousins states, he shares a cosmic sense with the Franciscans, an awareness of the vast sweep of creation and of the presence of God in all creatures. The divine immanence, which Bonaventure expresses through the exemplarism of the Word, Teilhard expresses through his doctrine of the cosmic Christ. As Omega of evolution, Christ is present in the entire cosmos, from the least particle of matter to the convergent human community. The world is like a crystal lamp illumined from within by the light of Christ. For those who can see, Christ shines in this diaphanous universe, through the cosmos and in matter. The process of evolution that Teilhard describes, from matter to spirit, moves towards greater interiorization, toward a greater union in love. This process is effected by Christ who brings everything together into a union, a Christogenesis, or a coming-to-be of Christ.[125]

Bonaventure's Christocentrism is much more firmly grounded in the Trinity since the inner Word of God becomes the external Word in history in the person of Jesus Christ.[126] The world which is created through the Word is an exemplary world, a world which manifests the power, wisdom, and goodness of God, whereby Christ is the divine-temporal exemplar. Christ, the Word uncreated and incarnate, is the center of the Trinity and the center of creation, the center of all reality, and the archetype of creation. For Bonaventure, creation is linked to the Trinity through Jesus Christ. Just as creation emanates through the Word and is patterned according to the Word as exemplar, so it is destined to return to God through the Word incarnate. Unlike Teilhard, Bonaventure posits the integral link between the Crucified Christ and the Trinity, so that, through the Crucified, God is present in the world. By saying that Christ Crucified is the center of the world, the Alpha and Omega, Bonaventure indicates that only through Christ can the world return to God. Like Teilhard, he holds that all human persons are co-creators with God in the transformation of the universe insofar as they strive for mystical union with the Crucified. For Bonaventure, compassionate or crucified love is the drawing force of the return to God. The realization of universal completion in Christ is contingent on the perfection of the human person in Christ which means conformity to the crucified humanity of Christ.

Although Bonaventure, unlike Teilhard, does not explicitly identify the role of cosmic love, his writings point to the fact that love moves the material universe to its fulfillment in Christ. Compassionate love, the love of the Crucified, is the dialogue between God and the world. Through the self-diffusive love of Christ on the cross, the light of wisdom illuminates the whole created world and moves the world toward its destiny, its consummation in God. In Christ, all reality is completed and brought to perfection. The world, therefore, like the soul, realizes its fulfillment in God not through knowledge but through love. Bonaventure's emphasis on the Crucified Christ as the center of the world, the revelation of God in the world, and the love of God that moves the world to completion, illuminates God's relationship to the world. In light of the Crucified, we see that God's omnipotence is his suffering love, his omniscience is the wisdom of the cross. The world moves toward its completion not because God stands "over" the world with almighty power but because God is humble and, in the poverty of the cross, stands "with" the world, intimately united to it through crucified love. One who, like Francis, is in union with Christ Crucified helps to move the world toward its final consummation in God.

Union with Christ, Embracing the World: Bonaventure's World View

In an illuminating study on Bonaventure's theology entitled, "The Two Poles of Theology," Ewert Cousins remarked that "one wishes that as a companion piece to the disputed questions *De scientia Christi* one could find a series *De Christo medio*. If Bonaventure had given his Christocentricity such an analytical treatment, his synthesis would have been more complete."[1] The almost labyrinthine structure of Bonaventure's thought with its various ideas interwoven into a cosmic quilt could easily impel one to search for a manuscript that "ties all together" with Christ as center. But indeed, no such manuscript has been found and it is unlikely that such a discovery will ever be made. The new direction of Christocentricity that begins with the *Itinerarium* is not one that easily lends itself to objective analysis such as one finds in the *quaestio disputata*. Rather, what Bonaventure's *Itinerarium* brings to light for the first time in his writings is the *absolute* centrality of Christ. The Christ that he presents is not some generalized symbol of a "mystical" Christ, but the brutal concreteness of the Crucified Christ.

Bonaventure's insight to the mystery of the Crucified Christ on mount La Verna was not simply a momentary thought, a fleeting idea; rather, it was an inspired "vision" similar to what Francis himself expressed on the same mountain thirty three years before—a transforming vision. As Bonaventure writes in the prologue: "I saw at once that *this vision* represented our father's rapture in comtempla-

tion and the road by which this rapture is reached."[2] Doyle sympa-
thetically remarks that Bonaventure descended the mountain "interiorly stigmatized,"[3] an idea well worth pondering, for after the
Itinerarium the Seraphic Doctor seems to turn his entire attention to
the mystery of the Crucified. The *Hexaëmeron*, his final masterpiece
left unfinished by an untimely death, is perhaps what the Seraphic
Doctor had intended as his *summa* on Christ the center. That these
lectures emerged at the end of his life underscores what Cousins
claims, namely, that Bonaventure's Christology *evolved* into a doctrine of universal proportions. He did not see the whole mystery in a
single moment but the mystery grew and developed, probably with
the maturity of his own religious experience, until it acquired
dimensions that corresponded to all aspects of reality. Never, however, did Bonaventure lose sight of the stigmatized Francis. The poor
man of Assisi, bearing the wounds of Christ, was the model he continuously placed before him and his followers. Even in his final lectures on the *Hexaëmeron*, Bonaventure held up Francis as the model
of the final age of peace.[4]

Without trying to impose a structure on Bonaventure's thought,
I think it is possible to construct a distinctly Franciscan world view
based on his theology. With Francis as a model, we can describe this
world view with regard to God, humanity and creation. Taking the
last chapter of the *Itinerarium* as our starting point, we can say that
Bonaventure formulates a world view with an authentically Christian
metaphysics, the center of which is the Crucified Christ. Although he
uses the language and basic scheme of Neoplatonism (see Appendix
One), he transforms Neoplatonism by his radical Christocentricity
and describes a metaphysics whereby love, as the highest form of the
good, becomes the basis of all reality in the created world. In
Bonaventure's vision, the created world is loved into being and recreated in love through the suffering and death of Jesus on the cross.
Since love by its very nature is relational, Bonaventure's view of the
world is fundamentally relational, and he envisions the consummation of the world in union with Christ Crucified who is center.

Relationship is the key to the fulfillment of all life in
Bonaventure's vision. The journey to God is a growth in relationship
with God through union with Christ Crucified. It is a growth in the

knowledge of God through conformity to Christ and at the same time, moving beyond this knowledge to the hidden depths of divine love through the fire of the Spirit. The journey, therefore, is a dialectic of knowledge and love until at the final stage of the journey, love alone draws the soul into the fullness of the divine mystery. Jesus Christ, the Word incarnate and Crucified, is the one to whom and through whom we continuously make the journey into God.

Bonaventure describes the spiritual journey in the life of Francis as an ascent and descent; as we ascend to God, we descend to our neighbor (cf. *LM* 8, 1). This two-fold nature of the journey corresponds to the idea of image and expression. As we are restored in the image of Christ and thus conformed to him, we are impelled to express the image in our relationship with others, since form or content acquires meaning not in itself but in the expressed image which is manifested in relation to the other or the object of one's love.

Bonaventure, as we have seen, places a firm emphasis on the suffering humanity of Christ. To be sure, he does not deny the ascension of Christ; indeed, he describes the completion of Christ's work in his passion, death, resurrection, and ascension.[5] Rather, it is precisely *because* Christ Crucified has ascended that his suffering and death on the cross fully express divine love and thus are worthy of imitation. To ascend with Christ is to plummet into the depths of Christ's passion and death on the cross; it is to become cruciform in love.

The notion that compassionate love is the highest love, by which one descends below oneself, lies at the heart of Bonaventure's doctrine of mystical union. Richard of St. Victor states that in the fourth or highest degree of love, the soul is transformed into a servant. The contemplative who transcends to the glory of God is conformed to the humility of Christ. Whereas in the third degree of love the soul is conformed to the likeness of God, in the fourth degree "she begins to empty herself, taking the form of a servant," following Christ in his passion.[6] In the highest degree of love, he states, "the soul goes forth on God's behalf and descends below herself. . . because of her neighbor."[7] Suffering compassion and the humble descent below oneself is a higher degree of love than the love by which the "soul is absorbed in the consuming fire in the furnace of divine love."[8] Thus, to acquire the spirit of burning love like Christ is to descend below oneself, to become the humble servant of our neighbor.

Bonaventure expounds the ideal of compassionate or crucified love in the *Triplici via* where he recounts the six degrees of love: sensitivity, avidity, satiety, ebriety, security, and tranquility, highlighting the nature of perfect love as compassionate or agapic love.[9] The fourth degree, ebriety, he states, consists of a love of God that is so great that "one is not only disgusted with consolation, but instead of it, loves and seeks the cross. Out of love for the Beloved, s/he rejoices like the Apostle, in pain, abuse and scourging."[10] In the fifth degree, security, he states, "the soul feels that it loves God so much that it would happily bear for his sake every punishment and every shame, fear is readily expelled, and the soul conceives such hope in the divine assistance that it believes no power could cut it away from God."[11]

As one progresses in the perfection of love leading to ecstatic union with the Crucified, the spirit of love conforms one to the likeness of the beloved giving rise to the desire for martyrdom, since the spirit which is impressed is expressed in imitation of the Crucified. Bonaventure describes the Stigmata of Francis as the mark of his desire for martyrdom which he attained not by martyrdom of the flesh but by the ardent love of his heart: "As Christ's lover . . . he was to be transformed into the likeness of Christ crucified, not by the martyrdom of his flesh, but by the fire of love consuming his soul."[12] Describing Francis' sojourn among the Saracens as a journey impelled by the desire for martyrdom, Bonaventure writes:

> In the fervent fire of his charity he strove to emulate the glorious triumph of the holy martyrs in whom the flame of love could not be extinguished nor courage be weakened. Set on fire, therefore, by that perfect charity which drives out fear, he longed to offer to the Lord his own life as a living sacrifice in the flames of martyrdom so that he might repay Christ, who died for us, and inspire others to divine love.[13]

In the *Triplici via* Bonaventure states that, at the highest level of love which is ecstatic union, one is willing to die for one's neighbor in order to please God.[14] As Daniel notes, it is not the attainment of martyrdom itself but the *desire* for it that imparts an active component to mystical union.[15] Desire, as Bonaventure writes in the *Itinerarium*, is "the fire of God which Christ enkindles in the heat of his burning passion."[16] The desire for martyrdom, the perfect love of Christ, means to be consummed by the fire of the Holy Spirit.[17] It is as Francis showed in his own life, a mystical death of love.

There seems to be a link, albeit, without any explicit connections, between Bonaventure's Christ mysticism and the visionary mysticism of Franciscan women mystics. There is a striking parallel between what the Seraphic Doctor describes as mystical union and that which Franciscan women sought. Studies on medieval women mystics in general show that, for women, the experience of God was formed largely by visionary experience of the life of Christ and participation in his passion.[18] Women perceived that the passivity of Christ's wounded flesh became the powerful means of spiritual healing in the world. By identifying themselves with the Crucified and becoming crucified with Christ, women were empowered to break out of traditional restrictions and began to work in the world with a new determination, assertiveness, and inspiration in the face of the ambivalence and hostility toward women. Many gave their goods to the poor, begged in order to feed them, and worked for their food and clothing.[19] Others worked among lepers sharing their life and even going so far as to drink the water in which those afflicted had been bathed.[20] For medieval women, suffering and service became one in the imitation of Christ.

Although there is little evidence to suggest that Bonaventure influenced the spirituality of women mystics, they do exemplify the type of mysticism that Bonaventure articulates in his writings. Women such as Angela of Foligno, for example, manifested a spirit of "burning love" not only in their spiritual lives but also by changing their lives physically and patterning them after the Crucified. The spirit of crucified love impelled women like Angela, to act in extraordinary ways, as in the care of lepers. To become crucified with the Crucified, as Bonaventure taught, is to live in the spirit of cruciform love, to act with a wholehearted commitment of one's life for the healing of others.

Women's relationship to Christ, however, was not simply a new empowerment or reversal of roles. While the link between women and the Crucified Christ was grounded in compassion or suffering with Christ, the suffering humanity of Christ was not simply reflective of womens lives. Rather, women perceived Christs sufferings as a manifestation of divine love. As the eighteenth century mystic Veronica Giuliani states, suffering and love are the same thing.[21] Clare of Assisi referred to Christ Crucified as a mirror (3 LAg) in which one could see ones true image. To see Christ Crucified as ones true self, to enter into this self grounded in divine love, and to be bodily marked with suffering as a sign of Gods presence constituted the lives of Franciscan women such as Clare, Angela, and Veronica. The experience of love in union with the suffering Christ led these women into the depths of the divine self-diffusive good so that they came to see all created reality permeated with the good.

In light of the experience of women mystics, we can say that Bonaventure's mysticism is a mysticism of love based on relationship with the suffering humanity of Christ. It is a mysticism of utter relationship with Christ in which one becomes a source of healing and life for others. To be restored in the image of God is to love God with the same intensity as Christ loved, to offer one's life, soul and body, in compassionate love. Just as the Father pours out his love in the suffering of the Son, so too the Son loves the Father with all that he has and all that he is. In the inner life of the Trinity, this love is bonded in the Spirit. In creation, the Spirit draws the believer into the life of the Crucified Christ, inspiring the believer to love with the same intensity that Christ loved. To to be united to the love of God in Christ, therefore, is to become cruciform in love.

Ecstatic union with the Crucified, expressed as the desire for martyrdom, means that one is willing to suffer or die for the love of one's neighbor. It is the summit of love where charity reigns. As the highest state of perfect love, it is the state of peace where the soul is in a state of tranquility "as if in Noah's Ark where nothing can disturb it."[22] This peace, Bonaventure indicates, means perfect concordance between all things—God, the soul, and creation.[23]

The Created World

While Bonaventure holds up relationship with Christ Crucified as that which undergirds the unity of humankind, he also maintains that union with Christ, the Crucified center, brings about a *re-creatio*, a renewed relationship to the created world. In the *Legenda Major,* he describes Francis as one who was restored to original innocence because of his intimate relation to Christ. As one conformed to Christ, Francis was drawn into the beauty and order of the world, perceiving creation in its proper relationship to God and experiencing the harmony with creation that the first Adam enjoyed. Bonaventure writes:

> True piety . . . drew him up to God through devotion, transformed him into Christ through compassion, attracted him to his neighbor through condescension and symbolically showed a return to the state of original innocence through universal reconciliation with each and every thing.[24]

Bonaventure's Christ-centered world means that one who is in union with Christ stands with Christ at the center of the world, intimately related (*pietas*) to the world in all its createdness. Francis is the model of one who, because of his conformity to Christ, was restored in right relationship to the created world. Bonaventure describes Francis' encounter with the Crucified Christ as an encounter with the beauty of divine wisdom, the light of true knowledge. The beauty of wisdom, he states, appeared to Francis in the form of the crucified seraph: outwardly it appeared disfigured and distorted; inwardly it was illuminating. The passover through "ecstatic elevations of Christian wisdom" that Bonaventure describes in the *Itinerarium* underscores Francis' intimate relationship with God and the world in Christ. For Francis creation was sacramental, an encounter with God. Nature spoke of God by serving as the means of self-communciation. All created things pointed beyond themselves to their Creator. Bonaventure writes in the *Legenda Major*:

> Aroused by all things to the love of God, he rejoiced in all the works of the Lord's hands and from these joy-producing manifestations he rose to their life-giving principle and cause.

In beautiful things he saw Beauty itself and through his vestiges imprinted on creation he followed his beloved everywhere,
making from all things a ladder by which he could climb up and
embrace him who is utterly desirable. With a feeling of
unprecedented devotion he savored in each and every creature—as in so many rivulets—that goodness which is their
fountain-source.[25]

Just as Francis understood the descent of the Word into creation,
so too, he saw humanity not as the highest rung of the ladder but as
a part of creation. Thus his nature mysticism is one of a descending
solidarity between humanity and creation: "When he considered the
primordial source of all things, he was filled with even more abun-
dant piety, calling creatures, no matter how small, by the name of
brother or sister, *because he knew they had the same source as himself.*[26]
Instead of using creatures to ascend to God (in a transcending manner) Francis perceived that all creatures are brothers and sisters mutually dependent on God. He expressed solidarity with the lowliest of
creatures because he recognized that they had the same primordial
source as himself.

E. R. Daniel states that Francis's Christ mysticism is the source
of his nature mysticism: "the same *pietas* which raised Francis to
God and transformed him into Christ, drew him toward his neighbor
by condescension and remade him into a state of innocence by a universal reconciliation with individual things."[27] As Bonaventure notes,
Francis' piety renewed in him a *status innocentiae*. Christ gave him a
new relationship to nature, one in which grace and innocence pre-
vailed, not sin and conflict. Being transformed into Christ repaired
the relationship between Francis and created things. By conforming
himself to Christ Crucified, Francis attained a harmony between his
flesh and spirit and between his spirit and God's such that God
ordered nature to obey him.[28] The harmony of his own flesh and
spirit in union with Christ enabled his union with the spirit of God,
the Creator and Sustainer of all nature.

It was from this union that the created world provided for
Francis in miraculous ways. In his sermon on Francis, Bonaventure
elucidates the cure of a fatal epidemic through the sprinkling of
water which Francis had touched.[29] In the *Legenda Major,* Bonaventure

describes Francis' edenic relation with all of creation by recounting numerous animal stories and miraculous events of creation. Francis, for example, not only subdued a ravenous wolf (*LM* 8, 11), but he could also draw water from a large rock to quench the thirst of a poor beggar (*LM* 7, 12). Francis' piety was of such remarkable sweetness and power, Bonaventure states, that he could tame brute beasts that had rebelled against fallen humankind. Francis' relation to the created world is best described by the word "piety" (*pietas*), for piety means "blood-related," being intimately united in a familial sense.[30] Because Francis was united to Christ, his brother, spouse, and mother (cf. 1 *Ep Fid*), he was intimately united to creation as well. By joining with Christ and, moreover, with Christ Crucified, Francis became intimately related with the entire created world.

Although Francis does not draw a connection between the imitation of Christ Crucified and the renewal of a *status innocentiae*, his *Canticle of Brother Sun* is a testimony to this very interrelatedness. Composed in 1225, one year after the Stigmata and one year before his death, the *Canticle* is Francis' Christ-centered hymn. At the time of its composition, Francis was blind and living in a dark hut behind the convent of San Damiano.[31] Although he had reached the height of his mystical union, reflected in the Stigmata, he still suffered physically from his weakened body. In the *Legenda perugina*, the author indicates that while Francis was asleep God spoke to him in a dream and asked if he would like to exchange his earthly infirmities and tribulations for an earth of pure gold. Francis responded affirmatively. Then the voice added, "rejoice as if you were already in my kingdom." Francis awoke and composed the *Canticle*. What is remarkable about this work is that it is a hymn filled with light. Although the words Jesus or Jesus Christ are not mentioned in the Song, the mystery of Christ permeates the entire work as Eloi Leclercq states, and it is through Christ that Francis joins in the praises of God through the works of creation. Francis gives expression to a cosmic incarnation in which the elements of the universe are in union with "brother sun," a symbolic reference to Christ,[32] together with brother wind, sister water, brother fire, sister mother earth. Leonhard Lehmann interprets the *Canticle* in terms of the cosmic Christ who, as high priest, offers up everything to the Father; all of creation is a cosmic liturgy.[33]

Humanity and creation join together with Christ to offer to the Father praise and thanksgiving. Leclercq interprets the *Canticle* as an expression of Francis' interior life, transformed in Christ, now manifested in the cosmos where Christ is the center of all reality. Francis' transformation into Christ Crucified enables him to see the earth as "pure gold" or as the new paradise since Christ is the new Adam in whom paradise is renewed. Bonaventure highlights this point in the last chapter of the *Itinerarium* where he quotes from the gospel of Luke: "Today, you will be with me in paradise."[34] In Bonaventure's vision, the person, like Francis, who is in union with Christ, enters into the unity of all things in Christ who himself is the heavenly Jerusalem (cf. *Hex.* 23, 22).

The *Canticle* underscores the harmonious relationship between humanity and creation; yet, it also underscores the fact that the destiny of creation is intertwined with that of the human journey. As Bonaventure notes, the world shares a common fate with humanity since the greater material world is made for the sake of the smaller world (the human person) and is affected in its inner condition by the human condition: innocent with the innocent, fallen with fallen humanity, shaken, judged and purified.[35] This means that the relationship of the person in union with Christ is at the same time the relationship between the person and the created world. How we live in relation to Christ is how we live in relation to the world.

Bonaventure's World View

The Seraphic Doctor sees Francis as the model of one who lived in the unity of God, humanity and creation through Jesus Christ, the Crucified center. The bond of interconnectedness is the spirit of burning love, the spirit that inflamed the heart of Francis and forged him into the likeness of the Crucified. It is not surprising that in the upper basilica of Assisi the artist painted the fresco of Pentecost opposite to the fresco of Francis striking the rock, for as Gregory Alhquist has shown, the artist intended to portray the Poverello as one filled with the Spirit.[36] The Spirit sent by the crucified and glorified Christ upon the church is the same Spirit that inflamed the heart of Francis. All gifts of grace flow from Christ's sufferings,

Bonaventure states; Francis, who bore the cross of Christ, was filled with the gifts of the Holy Spirit.[37] The spirit of love imbued in his heart flowed from his love of the Crucified. In his sermon on Francis, Bonaventure writes:

> Love embraces all that love commands, but such love is found only in the virtuous. It was through love that the divine nature was united to flesh and through love that Christ humbled himself and underwent death. The Book of Sirach tells us: "Look upon the rainbow and praise him who made it." What is this rainbow except the cross of Christ? Therefore, the sign of Christ's cross had to be found on this man of heavenly virtue, St. Francis, whose love was boundless. He had love without limit for everyone. Love spends itself for sinners without counting the cost.[38]

Bonaventure continues by saying that the cross imprinted on Francis' body symbolized his love of Christ Crucified, and by the flame of that love he was totally transformed into Christ. Francis' conformity to the Crucified enabled him to become a *sacramentum Domini*, a sign of God's perfect works and deeds, so that his love for God reflected itself in love for neighbor and creation. As Bonaventure states: "He shed light on his neighbors by his manifest virtues; refreshed them with living waters by his exemplary holiness; inflamed them with ardent love by his devout prayers; and filled them with wonder by the miracles wrought through his holiness and goodness."[39] The model of Francis that inspires Bonaventure's Christocentric world view shows that relationship is essential to a unified world.

Bonaventure's decisively Christocentric Franciscan world view is integrative, unlike the hierarchical world view of the monastic tradition with its Neoplatonic ascent (see figure 1, p. 136). The soul that is set in the order of charity and inflamed by the Spirit passes over in ecstatic union with the Crucified, and this union brings the whole created world into ordered love which is peace. Union, in this context, does not mean only the act of union but a transformation of being. The ascent to God through union with Christ means being transformed in Christ and thus into God. It does not draw one

WORLD VIEWS

Monastic

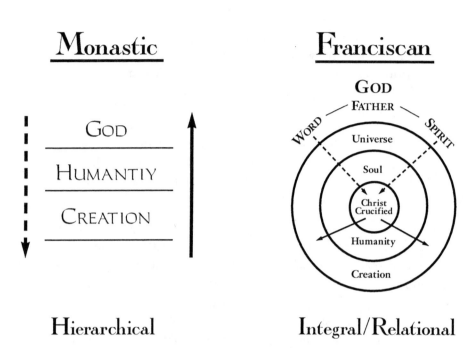

Franciscan

Hierarchical

Integral/Relational

Figure 1.   A comparison of world views between the monastic tradition and the Franciscan tradition based on Bonaventure's theology. The monastic journey follows the Plotinian introversion and ascension pattern whereby the desire for union with God means detachment from the world and interior perfection of the soul. The ascent is hierarchical, in the form of a ladder, in that the soul moves toward the transcendent God, aspiring to contemplation in the heavenly Jerusalem. In the Franciscan tradition, emphasis is placed on the incarnate Word who takes on human nature and thus unites to all creation. To ascend to union with God is to be conformed to Christ in soul and body. While the spiritual journey follows the pattern of introversion and ascension, the hierarchization or perfection of the soul necessitates a detachment from the world of sin but not from the created world itself. Rather, at the highest stage of mystical union one becomes the servant of all, expressed through compassionate love, which is an outward movement of crucified love for neighbor and a filial relationship to the non-human world of creation (indicated by the solid arrow).

KEY: Incarnation   Human ascent to God

upward beyond the world like the Plotinian flight of the alone to the Alone. Rather, in union with Christ one is drawn into the heart of the world where Christ is center.

Union with Christ not only bears significance for humanity but, in Bonaventure's view, the material world has spiritual potency and "cries out" for perfection. In other words, the fate of creation is intertwined with the human journey. If the relationship between the human person and God is disrupted, so too, is the relationship between God and creation disrupted. Only when the human person is conformed to the poor and humble Christ does one stand in a relationship of poverty and humility both to the created world and to one's neighbor. Union with Christ Crucified means that rather than standing in power over others and creation itself, one stands "under" or united to others in a stance of humility and servanthood, like Francis, "burning in love" for Christ and for one's neighbor.

Bonaventure's world view is an integrative world view, one that moves toward a unity of relationship between God, humanity and creation precisely because Christ is the center. The basis of all relationship is trinitarian, the Father and Son united in the Spirit—in union with the Son, one is in union with the Father and Spirit. The importance of relationship rests on the fact that the Trinity is relational. The Trinity is grounded in the relationship of the self-diffusive good which is essentially a relationship of love. The incarnate Word who manifests the Trinity in a unique way embodies the divine good in the created world. In light of this, one can say that Christ truly expresses the love of God in the world. To be in union with Christ who is center, therefore, is to participate in the divine diffusive creative love. Just as Bonaventure sees Francis' journey to God as a two-fold movement, an ascent to God and a descent to neighbor (*LM* 8, 1) or an inward spirit of love expressed in the desire for martyrdom (*LM* 13, 10), he clearly sees that the world is dynamic, sustained by the self-diffusive goodness of God. To participate in this creative goodness through conformity to the Crucified is to become co-creative with God, transforming the world in divine goodness and bringing the world closer to its consummation in God. The passion of Christ is God's perfect communication of love because love gives of itself freely and totally to the other. To become one with Christ in his passion is to become self-diffusive in love.

Catherine LaCugna in her insightful book, *God For Us*, argues that a truly Christian understanding of the Trinity and, correspondingly, authentic Christian living, was lost early on in the Church when the doctrine of the Trinity was never fully integrated in the Christian life. This led, she indicates, to a type of ditheism whereby Christians professed a belief in the Trinity but acted as if God was purely monistic. Commenting on Karl Rahner's theology of the Trinity she states:

> At least two factors prompted Rahner to fomulate the axiom on the identity of the economic and immanent Trinity. First was *the isolation of the doctrine of the Trinity from piety and theology*. Apart from a few studies in the early part of this century, trinitarian doctrine has had negligible influence on Christian life and piety. Certainly the patterns of liturgical prayer—baptism into the threefold name of God; the trinitarian structure of doxologies; eucharistic prayers offered to the Father through Christ; the threefold design of creeds—are constant reminders of the trinitarian pattern of the economy of redemption. But, in Rahner's estimation, in their practical life most Christians are mere 'monotheists'. In fact, Rahner comments, "should the doctrine of the Trinity have to be dropped as false, the major part of religious literature could well remain virtually unchanged.[40]

Bonaventure's doctrine of the Trinity which gives rise to a world view with Christ as center rectifies this malady of the Christian faith that has persisted through the centuries. In the created world there can be no other way to live in the heart of the Trinity than by living in Christ. Christ *is* the heart of the Trinity in the created world. Bonaventure underlines the fact that it is Christ's humanity and, in particular, his suffering humanity, that manifests the love of the triune God in the world. There is only one way, therefore, to live in the Trinity of love and that is to live in personal relationship to Christ Crucified in whom the Trinity is expressed. The relationship between the Trinity and Christ is the essential meaning of the *Itinerarium*. The journey into God is the journey into Christ in whom the triune God is expressed. It begins when one desires God wholeheartedly and prays to God through an outcry of prayer. The journey is a growth in knowledge of God by coming to know the person of Christ as truly divine and human, and a growth in love of God by coming to love Christ. It is a journey of moving ever closer to the mystery of God through knowledge and love in union with Christ. It is union with Christ that leads one into the heart of the Trinity.

For Bonaventure, the journey to God is not simply a journey *to God* but a journey *into God* who pours himself out into the world in the cross of Jesus Christ. Thus, it is a journey into the world and into God. The way each person lives in relation to the Crucified influences the destiny of the world. Bonaventure does not uphold a *fuga mundi* in a hierarchical sense, a rejection, separation or subordination of the material world. Rather, his is an intentional flight, a *fuga affectorum mundi*, effected through union with Christ and the grace of the Holy Spirit whereby the world ceases to serve as an end in itself and is instead restored to its true role as a means—*the* means, the truly *human* means—to God. The Seraphic Doctor has a profound grasp of the unity of the human person as a multi-dimensional nature of sensual, spiritual and contemplative modalities, so that the journey to God is never a linear progression of transcending the world. Rather, it is a simultaneous process of ascent and descent. One never leaves the world precisely because it is part of humanity's God-given nature to be *in* and oriented *toward* the world. However, sin disrupts our right relationship to the world and, since Christ alone restores the ladder broken in Adam, our relationship to the world is restored only in union with Christ. Bonaventure's modification of the Pseudo-Dionysian emanation/return scheme shows that the closer one is drawn to God through union with Christ Crucified, the closer one is drawn to the created world. As von Balthasar states, in Christ the world has been grasped by God.[41]

Mysticism of the Human Person

This brings me to my final point with regard to Bonaventure's world view. We have identified the center of this view as Christ Crucified sustained by a metaphysics of the good. By this I mean that love is the very basis of created reality insofar as the self-diffusive divine good is embodied in the Crucified Christ. However, I would argue that it is not Christ but the human person, the mystery of the human person who is *capax Dei*, who rests at the base of Bonaventure's mysticism. Turning to the prologue of the *Itinerarium* and the beginning of that new direction for him on the mount of La Verna, we see that his spontaneous insight is not at first the Crucified Christ but the stigmatized Francis. What initially impresses Bonaventure is not what God has done for us in Christ but what Francis *has become* in Christ and how his transformation in Christ has transformed the world around him. He sees Francis as one who reached the height of heaven, as one who became a sacrament of God in the world, and as one who, conformed to Christ, helped restore the world in rightful relationship. Bonaventure's relevance to the contemporary world rests precisely on this point—that every person is to be transformed in Christ if the world is to reach the final age of peace and consummation in God. Each person must participate in the good and become self-diffusive goodness which means interacting with humanity and creation on the basis of compassionate love.

In his sermon, "Christ the one Teacher of All," Bonaventure states that, in the incarnation, Christ perfected the world,[42] yet, the world remains incomplete. It is perfected and not perfect; it is consummated and not completed. He views Christ, the most noble perfection of natures, as the center of a consummated world; indeed, it is because of the incarnation that "potency is reduced to act and the perfection of the entire created order is realized."[43] Christ enables perfection of the created order and exalts human nature by uniting it to the divine. Although Bonaventure extols the wonder of the incarnation, his attention seems directed to the nobility of human nature made fit "to be united in a unity of person with the divine." As he states: "When God became man the works of God were brought to perfection . . . but the last among the works of the world is man."[44] What the figure of the stigmatized Francis exemplifies for the Seraphic Doctor is not only the divine height to which our noble human nature may reach but the breadth, length and depth of that union with regard to the whole created world. We might say that undergirding Bonaventure's Christocentric world view is a "mysticism of the human person" whereby he sees the perfection of the created order intertwined with the perfection of the human person in union with Christ. The model of Francis shows that in union with Christ Crucified, compassionate love unifies the relationship between God and the world. Without being too bold in my speculation, I might say that the created order is perfected in Christ when the human person is perfected in Christ. Simply put, the destiny of the created order depends on humanity and humanity's relation to Christ the center. Anthropology is bound up with Christology. Francis is not only the model, but he also reveals the profound role of the human person in the created world—a dynamic role that is kindled by the compassionate love of the Crucified. The role of the human person is to transform the world by participating in the good and becoming good, that is, self-diffusive in love. It is to become Other-centered whereby the person finds his or her truest self in relation to the Other, to Christ, and to the neighbor redeemed by Christ. It is to become compassionate in love, humble in stance, and expressive in action. To find one's truest self in Christ means to risk all in the name of love.

The mystical relationship of the human person to God through the burning love of the Crucified leads one to the heart of God—the burning love of the Trinity whose love burns in the world through the cross of Jesus Christ. Although Bonaventure maintains that God is immanent in the world without being dependent on it (*Itin.* 6, 2), it seems that God, in a mysterious way, needs *us*; that God's world is incomplete without *us* because we are made in the image of the Son. In the created world, even the Trinity is incomplete without humanity.[45] What Bonaventure illuminates in the life of Francis is that God, present in the world, calls out to us from the cross. He calls out to us that we may find him, and in finding him, love him, and in loving him, that we may love the world in him. As he writes in the *Soliloquy*: "Christ on the cross bows his head, waiting for you, that he may kiss you . . . that he may embrace you . . . that he may enrich you . . . that he may give himself totally."[46]

Thus, while I agree with the position that Bonaventure's theology is Christocentric, I would qualify this by saying that it is anthropologically Christocentric. While the weight of the mystery rests on the part of the divine, it rests equally on the human nature that

God has humbly bent down to lift up as his own. The figure of the stigmatized Francis reminds each of us of our Christian vocation: to be another incarnation of the Word in all its mystery. Through the burning compassionate love of the Crucified, we are called to reenact the mystery of the Crucified in our own life. Until we enter into that mystery and express that mystery through compassionate "burning" love, for our neighbor and for creation, the world remains incomplete.

8

The Contemporary Relevance
of Bonaventure

To study a philosopher, theologian and spiritual writer such as Bonaventure is to engage in a continuous stream of rich thought that unifies all reality—God, creation, and the universe—in a comprehensive vision. Perhaps what enabled Bonaventure to formulate such a comprehensive synthesis was the fact that he lived in the Middle Ages, a time when the harmony of heaven and earth seemed so synchronous that the whole universe resounded "like an immense zither," as Marie-Dominique Chenu once stated.[1] The idea that the macrocosm or the world was contained in the microcosm or human person was not a radical idea but one quite common among many writers. The earth was the center of a hierarchically ordered universe, sealed by the heavens. In this medieval world where the figure of the suffering Christ as personal Savior predominated, a unified world view with the Crucified Christ as center was not totally unthinkable—although perhaps radical for its time.

One might say that, Bonaventure was a radical thinker, radical not in an overt intellectual sense but rather in the sense that his thought emerged from radical love, a love that entered deeply in the mystery of the Crucified Christ. His profound insights to the mystery of the Crucified enabled him to formulate a view of the incarnational view of the world with Christ as its center, indicating that the world is grounded, metaphysically, in the self-diffusive good or love of God. In this respect, his doctrine of the Crucified Christ is relevance to our contemporary world in which individualism, autonomy and self-sufficiency, in addition to a spiral of violence, predominate. The basis of his doctrine is the notion of relationship. Relationship is fundamental to Bonaventure because God is essentially relational. God is not simply relational in the sense of personal being, but rather God is relational in terms of dynamic exchange—the self-diffusive goodness of God. By his very nature, God pours out his goodness to others; in the Trinity, the Father, diffuses goodness to the Son and Spirit. In creation, the self-diffusive goodness of God gives rise to created reality. Just as the Son, the Word, emerges out of the depths of divine goodness, so too, everything created through the Word arises from the goodness of God and therefore reflects the love of God.

The dynamic outpouring of divine goodness in the world is made possible precisely because the Word is center. Through the Word God communicates all that he has and all that he is. The Word indicates to us that God is not a being of monologue but God is dialogic, interactive, one who "speaks" in the variety of createdness. Bonaventure uses the analogy of language to describe the relation of the Word to the Father.[2] Just as language involves activity and interaction, so too, God continuously acts in the created world through the Word. The richness of Bonaventure's doctrine of the Word corresponds to the Gospel of John where the Word made flesh is placed at the center of divine life, the act of creation, and the whole of human history. The story of this Gospel, as John Lakers states, recounts metaphors of intimacy, culminating in Jesus' prayer that all be one in him as he is with the Father by loving one another as he loves them.[3]

While the notion of center is fundamental to Bonaventure's theology, such a center seems to be lacking in the complex world of today, a world that orders itself according to power and domination. It is difficult to say what has happened to the center of our world; or if indeed there ever was a center, as evolutionists would argue. Yet, for Bonaventure, a center is a metaphysical absolute because God himself is "centered" in the Word. Jesus Christ, the Crucified Word, is the center of communication between God and the world. Such communication is not simply an acquiring of knowledge, but an act of love.

Bonaventure's theology of the Word is immensely rich for us today because it underscores the fact that God speaks to us in the mystical language of love. God is not the unmoved Mover of Aristotle but the dynamic lover revealed in Christ. God communicates to us in the language of love, a love which does not rest on language alone but on deed, on act. "God so loved the world that he sent his only Son" (Jn 3:16). Love, according to Bonaventure, means going out to the other and uniting oneself to the other.[4] For the Seraphic Doctor, God is intimately involved with the world because God is love. God, by nature of his self-diffusive good, communicates to the world all that he has and all that he is. To say that the world is created by God is to say that the world is sustained by the divine goodness, that is, God's eternal, self-diffusive love. This is not an abstract concept for Bonaventure but a concrete act in which divine love is visibly manifested in the Crucified Christ. God reveals his diffusive goodness, his love, on the cross.[5] In Christ's passion and death, God communicates the entirety of God's love to us; and because communication, by its very nature demands receptivity and response, Bonaventure impels us to respond by conforming ourselves to Christ. As he writes: "He withstood all these sufferings in order to set you aflame with love for him; in order to move you, in return, to love him with all your heart, all your soul, and all your mind. . . . We are invited to love him, and in loving him, to follow his example."[6]

Bonaventure's doctrine of Christ the center means not only that Christ is the center of all knowledge but that through the Word, God is intimately involved in the created world; all of the world, including nature itself, flows from God's goodness and, in some way, is related to God. Creation is not inert matter, a series of physico-chemical reactions; rather, it is "spiritualized matter," reflecting the divine presence and destined for consummation in God. Creation flows out of the self-diffusive goodness of God *ad extra* and therefore is related to God.

The fact that God is intimately united to creation as the divine good corresponds to the idea that God is perceived *altissime et piissime*. It is precisely because God is Most High that God is most intimately united to the created world; for the nature of God is such that nothing can exist outside him without in some way being related to him. God is by nature a coincidence of opposites, a divine mystery which is grounded in the Word as center. When we contemplate the mystery of Jesus Christ, Bonaventure states, we see that he is "the first and last, the highest and lowest, the circumference and center, the alpha and omega, the caused and cause, the Creator and creature, the book written within and without."[7] Thus, because of Jesus Christ, the Word uncreated and incarnate, nothing that exists, or that has existed or will ever exist, exists outside the overflowing goodness of God. This is a point to ponder in our modern scientific world.

For Bonaventure, the divine love in the world manifested to us in Jesus Crucified is the revealed goodness of God. We are called to participate in this divine goodness because we are made in the image of God and, therefore, like God, we are called to be in relationship to God, our neighbor and creation. We are called to reciprocate the communion of God's love. According to Bonaventure, relationship with God can only come about through Jesus Christ who, as mediator, unites God and humanity in a single center. Such relationship is not static or passive; rather, it is a dynamic interaction just as God dynamically interacts with the world through the Word and, in a particular way, through the Crucified Word. The journey to God is a journey through imitation of and conformity to the Crucified Christ—it is a journey into a deeper relationship with Christ. Union with the Crucified brings about a right relationship of the human person to God and the world by restoring the divine image in which we are made.

In contemporary terms, we can describe the restoration of the human image in Christ in three ways: as a decentering of self; as an empowering of self; and as a growth in compassion. The "decentering of self" refers to our search for authentic identity today in a world saturated with images. Bonaventure assures us that by joining oneself to Christ through imitation and conformity, one finds one's truest self in Christ. He viewed the stigmatized Francis as a "true image," because Francis became his truest self in the image of Christ. Describing Francis after the Stigmata, Bonaventure writes: "When the true love of Christ had transformed his lover into his image and the forty days were over . . . the angelic man Francis came down from the mountain bearing with him the image of the Crucified."[8] For Bonaventure, mystical union is not an absorption of self in God but a de-differentiation, a true becoming of self in relationship to the Other, to Christ. By fully uniting oneself to Christ in flesh and spirit, one acquires a new power to act in the world which s/he did not have otherwise. We can describe this effect of union with Christ as an empowering of self. Francis became "filled with the spirit" and was able to prophesy, to perform miracles, to heal and restore broken relationships in the world. When we find our true self in God through conformity to Christ, we begin to acquire the spirit of Christ, the spirit of love that impelled Christ to suffer and die on the cross. Union with the suffering humanity of Christ enkindles the flame of burning love within, the flame of compassion, enabling one to act with compassion in the world, just as Francis did in his relation to humanity and creation. As we grow in love through conformity to the Crucified, we acquire the form of crucified love which, according to Bonaventure, is to be expressed in the desire for martyrdom, the desire to lay down one's life for another in the spirit of Jesus Crucified. Thus, in light of Francis, we can say that relationship with the Crucified Christ enables us to become authentically human—to become "all that we can be"—not in a superficial sense of acquiring power and possessions but in the deepest and truest sense of being an image of God in the world.

If relationship is the underlying key to Bonaventure's mysticism of the Crucified, the center of unity of God, humanity and creation, then how do we find this center in a century that "boasts" of more wars and violence than any other has experienced? According to Bonaventure, we find the center first within us, within the depth of our soul where Christ Crucified is center. But the discovery of the center and the journey to union with Christ necessitates that we move outward, to our neighbor and to the world of creation. Union with the Crucified is not a private I—Thou relationship, for the union by its very nature seeks expression. Thus, as we grow in the love of God through conformity to Christ, we mature in the love of our neighbor redeemed by Christ. Love of God and love of neighbor are two axes of the same center so that as we "ascend" to God we "descend" to our neighbor in compassionate love. This twofold movement that Bonaventure describes in union with the Crucified is the path to peace. His doctrine of union with the Crucified, as the path which leads to mystical peace, speaks to a world of violence. There is no other way to peace, Bonaventure states, than through the burning love of the Crucified.[9]

From Violence to Peace

Bonaventure's doctrine is illuminated by the work of the contemporary scholar René Girard. Through extensive analysis of literary works, Girard has shown that only the Crucified Christ can break the spiral of violence that has embedded itself in the human matrix and, through unconditional love, lead to peace.[10] While violence seems indigenous to humankind, its origin lies at the beginning of humanity. According to Girard, we are existentially mimetic, created by God, in the image of God, so as to imitate God. Our original desire for God was itself our imitation of God since all desire is a form of imitation. Gil Bailie states that the story of the fall is the story of contagious desire, a type of desire awakened by that of another's desire. In the story of Genesis, the serpent inspired Eve to desire the fruit of the forbidden tree. Behind this was Eve's desire to be God-like. The fall, according to Bailie, is the moment when our desire ceases to be directed toward God and becomes directed toward other things.[11] The effects of the fall distorted true mimetic desire and transformed it into mimetic rivalry. This dual mechanism of mimetic-desire mimetic-rivalry has given rise to a spiral of violence in the history of humanity. Through a literary reading of the Scriptures, Girard has discovered that the spiral of violence is broken only in the cross of Jesus Christ, since Jesus confronts violence with the truth of the unconditional love of God. Although Girard approaches the cross from an anthropological and not a theologial view, his work underscores the fact that it is only in union with Jesus Crucified that one can attain true peace.

Bonaventure, in a sense, anticipates Girard by over seven hundred years by discovering the way to peace through the burning love of the Crucified. By exhorting Christians to imitate and conform themselves to the crucified humanity of Christ, Bonaventure helps redirect human desire to its proper end, to the God who is peace.

Participation in the life of Christ through imitation and conformity reestablishes authentic human desire, the desire for peace and happiness which can only be found in God. Bonaventure advises a Poor Clare nun, for example, to "desire nothing else other than to be able to die with Christ on the cross."[12] Since this desire is enkindled in us by the Holy Spirit, true desire is the work of the Spirit—the Spirit of love.[13] For Bonaventure peace is the fruit of love. True peace, he states, cannot be attained without charity. "As soon as we acquire charity, all that pertains to perfection becomes easy: acting or suffering, living or dying. We must advance, therefore, in perfect love, for perfect love leads to perfection in all else."[14] He claims that the summit of love which leads to peace is attained in union with Christ Crucified which means that one is to become like the Crucified, nailed to the cross. The term "nailed to the cross" seems like a harsh admonition and, yet, what it means is to put those things that stand in our way to union with God (personal wealth, family, nation, power) in proper relationship. Bonaventure's path to peace through the Crucified is the fruit of his meditation on the stigmatized Francis. The poor man of Assisi who converted from power and wealth to suffering and compassionate love, by conformity to the Crucified, became a man of peace. As Bonaventure writes:

> This is the peace proclaimed and given to us by our Lord Jesus Christ and preached again and again by our father Francis. At the beginning and end of every sermon he announced peace; in every greeting he wished for peace; in every contemplation he sighed for ecstatic peace—like a citizen of that Jerusalem of which that Man of Peace says, who was peaceable with those who hated peace: Pray for the peace of Jerusalem. For he knew that the throne of Solomon would not stand except in peace, since it is written: In peace is his place and his abode in Sion.[15]

For Bonaventure, ecstatic union with the Crucified, leads one to the highest stage of love because it leads one to the heart of the Trinity, the heart of peace. To enter into the mystery of the cross in one's own life, therefore, to become crucified with the Crucified, leads to mystical peace. Through conformity to Christ Crucified, the soul becomes interiorly free to enter into the fullness of God's love.

Imitation of Christ and participation in his life, in a sense, "resets" our mimetic desire, orienting it to its proper end which is God. By becoming crucified with the Crucified, the violence within us is overcome and we can be drawn by true mimetic desire into the silent mystery of God where the fire of divine love envelops us in peace. The God who is love is peace.

If the beginning of violence is, as Girard claims, due to a perversion of our desire, then a fundamental question we should ask ourselves is, what do we desire? For sin is the consequence of falling away from God, of desiring to be like God, and contagiously desiring what our neighbor possesses. If our desire is not first for God, then all our desires are necessarily distorted—they are "broken" desires which ultimately lead to violence within ourselves and in our relationships to others. As Girard points out, a distortion of mimetic desire leading to mimetic rivalry is the basis of a spiral of violence in humanity. Bonaventure clearly sees desire at the base of our rightful relationship to God and the world. In the prologue to the *Itinerarium*, for example, he writes:

> No one is in any way disposed for divine contemplation that leads to mystical ecstasy unless like Daniel he is a *man of desires* (Dan 9:23). Such desires are kindled in us in two ways: by an outcry of prayer that makes us call aloud in the groaning of our heart and by the flash of insight by which the mind turns most directly toward the rays of light.[16]

Similarly, in the prologue to the *Lignum vitae* he writes: "The true worshiper of God and disciple of Christ, who *desires* to conform perfectly to the Savior of all crucified for humankind should, above all, strive with an earnest endeavor of soul to carry about continuously, both in his soul and in his flesh, the cross of Christ."[17] And in the *Legenda Major* Bonaventure writes that Francis became a perfect follower of Christ because "the flame of *heavenly desire* was fanned in him by his frequent prayer, and his desire for his heavenly home led him to despise as nothing all earthly things."[18] The desire we must possess, according to Bonaventure, is essentially the desire of the heart for the good. What would Bonaventure say to a contemporary world that upholds money, wealth, power and prestige, as the principal desires? His answer would probably be that given to the Poor Clare Nun: desire God alone. Pure desire is what Bonaventure teaches and his advice on how to strive for this is simple: one must turn one's *entire heart, mind and soul to God.*[19] Since that which brings happiness and peace rests in God, only the desire for God can lead to happiness and peace. This is not merely an exhortation of medieval piety but an idea rooted in the fact that, in the incarnation, God has turned his entire being, all that he has and all that he is, to us. Should God expect any less of us than what God has given and continues to give to us?

For Bonaventure, desire is closely associated with prayer; indeed, it is enkindled by "an outcry of prayer." No one can rightly turn to God without desire and prayer. "Prayer," he writes, "is the mother and source of ascent."[20] Prayer is the lifting up of our heart to God, the opening up to God of one's entire being. Prayer, according to Bonaventure, is rooted in our existential poverty, our absolute dependency on God. It seeks the grace which will "bring the soul to the point where it is re-oriented completely toward God."[21] Prayerful desire is the desire of the heart for the good; it makes one cry out "in the groaning of the heart and impels one, by a flash of insight, to turn the mind directly and intently toward the rays of life."[22] Desire itself is a type of unceasing prayer. Bonaventure maintains that spiritual desire is opposed to corporeal or temporal desire and is experientially grounded in the ever deepening enjoyment and possession of the most high good—that is, the possession and enjoyment, albeit imperfect, of God. It is a type of love that yearns to cling to God; the type of love shown by the Apostle Paul who longed with desire to depart from the world and be united to Christ.[23] It is love which longs to possess completely the beloved. In his *De regimine animae* Bonaventure writes:

> Desire intensely that God be well-pleased through a generous imparting of the Holy Spirit; desire more intensely to conform to God through an exact imitation of Christ Crucified; desire most intensely to know God by seeing the eternal Father face to face, so that you may truly sing with the prophet: "Athirst is my soul for God the living God. When shall I go and behold the face of God?"[24]

Unlike Gregory of Nyssa who spoke of insatiable desire that continues even in eternal life,[25] Bonaventure sees fulfillment of spiritual desire in Christ. As he indicates in the *Itinerarium*, it is desire that draws the soul upward in its ascent to God where, in union with Christ, the soul passes over in him to find its ultimate and total fulfillment in God. It is Christ, therefore, who answers the prayer of our desire for God. Bonaventure maintains that we "should turn our heart, mind, and soul to Christ" if we truly desire the love of God, that love which leads to peace. Bonaventure's doctrine of desire serves as a spiritual antidote to what Girard has identified as the fault of mimetic-desire mimetic-rivalry that lies at the base of humanity's violence. Only in Christ can our desire be healed of its self-centered mechanism and become oriented toward its fulfilling end in God. Once our desire is oriented toward its proper end can we hope for a unified world of peace in Christ the center.

Bonaventure and Postmodernism

The movement to overcome a fragmented world, a world of violence, and to strive for unity underscores the trend in Postmodern spirituality. Postmodernism rises from the ash heaps of the death camps of World War II and the failure of reason alone to save humankind. It is an attempt to overcome a fractured world ushered in by modernity and the Cartesian turn to the subject. With the dualism of soul/body, spirit/matter, grace/nature, modernity sanctioned a denial of the human self as internally related to other things, including one's own body.[26] God was pushed out of a world that seemed to regulate itself according to its own internal laws. Ewert Cousins claims that by divorcing spirit from matter, modernity stripped the created world of the divine good.[27] Postmodern spirituality seeks to organically integrate the human person into the world created by God, to overcome all dualisms and separations by striving for unity.

Massive destruction in this century due to war has impelled Christians to reconsider the presence of God in the world. The prophets of Postmodernism are those such as Dietrich Bonhoeffer, Joseph Kentenich, Chiara Lubich, and Simone Weil, who were either incarcerated in concentration camps or endured camp-like conditions.[28] Postmodernists speak of an incarnational spirituality, the absent wholly other God of modernism returns, descends, and takes on flesh anew. As Ann Astell writes: "That return and enfleshment necessarily calls attention to the people, things, places, tasks, and events in our lives, and the way they mediate between God and humankind and among the members of a community to represent the unrepresentable."[29] Postmodernism is a return to the exemplary world that Bonaventure so eloquently described in his writings. As Astell states:

> God bridges the distance between himself and the world through sensible reflections of Christ (*Abbilder*), the *Logos* or *Urbild* of all creation, who in the fullness of time stripped himself of glory and became human. These creaturely reflections of Christ . . . condition our faith, represent God to us through a kind of transference, allow us to experience his love, capture our hearts, and finally allow for the organic transmission of our affections to the God we cannot see.[30]

Mediation, as Postmodernists tell us, is the basis of the relationship between God and the world. Bonhoeffer speaks of Christ as "the mediator not only between God and man, but between man and man, between man and reality."[31] Weil emphasizes Christ as the *Logos* and affirms the necessity of creatures as *metaxu* ("bridges") to God, affirming the possibility "for us to be mediators between God and the part of creation which is confided to us."[32] Kentenich speaks of creation as "the organism of attachments" that binds our hearts to God and to one another.[33] Mediation, therefore, is both vertical and horizontal; it is rooted in Christ the Word. Postmodern spirituality strikes a chord with Bonaventure's spirituality of a world created and sustained by the Word of God. Through the Word, the world is in God and God is in the world. Every created thing "speaks" and "reflects" God, so that creation is like a "ladder" which we may climb to God.[34]

Although Bonaventure clearly sees Christ as mediator, he also sees the human person conformed to Christ as a participant in mediation. Just as Christ reconciled the world to friendship with God, so too, the person, like Francis, helps reconcile the world to harmony and peace. The mystery of the human person, the one who is the image of God, reflects the mystery of Christ. The Christ center that Bonaventure describes becomes truly a dynamic center when it is discovered first within our own life and then in the world. He indicates that we cannot be mediators in the world unless we are first reconciled within our selves, and this means discovering the center of Christ within us.

For Bonaventure, the discovery of Christ is a spiritual program which he describes in the context of the soul's journey into God. The journey into God is not a flight from the world but a flight into the world, a grasping of the world in God just as the world has been grasped by God in Christ. To "grasp" the world is to grow in wisdom in union with Christ, attaining a right relationship with God, neighbor and creation, and living in the spirit of compassionate crucified love. It is to desire God with one's entire heart, mind, and soul by turning toward Christ and becoming "another Christ" in the world. The medieval theme of *alter Christus*, which Bonaventure describes in light of the stigmatized Francis, corresponds to the goal of Postmodern spirituality. As Astell writes:

> The themes of longing and desire predominate in Postmodern spirituality. Whereas premodern and modern spirituality (albeit in different ways) emphasized the soul's ascent to God, however, Postmodern spirituality simultaneously wills such an ascent and knows it to be impossible. Unable to "leave the world" as the monks of old did, Postmodern saints remain there and actively await the overshadowing of the Holy Spirit; at every moment, they welcome the *descensus Dei*, the "coming" of God into the world, as Mary did; expectant, they seek to discover God there, in the most unexpected of places, in the wasteland and the carnival. Indeed, they themselves naively set God present there, where he would not "be" without them, through their work, prayer, joyfulness and suffering. They themselves become God's instruments and points of in-break.[35]

The Postmodern concepts of the "descent" of God, spiritual motherhood, and becoming instruments of God's presence in the world are characteristically Franciscan themes. For Bonaventure, it is precisely the descent of the Word into the world that impels one to seek God in the world by uniting oneself to Christ, thus mediating the divine presence in the world by regenerating the divine goodness through compassionate love.

Bonaventure's journey to God through the Crucified Christ underscores what Postmodernists call a deconstruction and reconstruction of the self. For Postmodernists, the self is not autonomous but is formed by being perceived by the Other who is fundamentally different from the self and thus the object of desire. The Other in Bonaventure's view is the Crucified Christ. As he describes union with the Crucified in the life of Francis, we see that this total turning to Christ, the Other of the self, means a gradual process of conversion whereby one's center of gravity is no longer in one's self but in God. It is interesting that Bonaventure structures his biography of Francis according to the seven visions of the cross. At the beginning of his spiritual journey, Francis encounters the cross in which the Crucified speaks to him; at the end of his spiritual journey, he becomes a living icon of the Crucified, bearing in his flesh the mystical wounds of Christ. As Bonaventure writes:

> Behold these seven visions of the cross of Christ, miraculously shown and manifested to you or about you at different stages of your life. The first six were like steps leading to the seventh in which you have found your final rest. The cross of Christ given to you and by you accepted at the beginning of your conversion and which from then on you carried continuously in the course of your most upright life, giving an example to others, shows that you have finally reached the summit of Gospel perfection.[36]

To become one's true self in God for Bonaventure means to become restored in the image of God, to become an image of the Son, and thus to acquire the spirit of the burning love of the Crucified. We might say that Francis' conversion and growth in Christ was a deconstructing of self and a reconstructing of self as self because of his total turning toward Christ Crucified. This "restructuring" of self in Christ enabled Francis' entire world to be restructured and transformed. Bonaventure describes his ardent love for neighbor and creation, his desire for martyrdom by preaching the

Gospel among the Saracens, and his patience in trials and physical suffering. Francis' perfect conformity to the Crucified did not release him from the world; rather, as Bonaventure writes, his love for God's world—humanity and creation—intensified. He writes: "Now fixed with Christ to the cross, in both body and spirit, Francis not only burned with a Seraphic love of God but also thirsted with Christ crucified for the salvation of men."[37]

In light of Francis' conformity to Christ, Bonaventure indicates that relationship with Jesus Crucified is essential to mediating God's presence in the world. We become points of God's "break-in" when we are conformed to the Crucified. This idea undergirds the spiritual journey as a journey into God and a journey into the world grasped by God in Christ. It is the twofold movement of ascending to God and descending to neighbor, the type of journey that Postmodernists advocate. Bonaventure's theology both complements and contributes to Postmodern spirituality by indicating that the "restructuring" of self in Christ must be visibly expressed. Since we are images of God, the image by its very nature expresses the original of what it imitates. In the Stigmata, Francis was "stamped" with the otherness of Christ, the burning love of the spirit, and became an example of authentic Christian living and Gospel perfection.

For Bonaventure, as for Postmodernists, the cross stands at the center of God and the world. It is the fundamental ground of vertical and horizontal mediation. The German theologian and martyr, Dietrich Bonhoeffer, discovered in the universality of human suffering, "the sufferings of God in the secular life," the sufferings of Christ who died for all people without exception and whose cross reconciles Christians and pagans alike.[38] Simone Weil described the cross as the center of creation and the foundation of the world. The very act of creation, she indicated, reflects something of a "divine crucifixion"; for in creation God renounces his power and this renunciation of divine power is the self-diffusion of the divine good, that is, the total love of God for the world.[39] Like these Postmodern Christian mystics, Bonaventure sees the Crucified Christ as the physical and metaphysical center of the world—the absolute center through whom one must "pass over" to the fullness of life in God. The cross of Christ is precisely that which reconciles humanity's broken relationship with God, extending even to the depths of the underworld so that nothing is beyond the reach of God's love. It is by following Christ that the believer can welcome God's descent into the world. The follower of Christ becomes the point of God's break-in, even in suffering and abandonment, which is seen not only as the invincible ground of union with God but also of loving unity with others.

While Bonaventure firmly emphasizes God's presence in the world, Postmodernists maintain that God is both present and absent. God's presence is his absence. Rather than confusing an experiential with a metaphysical absence, however, Postmodernists find another form of God's mysterious presence and activity even in the midst of suffering. Kentenich reminds us that the suffering of the present enables us to share in Christ's ongoing work of redemption while Chiara Lubich, foundress of the Focolare movement, discovers in human suffering a "oneness with Jesus forsaken" and thus the basis for perfect unity.[40] "In our time," Bonhoeffer wrote from prison, "God lets himself be pushed out of the world on to the cross. He is weak and powerless in the world and that is precisely the way in which he is with us and can help us. Only the suffering God can help. The human person is summoned to share in God's sufferings at the hands of a godless world."[41]

Jürgen Moltmann, in his book, *The Crucified God*, describes the mysticism of suffering in our contemporary world. He writes that anyone who suffers without cause first thinks that she or he has been forsaken by God. But anyone who cries out to God in this suffering echoes the dying Christ on the cross, the Son of God. God is not just a hidden someone set over against the human person and to whom the human cries. Rather, in Jesus Crucified, God cries with the human person and intercedes for him or her with his cross. Moltmann states that the human person suffers because that person lives and is alive because she or he loves. The person who can no longer love can no longer suffer, for she or he is without grief, without feeling, and indifferent.[42] Apathy, Dorothy Söelle claims, is the sickness of our times, a sickness of persons and systems, a sickness to death.[43] However, if suffering with the Crucified leads only to self-pity then faith is dissociated from the suffering Christ and he is seen as no more than a replaceable pattern for one's own sufferings. His suffering does not change anything nor does it change the human person who suffers. Rather, suffering is overcome by suffering and wounds are healed by wounds. For the suffering in suffering is the lack of love, and the wounds in wounds are the abandonment, and the powerlessness in pain is unbelief. And therefore the suffering of abandonment is overcome by the suffering of love which is not afraid of what is sick and ugly but accepts it and takes it to itself to heal it. Anyone who enters into love, and through love experiences inextricable suffering and the fatality of death, enters into the history of the human God, for his forsakeness is lifted away from him in Christ and in this way s/he can continue to love. Where we suffer because we love, God suffers in us. Where he has suffered the death of Jesus and has shown the force of his love, the human person also finds the power to continue to love, to sustain the suffering. Moltmann suggests that the more one loves, the more one is open and becomes receptive to happiness and sorrow; this may be called the dialectic of human life. We live because and insofar as we love, and we suffer and die because and insofar as we love. It light of Bonaventure's mysticism of the Crucified, we can say that the world is a mixture of joy and sorrow because *Christ Crucified* is the center of the world. The one who discovers God in the cross of Christ discovers the fullness of life as a mixture of joy and sorrow. Francis, who was a true lover of Christ "was flooded with a mixture of joy and sorrow" when he saw the vision of the crucified seraph. "He rejoiced because of the gracious way Christ looked upon him, but the fact that he was fastened to a cross pierced his soul with a sword of compassionate sorrow."[44]

For Bonaventure suffering is the historical expression of divine love. In the mystery of Jesus Christ, divine love entered into the world in the most profound suffering of poverty and humility. In the *De perfectione vitae* he writes, "from the first day of his life to the last, from the instant of birth to the instant of death, pain and sorrow were his companions."[45] In the *Triplici via*, where he links suffering with perfect love, Bonaventure indicates that to be conformed to Christ Crucified is to suffer; to express the spirit of burning love means to suffer in the body—to be "marked" by the wounds of Christ. Bonaventure sees suffering and love not as opposites but as synonyms; not the suffering of innocent victims but the suffering that comes when we turn to the Crucified in love. The love that is of God is a suffering love, a compassionate love, yet it is this love that leads to peace, happiness and eternal fulfillment.

To enter into this divine love, to be restored in the image of God, means to love with the love of the Crucified—to offer one's life, soul and body to the Other in compassionate love. To be united to Christ, for Bonaventure, is to become cruciform in love. It is the Spirit who draws the believer into the life of the Crucified Christ, inspiring the believer to love with the same intensity that Christ loved. In Bonaventure's doctrine, there is no place for autonomy or individualism; rather, one who is conformed to Christ Crucified inwardly is to express this spirit of conformity outwardly in compassionate love. The idea of expression means to be turned toward the other, Christ and our neighbor, in a whole-hearted manner. The expression of love as self-involvement becomes a sign of God's presence in the world. As J. Kentenich wrote: "What you are, the way you love affects others, determines their misfortunes and increases their happiness."[46] To be totally turned to the Other, Christ and our neighbor, in the spirit of burning love, a love that is willing to sacrifice one's life or suffer for another, is to mediate Christ's presence in the world; indeed, it is to make the center of Christ visible and audible so that, seeing and hearing, others may be drawn into the unity of love, the unity of Father and Son united by the Spirit.

By interpreting Bonaventure in light of Postmodern spirituality, one perceives that his theology serves as an antidote to an individualistic and privatized culture. Johann Baptist Metz argues that suffering proliferates in our era because of a privatization of religion, a middle class emphasis on personal salvation, indvidualism and personal autonomy.[47] Religion has become a private matter, it is no longer the expression of a primary need to be a subject but rather satisfies only cultural and social needs. The bourgeois person takes the Gospel under his or her own direction and uses it for one's own requirements and plans as a means of achieving one's self-preservation and self-defense. In a sense, Metz states, Christians bring their own futures to church to have it religiously endorsed and rounded off, anxious to have it protected and strengthened by religion.[48] The

messianic future then becomes a ritual rounding off and transfiguration of a "bourgeois" future already worked out here and into
eternity.

Bonaventure's mysticism of the Crucified Christ is not a privatized but a deprivatized spirituality. He calls us to turn our entire
being to Christ by first desiring Christ and then imitating Christ, so
that transformed in Christ, we may express the love of God in the
world. Union with the Crucified Christ is not only a personal transformation; it also has an influence on the world. All of creation suffers because all of creation has fallen. What happens to creation,
however, must happen first in the human person. When the soul and
body regain their harmonious relationship by being formed into the
image and likeness of Christ, then will relationships in humanity and
creation be restored; for when the Spirit of self-giving love takes root
within the human soul, then that same Spirit of love can heal the
world. It is in the turning toward the Other that love transforms. For
Bonaventure, this is the mystery of the Crucified Christ. When we
turn toward the image in which we are restored, then we turn toward
the One in whom we are healed. When we are transformed into the
Other of the Crucified, then are we able to turn to our world in a
spirit of healing, compassionate love.

John Lakers claims that in a world that rests on metaphors of
power and judgment we need a metaphor of intimacy. Intimacy
means to be passionately involved with a faithful love.[49] Individuals,
he states, who do not live within the metaphor of intimacy soon iso-
late themselves from a fully human involvement with one another
and with God. Intimacy with Christ means that interaction which
leads to a deepening involvement with him is revealing. God's love
for humans is a willingness to be fully and completely involved in
human reality in and through the incarnation. The Christian
promise of intimacy is seen as the ultimate realizable human purpose for human individuals.[50] Bonaventure's mysticism of the
Crucified Christ is a metaphor of intimacy. It means that God is passionately involved in the world and in the suffering of the world. God
does not stand over the world in power; God stands "united to" the
world in humility and compassionate love because God is by nature
humble and self-giving. God turns towards us as gift in the incarna-

tion. It is precisely because God is most high that he can be humbly and intimately related to us. Only God, who is absolute good, can give his goodness entirely to us without losing anything of God's own goodness. In this respect, God continuously calls us into relationship with him through compassionate love, to be self-giving goodness as he is. Only in this way can Jesus' prayer be realized, the unity of the Father and Son in the Spirit (Jn 17:22). This means living in and embracing the cross. When one turns toward God with all that one has and all that one is, then one turns toward the neighbor in a spirit of burning compassionate love. As we grow in love in union with the Crucified, we are led more deeply into the mystery of servanthood—of humanity and creation. As we "ascend" to God we "descend" to our neighbor and to the created world. The journey to God through the deepening of compassionate love in union with Christ helps us to unravel the spiral of violence—the violence within us and around us—and replaces the metaphors of power and judgment with the metaphor of love. It is this continuous movement toward union with Christ which makes Jesus Crucified "alive" as the center of the world, a center that can draw all humanity and creation into the powerful love of God, the unity of the Father and Son, the center of peace.

In the Middle Ages, the question was raised by theologians, "would Christ have come if Adam did not sin?" It seems that Bonaventure might have answered affirmatively, although he never officially responded to this question. Yet what he sees in the mystery of the Crucified is the profound love of God in the world, the diffusive divine goodness, a love that cries out on the cross to be received, to be loved. Christ Crucified has not only reconciled us to God; he has made possible for all eternity a love relationship with God that surpasses even that which the first Adam enjoyed.[51] Bonaventure's Christ mysticism offers hope to a world of suffering because the future horizon of eternal happiness and peace is already realized in the mystery of the cross.

Suffering persists in the world, and in the pain God may be silent. Yet, Bonaventure reminds us that God is a mystery of opposites, silent and communicative, hidden and present; for God is not simply the Word alone but the Word united to the Father and Spirit.

Although the Father is present in the Son, the Father himself, the fountain of eternal goodness, is always hidden. From a distance, the mystery of God as one who is immanent yet transcendent is inscrutable. But when we turn toward God with our whole heart, our whole soul and our whole mind, through imitation of and conformity to Christ, we discover the mystery in our own life; indeed, at the very center of our life. This mystery is the mystery of love, the love that is hidden since the beginning of the world, the love that moves the sun and the other stars, the love that draws us upward, beyond ourselves, the love that is eternal, dynamic and diffusive—that is of God and is God. Bonaventure tells us that we are invited into this love; indeed, God calls out to us, not from a distant world, but from the suffering of the cross. When we turn our entire being to God and enter within, when we join with Christ in the suffering of the cross, we enter into the depths of this mystery of love, the mystery of the Father:

> Let us die and enter into this darkness. Let us silence all our cares, our desires, and our imaginings. With Christ Crucified, let us pass out of this world to the Father, so that when the Father is shown to us, we may say with Philip: It is enough for us."[52]

At the same time we move, in a no less mysterious way, into the heart of the world where Christ is center. If our journey into God and our journey into the world is through the same Crucified center, that center which mediates our relation to God for all eternity,[53] then we may say that, even in this world of violence and suffering, heaven has been revealed; even here on earth, eternal life has begun.

9

Conclusion

Reinhold Seeberg, in his discussion on the theology of the Middle Ages, claims that Bonaventure's Christology is unoriginal, that the Seraphic Doctor faithfully receives and transmits what he has gleaned from the tradition but in an unimaginative way.[1] What I have tried to show here stands in contrast to Seeberg's claim. For I maintain that Bonaventure's theology not only provides something new but something radically new—radical in the very literal sense of the word (*radix*). Bonaventure has bared the root of the mystery of the divine Word as the mystery of relationship—the mystery of relationship of God with us and the mystery of our relationship to God.

The main inspiration of Bonaventure's theology is Francis, particularly the stigmatized Francis. It is *this* Francis who conveys to Bonaventure the mystery of the Word in all its richness. The Stigmata of Francis lift up Bonaventure's intellectual world above the level of a mere interweaving of the threads of the tradition to a cosmic vision of divine love. The influence of the stigmatized Francis plays a significant role in Bonaventure's writings between the years 1259 and 1274, that is, after his sojourn on the mountain of La Verna where in his reflection on Francis' vision of the fiery Seraph, he discovers the path to peace. Although Bonaventure does not abandon the tradition nor relinquish the ideas of his earlier writings, these take on new meaning in light of the stigmatized Francis. A perusal of Bonaventure's writings between the years 1259 and 1274 show ideas already contained in his commentary on the *Sentences*. What is different, however, is the refined focus of these writings on the mystery

of the Crucified Christ and the model of Francis as the exemplary
Christ mystic.

Bonaventure's thought on the mysticism of the Crucified underscores a development in his Christology although, at the same time,
such a development seems to correspond to his own growth and
transformation in the Crucified. While there is virtually no bio-
graphical evidence to suggest this, it is apparent that his theology
after 1259 is less speculative and reflects a greater emphasis on personal relationship to God as we see in his spiritual writings, for
example, his *Lignum vitae*, *De perfectione vitae*, and *Soliloquium*. Such
an emphasis seems to arise from an inner spirit rooted in God which
reveals itself in the language of ardent love.

What is the mystery of the Crucified Christ that Bonaventure
develops in such a profound way? The answer is, as I believe, grounded in his understanding of God as Trinity. While his doctrine is centered in the mystery of the Word, the eternal Word who is image and
expression of the Father; the incarnate Word in whom all things are
restored; and the inspired Word by whom all things are revealed (cf.
Hex. 3, 2), the significance of the Word is grounded in the Trinity.

The God who is Trinity for Bonaventure is not Trinity as sub-
sisting persons of relationship in the Augustinian sense; God is
Trinity as the self-diffusive good, distinguished in persons ultimately by the Father who is primal and the fountain source of goodness.
The Son is generated by the Father's very nature of the self-diffusive
good, and the Spirit is generated by the dynamic exchange of love
between the Father and Son. Bonaventure's Trinity, which follows the
Greek model, has certain distinguishing features: 1) God is a community of relationship formed by a dynamic exchange of love, since
God is by nature a self-diffusive good, and the highest form of good
is love. This love is a total self-giving to the other; 2) the self-diffusive good underscores a certain "poverty" in God, since the Father
who is primal, retains nothing for himself but by his very nature
gives all that he has and all that he is to the Son; 3) that the Father is,
by nature, oriented toward the Son and the Son, who is image of the
Father, is turned totally toward the Father, underscores a divine
humility; 4) the dynamic exchange of love between the Father and
Son, grounded in poverty and humility, is united in the Holy Spirit.

The reason why the Word becomes flesh is multifold for Bonaventure. He does not clearly articulate an Anselmian position of satisfaction, although the sin of humanity is a reason for the incarnation, albeit, not the first or foremost reason. Rather, the principal reason for the incarnation is to manifest the power, wisdom and goodness of God. He highlights the fact that, in Christ, the Trinity is expressed. However, there is sufficient reason to suggest that love is equally a principal reason for the incarnation. God is essentially a self-diffusive good which by its very nature seeks to share itself with an other. In the Trinity, sharing of the good is the basis of relation between the Father and Son. In the created world, the incarnate Word, particularly the Crucified Word, expresses the self-diffusive good or love of God. God gives himself to be known insofar as he gives himself to be loved. The horizon of God is the gift itself.[2] I have tried to show that the unity of God and the world is based on the relationship of love, the first relationship being that of the Father and Son upon which all other relationships are based. The Crucified is the diffusing center of God's love in the world whereby he reaches down to that which is furthest from him to draw all into his goodness and thus into the love of the Trinity. It is significant that Bonaventure unites the Trinity and Christ through the self-diffusive good, undergirding the fact that Christ Crucified is the fullest expression of God in the world. His thought is recapitulated in the words of Jürgen Moltmann:

> When the Crucified Jesus is called the image of the invisible God, the meaning is that *this* is God, and God is *like this*. God is not greater than he is in his humiliation. God is not more glorious than he is in this self-surrender. God is not more powerful than he is in this helplessness. God is not more divine than he is in this humanity.[3]

Thus, God who is love, and who loves by giving all that he has and is to the other, is expressed in the created world in the person of Jesus Christ. The mystery of Christ's humanity in his poverty and humility is the mystery of God. It is not accidental, therefore, or historical coincidence, that Jesus is born in poor and humble conditions and lives a poor and humble life which culminates on the cross.

Bonaventure sees that the incarnate Word is always the eternal Word. Since this Word is the Word of the Father, and expresses the Father's humble goodness, it is "fitting" that the Word become incarnate in poverty and humility.

If poverty and humility underscore the divine self-diffusive good, then it is again "fitting" that the fullest manifestation of divine love takes place in the cross. It is precisely because Jesus Crucified *is* God, that the Crucified is the fullest manifestation of God as love, as self-diffusive goodness, poured out in the poverty and humility of the cross—the *mysterium* of love. In this way, Bonaventure views the Crucified as the absolute way to God; there is no other path than through the burning love of the Crucified. Nowhere in the tradition do we find such a decisive emphasis on the Crucified, and I have argued that Bonaventure's insight to the Crucified enabled him to transform Neoplatonism into Christocentrism. Bonaventure "Franciscanizes" the Neoplatonic metaphysics of being and transforms it into a Christocentric metaphysics of the good. That which governs our relationship to God, our emanation and return, is the self-diffusive goodness of God, which is revealed to us in the Crucified Christ. Indeed, the Crucified Christ is preeminent in Bonaventure's theology because God is primarily good by nature. Being good by nature, God seeks to "give away" all that he has and all that he is to the other. God's being *is* his goodness and is given to us as gift in the incarnation of the Son and the gift of the Spirit.

While Bonaventure's doctrine of the Crucified is comprehensive in its inclusion of God, humanity and creation, there is one significant aspect of his mysticism that is so obviously missing in his writings that it calls for some comment. Although Eucharistic devotion gained prominence in Bonaventure's time, the feast of Corpus Christi being instituted around 1264, it is noteworthy that Bonaventure rarely discusses the Eucharist in his spiritual writings.[4] Michael Gaudoin-Parker, however, claims that Bonaventure may have composed a treatise for the feast of Corpus Christi, *De sanctissimo Corpore Christi*. In this treatise, Bonaventure down plays the ritual and external side of liturgical celebration but emphasizes the important sacramental symbols or signs of the liturgy for seeking an experiential knowledge of Christ. Since the Eucharist is the way *par excellence* to experience Christ, it recapitulates the purpose of the spiritual journey which is union with Christ.[5] The rare mention of the Eucharist in Bonaventure's writings can only be speculated upon but it seems to reaffirm the profound import of his theology of the Word. Since the Word is the center of all reality, when the Word becomes flesh, all of creation becomes a *sacramentum Domini*. Since the metaphysical center that gives meaning to all reality is the Crucified Christ, it is in this center that the diffusive love of God is manifested—that love which creates, sustains, and draws all things to itself. In this way, the eucharistic liturgy reflects the cosmic liturgy, since all of creation "speaks" of God and thus all of creation is a cosmic liturgy in which Christ Crucified is the high priest. We enter into liturgical celebration when we are conformed to the Crucified in body and soul. Conformity to Christ is true communion with God.

For Bonaventure, participation in the divine self-diffusive good underscores our return to God as well as the return of the whole created world to God. It is for this reason that I suggest that the Crucified Christ is the synthesizing principle of Bonaventure's theology, for this Crucified, self-diffusing center of goodness is what unites humanity, creation and the cosmos to the eternal God. Although Kevin Keane states that God's transcendence has no real "need" for the created world, Bonaventure sees that goodness "compels" itself to create a universe which can manifest and contribute to the perfect realization of his own goodness.[6] The Good is the diffusive center of the world as both the original fountain and the final end of all creatures and is expressed in the form of the Crucified Christ. Christ Crucified *is* the gift of God's self-diffusive goodness in the world.

In the created world, the goodness that is of God finds its ultimate significance in the human person who, as a union of spiritual and material natures, is not only the center of the created order but, moreover, an image of God. While at first this may not seem extraordinary, I believe it is the basis of one of Bonaventure's deep insights, the "mysticism of the human person." Here, the figure of the stigmatized Francis takes center stage. What impresses Bonaventure on the mountain of La Verna while he is there searching for peace is the figure of Francis marked with the mystical wounds of the Crucified, the sign that Francis had arrived at peace and the perfect contemplation of God. As he writes: ". . . there came to mind the miracle which had occurred to blessed Francis, the vision of a winged seraph in the form of the Crucified."[7] To be marked by a sign of God's love not only signifies a contemplative stance but it expresses God's presence in the world.

In light of Francis, Bonaventure maintains that to contemplate God is to attain that peace and happiness in the vision of God which the first Adam enjoyed, and which Francis attained through his conformity to Christ Crucified. Through Jesus Christ, the grace of contemplation is restored in a more perfect way, not merely as knowledge of God but as intimate love of God. Christ is exemplar and teaches both interiorly and exteriorly, that is, in his humanity and divinity. It is by conformity to Christ in his humanity that one arrives at true contemplation of God and this means imitation of and conformity to Christ in soul and body. Since it is Christ Crucified who restores the human image to its true likeness in God, Bonaventure sees that expression of the image takes on the form of crucified love—the love of the burning spirit within. As he writes of Francis:

> He was held up as an example for those who would be perfect followers of Christ . . .by the seal of the likeness of the living God, namely, of Christ Crucified, which was imprinted on his body not by natural forces or human skill but by the wondrous power of the Spirit of the living God.[8]

Bonaventure maintains that Francis not only arrived at the perfect contemplation of God but that he became an icon of Christ Crucified, manifesting the same spirit of compassionate love as did Christ, that spirit of love that is willing to suffer or die for one's neighbor. Francis demonstrated a type of love that ascends to God and descends to neighbor, a love that expressed itself in the desire for martyrdom and strove for unity with neighbor and creation. Francis, therefore, is not only the model of relationship with God but he models the relationship of the human person to others, to community, and to the created world. The Stigmata signify that Francis

attained the supreme love of God through his imitation of and conformity to Christ. Union with Christ Crucified, the center of all reality, enabled Francis to stand with Christ at the center of the world,
united to humanity and creation in solidarity, in the spirit of compassionate love—"burning" for love of God and love of neighbor
who has been created and redeemed by God. In light of the stigmatized Francis, we can say that the mysticism of the human person
means that in the human person, united to Christ, the self-diffusing
goodness of the Creator is clearly and perfectly manifested. Because
the human person is made as an image of the Son, she or he shares,
by grace, in his dynamic love, self-expression and creativity. In union
with Christ Crucified, God inter-penetrates one's being and imparts
a dynamic and creative presence that opens one to infinite possibilities—to be creative and to transcend oneself. "Participation" refers to
the way the human person can share in or possess the life of God. It
is goodness itself that provides the metaphysical basis for participating in the dynamic life of the Trinity. The human person must be
diffusive as his/her creation is diffusive, for this is what it is to be,
and no real *telos* is achieved in its absence. To be God-like is to join in
the intense generosity of goodness itself, a generosity that paradoxically grounds ever-more perfect intimacy in diversity.[9] Participation
in the good means to enter into the intimate love of the Trinity, as it
is revealed in Christ Crucified who is center.

The view that emanation of the good takes place principally for
the sake of a deep and personal relationship of love underscores
Bonaventure's world view. Although I have indicated that
Bonaventure never explicitly articulated a world view, still one is present in his writings when they are read with the Crucified Christ as
the hermeneutical key. His most comprehensive vision is presented in
the *Hexaëmeron* where Christ Crucified is described as the center of
knowledge, history and time. In these lectures, the figure of the stigmatized Francis enables the Seraphic Doctor to formulate a
Franciscan eschatology, one in which the final age of peace is contingent on mystical union with Christ Crucified. Bonaventure's world
view, with Christ Crucified as center, is an integral world view and
overcomes the hierarchy of domination that is inherent in the
Neoplatonic world view. Rather, Bonaventure maintains that in union

with Christ Crucified one is brought into union with the Father in the Spirit and into union with one's neighbor and the created world. This twofold movement toward God and neighbor is an ever-deepening of divine love as it overflows in one conformed to the Crucified. Unity and compassionate love characterize Bonaventure's world view and underscore a world that is authentically trinitarian—the relationships of the persons of the Trinity are the basis of relationships in the created world where the Word is center.

Bonaventure's holistic view of God, humanity, and creation is a systematic vision that resonates with our contemporary world. In a fragmented, suffering, and power-dominated world, Bonaventure offers a vision that is not only breath-taking in its comprehensiveness but metaphysically grounded in divine goodness and contingent on personal intimacy and relationship. It is a world view that is critically needed in our time. He offers the world the truth that the Word, the center of the Trinity, is the center of the world because through the Word all things are created. When the Word takes on flesh in the incarnation, everything in the created world, in the past, present and future, is united to God because the incarnate Word *is* the eternal Word. The world, therefore, is grounded in the Trinity through the Word who is center. As we have seen, this center is the Crucified Word because the cross reaches down to the depths of that which is furthest from God and reconciles all to God. As Crucified, Christ manifests to us the overflowing love of God. Bonaventure reminds us, therefore, that suffering is united to love in the cross of Christ. God's gift of compassionate love is a suffering love that gives of itself freely and unconditionally, even in the face of sin. It is *this* love that sustains the created goodness of all reality.

Bonaventure's mysticism of the Crucified complements a contemporary theology of hope and calls us from a privatized spirituality into the public scandal of the cross. The dangerous memory of the passion of Jesus, according to Johann Metz, must lead us into solidarity with our suffering brothers and sisters in the world—not in a passive way but through an active spirit of compassionate love—that love, as Bonaventure states, that is willing to risk one's life for another, for the sake of truth. Unlike contemporary theologians, however, Bonventure does not advocate a political theology but a theology of union, mystical union with the Crucified Christ. His is ultimately a theology of love that is grounded in the Trinity; it is a love expressed in union with God and with our neighbor. In a sense, Bonaventure's mysticism of the Crucified is more comprehensive than Moltmann's theology precisely because it is grounded in the Trinity and thus offers a divine ground for eschatological peace. The peace that is the fruit of union with Christ interiorly is the peace that Bonaventure envisions in the world when all Christians unite mystically to the Crucified and express their union in compassionate love. Peace is to mark the final age of this world. Union with the Crucified affirms the theory of René Girard that Christ Crucified has broken the spiral of violence in history. Only in union with the Crucified can we overcome violence to attain peace.

We can identify Bonaventure's mysticism of the Crucified within the context of Postmodern spirituality because it is a mysticism that draws its strength from mystical union. Such union overcomes all dualisms of soul/body, spirit/ matter, nature/grace, because Christ is the coincidence of opposites and reconciles all opposites in the unity of his person. In union with Christ, one is in union with oneself, one's world, and one's God and, indeed, draws God into the world at those places where God may seem absent.

Bonaventure sees union of love with Christ Crucified as the basis all unity because it is grounded in the relationship of the Father and Son united in the Spirit. His doctrine of mystical union with the Crucified, leading to the unity of all things in God, calls to mind the need for intimacy, the need to be personally involved with the Other, to give one's self totally to the Other and, in doing so, to find one's true self in relation to the Other. In a world that thrives on individualism and autonomy, the personal intimacy of love that Bonaventure puts forth, in union with the Crucified, is the necessary element that can transform our world.

Bonaventure's theological vision is highly relevant to our age; yet, it is a vision of unity that is so harmonious that one wonders how it can actually be realized. The answer is simply by discovering the burning love of the Crucified here and now, in the daily crosses of our lives. Many of the mystics claim that the incarnation is an act of divine madness, the radicality of God's love. God has not only loved us "wildly" but he has loved us to the point of suffering and death. To love like God is to suffer well, not to seek suffering much less to impose it on others, but to take on another's suffering or bear our own suffering as a way of loving. Bonaventure's world of love is a world of self-involvement, of truly finding one's self in the other through suffering, in union with Christ and our neighbor. By shifting the metaphysical basis of reality from being to the good, Bonaventure dismantles the age-old structure of ontological hierarchy and replaces it with a new system of relations in which the divine "first principle" is the most self-diffusive good or love, giving itself away completely to the point of becoming last. The first is truly the last through diffusion of the good. Because it is God who loves so completely, the ascent to God is the perfection of descending in love. The path is through the poverty and humility of Jesus Crucified who is our way, our truth, and our life. What Bonaventure calls us to is a participation in Christ's crucified humanity through poverty, humility, prayer and compassionate crucified love. We are to enter into the wounds of Christ and there find our happiness and peace because it is there that we find the diffusive love of God.

Our present age has taken the Crucified down from the cross and removed the cross from the center of the world. We are left with the painful suffering of human beings whose only form of redemption is to inflict pain on one another. Without the Crucified as center, violence and domination prevail. Bonaventure assures us, however, that the Word became flesh and was Crucified for us, that this Word is the Word of God eternally united to the Father and Spirit and that only in union with the Crucified Word can love triumph. It is the Crucified who has overcome all brokenness in the world through suffering love. All the wounds of human suffering are healed by his wounds, all the desires of love are filled by his love.

Do we truly desire a world of peace, a world of love, a world of mutuality and unity, a world where God can be at home and we are at home in God? Then we must become crucified with the Crucified, in our spirit and in our flesh. This is the way to perfect love of God and neighbor. There is no other way, neither in this life nor in eternity.

Appendix

Mysticism:
Metaphysical Foundations
and the Monastaic Quest for God

The Word Mysticism

To speak of Bonaventure's mysticism of the Crucified Christ as that which is central to his theology requires an understanding of the word mysticism, especially since this word did not enter the vocabulary of spirituality until after the Middle Ages. According to Michel de Certeau, the word mysticism was a product of seventeenth century France where it was used to identify the place of human effort in contemplative prayer.[1] Mysticism denoted "infused contemplation" which was an extraordinary gift of grace in contrast to "acquired contemplation" which was the fruit of human effort.[2]

Mysticism is a word originally associated with the mystery religions or mystery cults which abounded in the Greco-Roman world. Eleusinian, Dionysian and Orphic mysteries attracted a myriad of devotees to their esoteric rites and ceremonies. The mystic was one who was initiated into the privileged knowledge of divine things and in an oath of secrecy swore to be silent, or literally to keep his or her mouth shut (*myein*) with regard to the ceremonies of the rite.[3] The very term "mysticism," in its etymological meaning, suggests the limits of language, derived from the Indo-European root *mu* (imitative of inarticulate sounds). From this root are derived the Latin *mutus* (mute, dumb, silent) and the Greek verb *myein* (to close the eyes or lips), from which come the nouns *mysterion* (mystery) and *mystes* (one initiated into the mysteries) as well as the adjective/sub-

stantive *mystikos* (mystical, mystic).[4] Louis Bouyer notes that in the
pagan religions the term *mystikos* never had more than the general
meaning of "hidden." It was not used to characterize a spiritual experience nor was any proper religious sense attached to it.[5]

The word mysticism passed into Neoplatonism where it became
associated with shutting the eyes to all external things, a practice
which was central to Neoplatonic meditation. Both Plotinus and
Proclus used the verb *muein* to signify the closed eyes of one who is
rapt in profound contemplation.[6] In the Christian world, the word
mystikos was used in reference to the Scriptures, sacraments, and the
spiritual life. The first Christians to use the word *mystikos* were the
Alexandrians, Clement and Origen, who applied it to Scriptural exegesis and the discovery of the allegorical sense of the Scriptures.[7]
Origen considered exegesis as "mystical and ineffable contemplation,"
illuminating the "mystical sense" as the meaning hidden behind the
literal words of the text.[8] The Christian sacraments, particularly the
eucharist and baptism, were referred to as Christian "mysteries."[9] In
the writings ascribed to Macarius, the word *mystikos* came to modify
union or sharing in the life of God. According to Bernard McGinn,
this is the earliest appearance of the term "mystical union" in
Christian literature.[10] Robert Woods defines Christian mysticism as a
"hidden encounter with God, perceived by the eyes of faith and available to all who have been 'initiated.'"[11] McGinn defines it as "a direct
or immediate consciousness of the presence (or absence) of God."[12]

In the Middle Ages the word mysticism was not widely used, at
least with regard to perceiving spiritual realities. As in the early
church, it was associated with the allegorical interpretation of
Christian Scriptures, referring to the symbolic meaning of the
sacred text.[13] The common term for the phenomenon of mystical
experience in the Middle Ages was *contemplatio*, a Latin translation
of the Greek *theoria*, meaning "looking at" or "gazing at."[14] The word
contemplation described the personal relationship with God as a
"gazing upon" or experiential knowledge of God that could lead,
through grace and perfection, to mystical union. The word mysticism can be broadly conceived as contemplation insofar as one
encounters God either in a direct or indirect manner. In this study I
use the words mysticism and contemplation synonymously since the

word contemplation is frequently found in Bonaventure's writings, although the word mysticism appropriately describes the encounter with God hidden in the person of Jesus Christ which is the core of his mystical theology. When the term "mysticism of the Crucified Christ" is used, it means that God is hidden in the suffering of the cross. There he can be encountered.

Metaphysical Foundations: Plato

In order to understand the Christ mysticism of Bonaventure; indeed, to understand the roots of any Christian mysticism, it is important to understand the metaphysical thought of Plato and the adaptation of his thought in the form of Neoplatonism. Plato's metaphysics provide the most important foundation to the understanding of contemplation first as it relates to epistemology and second as Neoplatonism merges with Christian belief. The question of whether or not Plato was a mystic has plagued more than one scholar; however, there is no doubt that he was a philosopher. As a philosopher, Plato sought true knowledge. That knowledge which one could describe as changeless and true was not to be found, he claimed, from sensory experience but from innate insight into eternal truth. Plato set forth his ideas on the attainment of true knowledge in his "Allegory of the Cave" in which he describes the dim and illusory nature of life in the present world of shadows and the possiblity of a life lived in clear view of the supernal world of forms where the Good, the Form of forms, reigns like a supreme sun making all things visible. Since the soul is by nature divine, it seeks to return to its true home to contemplate true knowledge. Bernard McGinn summarizes the allegory as follows:

> One of the prisoners, chained from birth and condemned to watch mere shadows of images cast by firelight, can only with great difficulty learn to progress through the levels of contemplation to gaze eventually upon the sun itself. Were he to return to the other captives to try to instruct them and to release them from their prison, he would appear so strange and out of place that they would ridicule and perhaps even kill him, just as Socrates was killed. Nevertheless, the whole purpose of

the allegory, as later becomes clear, is to insist that such a return is the philosopher's vocation. He alone can guide the *polis* of blind captives toward a more just social order, just as most later Christian mystics will insist that the contemplative love of God must yield to active love of neighbor within the body of Christ as long as we remain in this life.[15]

According to Plato, the cave is the world revealed to us by our senses. It is a world characterized by unreality. And yet, it is the world we are used to, it is what we think of as "reality." The soul, which really belongs to the divine realm of Forms or Ideas has made itself at home in this world of unreality revealed to us through the senses. Plato's concern, then, is with the soul's search for true reality. The "Allegory of the Cave" shows us some of the problems that this search involves; the first of these is to see that we need to search for reality, and are not in touch with it already. The first stage, therefore, is an awakening to the fact that we are far from home, far from the soul's true abode, the realm of Forms. Once awakened, the soul must begin the gradual process of accustoming itself to true reality. A long and progressive detachment from false reality and attachment to, and growing familiarity with true reality is what Plato sees as the soul's ascent.[16]

Plato's metaphysics is a hierarchical construct of reality based on the notion of the Absolute Good. In the *Timeaus* he describes the formation of the cosmos by the Demiurge who fashions the sensible world based on the world of ideas or forms which in turn derive their perfection by their participation in the Absolute Good. The two worlds, spiritual and sensible, describe two realms of being: the intelligible world of true being which is the world of forms, and the sensible world of objects which are comprised of the image of forms and matter. While the world of forms is true reality, the corporeal world of sensible objects is not true reality but imperfect and subject to change. Thus, observation of the created world and true knowledge are in opposition. Since our physical senses in effect tie us down, the only path to true knowledge is through philosophical reflection. Although Plato portrays a rather negative attitude toward the created world with regard to true knowledge, he ascribes a limited value to the senses insofar as the physical senses can arouse us to seek the more noble forms. We can know Beauty, for example, from the physical beauty of the world. The beauty of creation or of a person can stimulate us to seek that beauty which is true and unchangeable—what we might call spiritual beauty. This is the goal of contemplation, according to Plato, to seek union with the supreme Good, and to desire to possess the Good. He describes this desire as *eros* which is a longing for something that is not possessed. *Eros* is "love for the good that seeks to possess the good."[17] It is an upward attraction that draws the soul back to its true home. It is a longing that begins on the physical level but has its end on the spiritual level since that which we experience here is limited and fleeting.

The *eros* or upward attraction that draws the soul back to its true home is what Plato describes as contemplation. Since like can be known only by like, it is the soul alone which ascends to the realm of the spiritual—the attainment of true knowledge. The body, being base and mortal, does not resemble the divine and therefore does not take flight with the soul in the pursuit of true knowledge. The soul, on the other hand, is like the divine, immortal, intelligible, uniform, indissoluble, and unchangeable.[18] The purpose of the body is to "house" the soul, fallen from its true home in the divine, and to enable the soul to contemplate the divine until it can be released from this earthly tomb and return to its true dwelling in the divine nature. Plato, therefore, envisions a hierarchical world of spirit and matter, soul and body, immortal and mortal, in which spirit, soul and immortality are superior to matter, body and mortality. To be divinized and gain immortality is the goal of the soul here on earth. As he states: "We should make all speed to take flight from this world to the other and that means becoming like the divine so far as we can."[19]

Plotinus

In the first few centuries of Christianity, Plato's metaphysics were revived from under the domination of Aristotelian metaphysics and interpreted in light of new philosophical insights. This revival of Platonism in the third century, referred to as Neoplatonism, claimed as its leader the pagan philosopher Plotinus.

Plotinus elaborated upon the metaphysics set forth by Plato and constructed a hierarchy of reality that consisted of the One, the Intellect (*nous*), and the Soul.[20] The goal of existence is to raise the lower soul or self to consciousness of its higher identity; the transcendent self is to enjoy identity with pure intellect and, through intellect, union with the unknown One.[21] For Plotinus, the One is the source of primordial unity—everything is derived from it and all things in existence flow out from the One. The realm of the intellect which exists below the One is the realm of true knowledge of differentiated reality. Beyond this is the realm of the soul where knowledge is the result of searching and the soul itself is distracted by its lack of unity. Beyond the soul is the material order which receives its coherence from the realm of the soul. Like Plato, Plotinus posited a fall of the divine soul. Having a form of "self-will" souls were subejct to evil and original sin. Although they were co-regent with the Soul, they "got tired of living with someone else" and turned away from the Soul, falling into the body. Therefore, in order to regain its divine status, the soul must liberate itself from its earthly bonds.

To appreciate contemplation for Plotinus is to appreciate the orderly metaphysical scheme he set forth, a scheme so impressive that many Christian writers adapted it to describe the spiritual journey to God. The basic construct of Plotinus' scheme is emanation and return; all things flow out of the One, the source of primordial unity, and all things return to the One. The outward movement of progressively diminishing radiation from the One, emanation, corresponds to a yearning (*eros*) on the part of all beings for unity or return to the One. Such return is a spiritual movement toward deeper inwardness, fostered by and expressed in contemplation.[22] Although the One is the goal, it transcends being and thought because it transcends essence. It is the source of all precisely because it is transcendent to all differentiation toward form.

The process of returning to the One involves a series of stages, according to Plotinus. In the first few stages, there is a separation from the realm of multiplicity, that is, the "here below" as well as from reasoning, since knowledge implies duality and prevents the soul from achieving its unity.[23] That which returns to the One is the intellectual portion of the soul, the *nous*, which is the higher portion linked to the realm of intelligence whereas the lower portion is linked to the material and sentient nature. Plotinus describes return to the One as the path of withdrawing from the multiple and lowest in us and ascending to intellect itself.[24] Withdrawal, therefore, is by way of knowledge so that in knowing oneself, one knows the "divine." The process of withdrawal and ascension requires introversion to the center of the soul, that part which is linked to the eternal source of being.[25] The idea of returning to the center of the soul is one of the hallmarks of Plotinus' doctrine which influenced later Christian writers who translated it as the *apex mentis*. For Plotinus, the soul does not find the One simply in itself, by stripping itself of all multiplicity, but by going beyond itself as well as beyond all knowledge; not simply becoming unified in itself, but in being united to him who transcends it. Thus, he presents a mystical dialectic of immanence and transcendence the purpose of which is to lead the soul to its ultimate liberation. The goal of existence is to raise the lower soul or self to consciousness of its higher identity; the transcendent self is to enjoy identity with pure intellect and through intellect union with the unknown One. This is what Plotinus calls the flight of the alone to the Alone.[26] The Neoplatonic ascent for Plotinus is one marked by desire (*eros*). The role of love in the soul's return to its source is among the most constant themes in Plotinus' thought.[27] The One is the source of the divine *eros* that burns in the soul and of which earthly unions are only a shadow. To love and be united with the One is to be divinized. The fulfillment of the soul's desire to be united to the One is the goal of return. The means to fulfillment of desire are accorded the soul by the intellect. By progressive elimination of what is multiple in operations of the intellect, one ascends to the point where there remains nothing but the ability of the intellect to be absorbed into the center of the soul, where the soul as desire becomes fulfilled and is caught out of itself.[28] Thus, by attaining union with the *nous*, the supreme intellectual principle, the soul becomes love itself.

Plotinus holds up the concept of ecstasy as the mark of union between the soul and the One. Mystical union is both a self-transcendence and a penetration to the soul's true identity. The process of deification, whereby the soul returns to the fatherland,[29] means a transcendence of oneself and the world, the renunciation of one's individuality and absorption into the One as undifferentiated unity. Mystical union is self-transcendence and penetration to the soul's true identity in the One.

Origen

Although Plotinus's doctrine of contemplation underscores a "privatized spirituality," his metaphysical scheme attracted followers among the Christians. One of the earliest systems of Christian Neoplatonic thought in which Plotinian elements can be identified is that described by Origen. A contemporary of Plotinus, Origen claimed to be vehemently opposed to the pagan philosopher's metaphysics; however, as scholars note, Neoplatonism permeated third century Alexandria. Henry Chadwick states that even though Origen wanted to be a Christian and not a Platonist, "platonism was inside him, *malgré lui*, absorbed into the very axioms and presuppositions of his thinking."[30]

According to Origen's hierarchical world view, the ultimate God, *ho theos*, the One, is the Father. The Word derives his divinity from contemplation of the Father. Similarly, the *logikoi*, the realm of spiritual beings, are divinized through contemplation of the Word. Contemplative union is the union of the highest point of the soul, the *nous*, with God through a transforming vision. Andrew Louth summarizes Origen's metaphysics which are described in his principal work, *On First Principles*:

> Originally all spiritual beings, *logikoi*, were minds, equal to one another, all contemplating the Father through the Word. Most of these minds (all except the future mind of Christ) grew tired of this state of bliss and fell. In falling, their ardor cooled and they became souls (*psyche*, supposedly derived from *psychesthai*, to cool). As souls, they dwell in bodies which, as it were, arrest their fall and provide them with the opportunity to ascend again to contemplation of God by working themselves free from their bodies and becoming minds, *noes*, again. As *nous*, the spiritual being can contemplate the Ideas and realize its kinship with this realm.[31]

Like other Neoplatonists, Origen posits a metaphysics of emanation and return. Originally, souls were in a pre-existent state of contemplating the Word but, through free will, fell from their sublime state into the created world. Although souls were originally in a spiritual state, the spirit became inert when the souls cooled. Souls fell, according to Origen, into bodies (*soma*) which, in a sense, captured fallen souls and prevented them from falling even further.[32] For Origen, the ascent to union with God means a purification of the soul in its ability to contemplate God as pure intellect. Material creation is not a punishment but an educational opportunity. Matter is not evil but a limited good. Contemplation is possible when the soul rises upward, transcending the body, to contemplate the Father in union with the Word.

Origen espouses a Neoplatonic doctrine wherein the second person of the Trinity is the spiritual activity of God, the world-principle.[33] Before the fall, he states, creation consisted of bodiless and immaterial minds that formed a unity by reason of the identity of their essence and power and energy. Originally all minds were equal to one another, all contemplating the Father through the Word. However, most of the minds (all except the future mind of Christ) grew tired of the state of bliss and fell. In falling their ardor cooled and they became souls. The Word became incarnate in order to restore them to the state which they had lost. Since humans are created after God's image to have perfect knowledge of and fellowship with him, the Christian is to journey to the true homeland in God and this necessitates union with Christ.[34] For Origen, to know Christ is the highest principle of the human being; but since humans are not only and ultimately flesh, Christian maturity involves a progressive detachment from the earthly Jesus. In his twenty-seventh *Homily on Numbers* he describes the spiritual journey from the purgation of vices and passions to the contemplation of and union with God.[35] Thus, knowing Christ in the flesh is a preparation but a necessary one for the true knowledge of the eternal Word.[36]

For Origen, attachment to Christ in his earthly life enables one to attain a more perfect knowledge of God. His doctrine is one of *gnosis* whereby only those who know God can contemplate (*theoria*) God. As he states: "The *nous* is deified in that which it contemplates."[37] Moreover, knowledge of God is bound up with understanding the Scriptures which he interprets as the model of the incarnation of the Word. Charles Kannengiesser states that imitation of Christ for Origen means a true understanding of the Scriptures:

> If the statements in Scripture incarnate the Word in their own way, whose perfect incarnation is achieved in Christ's humanity, the understanding of the Scriptures, in its turn, actualizes and universalizes this same mystery of the humanity of Christ in the "perfect." Their contemplation becomes, therefore, essentially an *imitation* of Christ, based on the Scriptures.[38]

Although Origen emphasizes the importance of knowledge in the contemplation of God, he also views Christ's humanity as essential to attain union with God.[39] Irénée Noye suggests that, for Origen, "the need to go beyond the visible, to read the invisible through the visible, led him to scrutinize the visible attentively."[40] In his scriptural homilies, Origen encourages his audience to consider themselves as if present during the events of Jesus' life and ministry. The faithful disciple is invited to consider him or herself as participating in the episodes of Christ's life.[41] Noye summarizes Origen's emphasis on the details of Jesus' earthly life:

> For Origen knowledge of the man Jesus is only one step toward the knowledge of God; for humanity is a veil, a shadow. It is a sign that must be transcended. . . . But this need to go beyond the visible, to read the invisible through the visible, led him to scrutinize the visible attentively.[42]

Origen indicates that the humanity of Christ is to lead one to the glory of contemplation: "He made his appearance this way in order to lead us through this knowledge to the contemplation of his very own glory, "the glory as of the only Son from the Father, full of grace and truth" (Jn 1:14).[43] Thus, identification with Christ in his humanity is necessary to move the person to love of God. Origen shows a tenderness with regard to the humanity of Christ, using such expressions as "my Jesus" or "my Lord, my Savior" frequently including the personal pronoun.[44] His personal sentiment for Christ is rare since in the early church the divinity of Christ was emphasized to a greater extent than the humanity of Christ, particularly with respect to the risen and glorified Christ.

Origen's doctrine of intellectual contemplation through contemplation of the Word follows the law of emanation and return in that the foundation of contemplation in this life is a return to that original state where the *nous* is in union with the Mind of God. The Logos is the model and artificer (Ideas and Demiurge) and the medium of return. The purpose of the incarnation is to awaken the *pneuma* to return. The Word became flesh in order to restore souls (minds) to the state which they had lost.

Since humans are created after God's image to have perfect knowledge of and fellowship with him, the Christian is to journey to the true homeland in God and this necessitates union with Christ. Knowing Christ in the flesh is a preparation for true knowledge of the eternal Word. Knowledge of Christ is important but not ultimate since humans are more than flesh. Thus, Christian maturity involves a progressive detachment from the earthly Jesus. The humanity of Christ leads one to the glory of contemplation as Origen states: "He made his appearance this way to lead us through this knowledge, to lead us to the contemplation of his own glory."[45] Love of Christ, according to Origen, is to foster love in the faithful Christian, that love which will draw one to follow Christ and arrive at the contemplation of God.[46] The soul is to be led away from material satisfaction and to be instructed by the Word to pursue the true object of its desire which is the knowledge of God.

The perfection of love between the soul and the Word of God can lead to mystical marriage, a theme developed by Origen in his commentary on the *Song of Songs*. Indeed, he was the first to write a (mystical) commentary on the *Songs* as an intimate union of love between bride and bridegroom, between soul and Christ, a love with breadth and length and height that could only be perceived by the spiritual senses. These senses enable the inner person to relate to the Word through taste, touch, hearing, smell, sight. At the beginning of his commentary on the *Songs*, Origen describes the union of the soul and Word as a wedding.[47] The contact that arises between soul and Word is not one of wills but of illumination in which the symbolic significance (mystical meaning) of Scripture is revealed in a perfect soul. The soul in its upward ascent and passionate desire attains union with the uncreated Logos and becomes divinized. The emphasis on spiritual perfection underscores the fallen nature of the world and the desire to pass beyond it. For Origen, the height of contemplation is not a flight of the alone to the Alone as Plotinus held but is rooted in the life of the Church.

Evagrius Ponticus

Origen's journey to God within a Neoplatonic framework was influential for Christian thought, particularly among monastic writers, since his mysticism is considered protomonastic.[48] His Christian Neoplatonism was taken up in the sixth century by the monk Evagrius Ponticus, the courtier turned hermit, whose doctrine of prayer provided an important Christian element in the journey to God.

Like Origen, Evagrius describes a preexistence of souls contemplating the Word, a fall due to freewill, and a return to God. In a distinct manner, however, he emphasizes prayer as the basis of contemplation. The path to prayer and purity of heart that he establishes is one that entails both the active and contemplative life which form the two parts of the spiritual life. Purity of heart, as a liberation from all sense images and sensible things that interfere with encountering God within, is related to the whole ascetic effort. The purpose of the active life, which is essentially a life of asceticism, is purification to prepare one for contemplation. Evagrius held that the goal of the active life is to purify the passionate part of the soul through ascesis and achieve the state of *apatheia* or passionlessness.[49] This state results in charity which then leads to the higher stage of contemplation. Thus, active life is preparation (anterior) for the contemplative life.

Evagrius set forth a method for attaining purity of heart through the sublimation and right ordering of the emotions or passions, as he referred to them. The spiritual life is first entered in the *praxis* or the ascetical practices. These consist in resisting the subtle temptations (the *logismoi*) of all evil spirits and in striving to spiritualize matter in an attempt to return to union with God through a *gnosis* or contemplative knowledge. He refers to the spiritualization of one's knowledge of created things as *theoria physike*, which is a lower type of contemplation. The monk, through purification of the passions of the body and the mind, attains a state of passionlessness (*apatheia*) or inner sensitivity to the presence of God, ultimately contemplating the blessed Trinity (*theologike*) which is the highest form of contemplation.[50] The ideal for the contemplative, according to Evagrius, is to move through purification from attachment to things and sin, and to enter into an angelic state of union with God without images. In analyzing the passions, he developed a theory of the eight principal thoughts, which passed into the western ascetic tradition through Cassian and eventually became known as the seven capital sins.[51] His program of purification can be identified as one of the earliest that concerns the discernment of the spirit. The goal of his spiritual program is to free the *nous* from falleness so that it may be "absorbed" into the intellectual sea of divinity. For Evagrius, the goal of union is to become like the angels, continually at prayer in the heavenly Jerusalem, not to be separated from all but rather to be united to all in continuous prayer and praise.

The doctrine of prayer established by Evagrius was highly influential on the western monk John Cassian who spent time with Evagrius and the desert monks. It is through Cassian's *Conferences* that the tenets of prayer, as the foundation for contemplation, made their way into the western monastic tradition. Saint Benedict of Nursia incorporated Cassian's doctrine of prayer in his monastic *Rule*.

The Pseudo-Dionysius

The complex development of Christian Neoplatonism can be identified in many writers of the patristic period; however, a rich synthesis of Christian Neoplatonism unfolds in the writings of the Pseudo-Dionysius, a sixth century monk whose personal obscurity remains one of the great historical enigmas of Christianity. The writings of this author, highly influential in the Middle Ages, have attracted the interest of contemporary scholars.[52]

It is to the Pseudo-Dionysius that the term "mystical theology" is attributed, arising from his treatise on the subject that deals with the mystical God himself. As Andrew Louth points out, the word mysticism became part of the Christian vocabulary in a distinct way through the writings of the Pseudo-Dionysius. In his treatise *De mystica theologia*, he associates mystical contemplation with the path to God by way of mystical darkness: ". . . and you, my friend Timothy, applying yourself with all your strength to mystical contemplations, abandon the senses and the intellectual energies and everything that is sensible and intelligible, everything that is, and raise yourself in unknowing (*agnostos*) toward union." [53]

Pseudo-Dionsyian mystical theology provides a fundamental basis to Christian mysticism particularly because it describes a dialectical view of the relationship of God to the world. The center of his theology concerns how the utterly unknowable God manifests himself in creation in order that all things may attain union with the unmanifested Source. The metaphysical scheme of the Pseudo-Dionysius follows the Neoplatonic emanation and return, although he clearly points out that emanation is not of divine necessity. From the Neoplatonist Proclus he adopts the idea of a theophanic triad. The unknown God always remains supereminently identical within himself (*mone*) while overflowing into differentiation in his effects (*proodos*) in order to regain identity by reversion (*epistrophe*).[54] Emanation gives rise to "divine yearning" or *eros* manifested in multiple theophanies in the universe.

The universe is a "thearchy," a word used to describe the direct relation of absolute dependence each individual reality has to God. Thearchy is the term the Pseudo-Dionysius uses for the triune God who communicates himself in creation. God as thearchy is the principle of the universe conceived of as hierarchy, that is, a multiple ordered manifestation of the divine. Thearchy is distinguished from hierarchy which means a sacred order, a state of activity close to divine. The goal of hierarchy is to enable beings to be like God and to be at one with him. Hierarchy is not a matter of position but a matter of how one grasps divine activity manifested in interrelation of the ordered whole.[55] The purpose of understanding hierarchies is to enable divinization. The Pseudo-Dionysius describes the return to God according to the stages of purgation, illumination, and perfection which are present in hierarchies of the created universe only because they are participations in the thearchy. His cosmic mysticism is based on being, goodness and the beauty of the universe and is less anthropological than spiritual—a point that corresponds to the fact that Jesus Christ plays a minimal role in the Dionysian return to God.

One of the most important concepts of the Pseudo-Dionysius that influenced Bonaventure is the idea of the self-diffusive good. In his work, *De divinis nominibus* he identifies the principal name of God as Good. This essential Good extends goodness to all things and is described under the metaphor of light.[56] According to Dionysius, creation is an erotic outpouring of divine goodness by which the One (God) comes to stand outside itself (*ekstasis*) in the multiple differentiations of the created world while still retaining its apartness in its self-possessed One.[57] This essential Good is *eros* or yearning and has the power to move all things as final cause—it is (in Aristotelian terms) efficient cause and final cause. Thus, all movement in the universe comes from above and is erotic. Dionysius does not distinguish between *eros* and *agape* but like Origen views both *eros* and *agape* as the same reality. *Eros* is ecstatic—God can go out of himself in complete self-giving and yet remain absolutely within himself. The Pseudo-Dionysius, as we have noted, uses Proclus' terms of emanation, remaining and reverting to describe this movement. Because God's *eros* is cosmic, the whole universe is drawn to God, although God's being remains utterly transcendent. God is both hidden and revealed and there is no access to the hidden God except by way of God manifested in creation.[58] Thus, all theology begins with consideration of the relationship between God and world: thearchia and hierarchia.

The hallmark of the Pseudo-Dionysius' mystical ascent is his dialectic of positive and negative theology or what is known as cataphatic and apophatic theology.[59] God can be known in the created world, he states, and can be described under metaphors such as light and good, but God is greater than anything that can be known in this world. As one ascends to God or "rises higher" in the spiritual life, that which can be said of God (cataphatic) must be negated (apophatic) since God is greater than anything which can be said of him. The process of spiritual ascent, therefore, is a process of negating the negation—negation supercedes affirmation. In the *Celestial*

Hierarchy, God is revealed both through similar and dissimilar symbols, but negation has priority over affirmation ("dissimilar similarity").[60] The cataphatic moment—immersion in universe—shows the apophatic truth, that God is more than we can conceive. God is known through all things and distinct from all things.[61] The Pseudo-Dionysius uses the theme of divine darkness to signify God's unknowability, indicating that we attain union with him only through unknowing. By using "hyper" terms to describe God (for example, hyperessential, hyperluminous), he indicates that God is not only unknowable but more than unknowable; he is the unknowable unknowable. Thus, both negation and affirmation must be surpassed to reach union with God.

The goal of the Pseudo-Dionysius in the ascent to God is to seek the face of God (Ps 24:6). But this ascent takes place through unknowing (that is, mystical darkness) since God is ultimately a hidden God. The dialectic of knowing and unknowing leads to a self-transcendent union of vision. The type of mysticism the Pseudo-Dionysius espouses is more objective than personal. Contemplation is rooted in God himself and is a mystical darkness. In *De mystica theologia* he writes: "As we plunge into that darkness which is beyond intellect, we shall find ourselves not simply running short of words but actually speechless and unknowing."[62] Dionsysius speaks of *ekstasis* or the radical rupture of God into the world through the power of love. To be united to God, one must, in turn, "break through" the sensible world and pass beyond the human condtion to be divinized. Thus, we are to move from knowing to unknowing, from knowledge to love.

While love and knowledge have essential roles in the ascent to God, that of love is greater.[63] Mystical union is not one of knowledge but of love; however, the Pseudo-Dionysius affirms that mystical union is not to be separated from its liturgical context. This anagogical movement or uplifting is not a flight of the alone to the Alone in the Plotinian sense but ecclesial and liturgical involving scripture, rituals, and ecclesiastical hierarchy. Although Christ is rarely mentioned in the ascent to God, the Pseudo-Dionysius is not without a sense of personal devotion. Jesus is the source and perfection of every hierarchy since he is the perfect Hierarch. The incarnation, he reassures us, is a work of divine love.

The Monastic World

The writings of Origen, Evagrius, the Pseudo-Dionysius and others show that the spiritual journey to God is supported by a metaphysical scheme transposed from pagan Neoplatonism to Christianity. Christian writers used this scheme to give spiritual meaning to the Christian life, as one created by God and destined to return to God.

It is not surprising that the majority of Christian spiritual writing was done by monks since the monastic life provided the ideal enviornment to embark on the spiritual journey to God. Monks, in general, viewed the contemplative life synonymously with the monastic life, although in the principal rule of western monasticism, the *Rule of St. Benedict*, there is no mention of contemplation and, Jean Dechanet states, the idea itself is absent.[64] Gregory the Great, however, claimed that contemplation, while open to all Christians, is higher than the active life and thus, by its very nature, can only be attained in the monastery. Although he perceived a mutuality between action and contemplation, he distinguished between the active and contemplative life in a manner similar to Evagrius. The active life is love or compassion toward neighbor and can join us to God, preparing us for contemplation or the vision of God. Contemplation is an anticipation of union with God in heaven. It begins with the Word who became incarnate to restore Adam's contemplative vision to humanity; however, it is attained in eternal life.[65] Gregory is one of the first to view the carnal love of Christ as the foundation for the spiritual love of God, joining love and knowledge in the pursuit of union with God (*amor ipse notitia est*).[66] His emphasis on the monastic life as the "greenhouse" of contemplation underscores the fact that God is not to be found in the things of this world. In order to reach God one must, as Augustine said, enter within and rise above.[67]

Principal Themes in the Monastic Spiritual Life

The notion of the monastic life as the ideal environment for contemplation corresponds to the fact that the Christian Neoplatonic ascent depends on prayer and solitude which are essential to the contemplation of God. Although the primary purpose of the monastic life is to seek God (*quaerere Deum*), the structure of the life according to the themes of solitude, silence, prayer, meditation, and contemplation enable the monk to aspire to the highest goal of the spiritual life: union with God. It is worthwhile to examine these themes in more detail to see how they aid the goal of contemplation.

The notion of solitude and silence in the monastery is contingent on the concept of *fuga mundi* or flight from the world, that is, an abandoning of worldly values and taking on of ascetical practices. The monastery was viewed as a renewal of the "true paradise" lost in the fall and, thus, the only place where Christian perfection could be attained.[68] The solitude of the cloister was linked to fitting silence which was thought to be necessary to attain mystical contemplation, that is, to experience the presence of God. Silence was not simply the absence of noise but a form of activity, a special attentiveness to God. Corresponding to this "paradise" was the idea of the angelic life, the unceasing life of prayer in the heavenly Jerusalem. The theme of angelic life is consonant with the eschatological direction of monastic life and the desire for heaven.[69] Jean Leclercq speaks of the eschatological aspect of the monastic life and states that the Jerusalem above is the end that the monk strives for. He adds that it is the place where far from the world and from sin, one draws close to God, the angels and the saints who surround him.[70] According to André Vauchez, monks strive to live the angelic life not in the sense of being equal to angels, but in being, like them, continuously at prayer in the heavenly Jerusalem.[71] The monastic life anticipates the life of heaven where the angels enjoy the vision of God.

The solitude of the monastic life is nourished by the *lectio divina* or prayerful reading of Scriptures. In the Middle Ages, as in antiquity, reading was done aloud, pronouncing the words of the text and listening to them; *legere* meant at the same time *audire*. Although reading in silence was not unknown, the word *legere* used without further explanation, meant an activity like chanting or writing, which required participation of the whole body and whole mind.[72]

The *lectio divina* consists of two phases: *lectio aperta* or reading the text out loud and *lectio tacita* or reading the text in silence and reflecting on it. The purpose of the *lectio*, states Leclercq, is to bring about compunction; it is to move the heart to greater love of God and to understand divine things.[73] As a method of prayerful reading, the *lectio divina* could lead one to contemplate God according to the discipline with which it was carried out. It is to be neither a haphazard nor a random reading of Scripture and is to be regularly practiced; only in this way can it lead the soul to the level of pure prayer.

As a method of prayerful reading, the *lectio* is very close to the *meditatio*. In Scripture, *meditatio* generally refers to the act of making a biblical text one's own by "meditating on the law of the Lord day and night" (Ps 1:2). It means to ponder a text and to fix it in the memory in a way comparable to the digestion of food. It is what inscribes, so to speak, the sacred text in the body and in the soul. To meditate is to attach oneself closely to the sentence being recited and weigh all its words in order to sound the depths of their full meaning. Guigo II, the Carthusian, in his *Scala claustralium* describes the four stages, reading, meditation, prayer and contemplation, as a ladder by which the monk is lifted from earth to heaven. He summarizes these as follows:

> Reading is the careful study of the Scriptures, concentrating all one's powers on it. Meditation is the busy application of the mind to seek with the help of one's own reason for knowledge of hidden truth. Prayer is the heart's devoted turning to God to drive away evil and obtain what is good. Contemplation is when the mind is in some sort lifted up to God and held above itself, so that it tastes the joys of everlasting sweetness.[74]

Guigo defines the functions of the steps with a decided emphasis on the rational character of the process. The careful investigation of the Scriptures requires the attention of the mind. *Meditatio* is the studious action of the mind, investigating the knowledge of hidden truth under the impetus of one's reason. *Oratio* is defined in terms of the heart and *contemplatio* in terms of the traditional imagery of taste, but through the elevation of the mind to God.[75] In the Middle Ages, *lectio divina* became more interiorized and intellectual with a greater emphasis on remembrance as an interior operation, corresponding to the mysteries of Jesus. The focus on the reflective dimension of meditation indicates that it is not only concerned with the text itself, but, as an activity of reflection and investigation, it orients one's life to the message of Scripture and toward contemplation.

In addition to the prayerful reading of Scripture, prayer itself is an essential aspect of the monastic life, since the life is oriented to seeking God. The directives on prayer in the *Rule of St. Benedict* provide an important foundation for contemplation, especially since they are influenced by the *Conferences* of John Cassian. The basic principles are incorporated in two short passages (*RB 20; RB 52*). In his instructions on private prayer in Chapter 20 Benedict states:

> We must know that God regards our purity of heart and tears of compunction, not our many words. Prayer should therefore be short and pure, unless perhaps it is prolonged under the inspiration of divine grace.[76]

Although the *Rule* does not say much with regard to private prayer, Benedict succinctly presents the distinguishing characteristics of prayer: brevity of prayer, purity of heart and compunction. The first, brevity of prayer, can be associated with the eastern hesychast prayer as well as the scriptural injunction to "pray unceasingly" (1 Thess 5:17). The word *hesychia* is a Greek word that means tranquility or peace.[77] The pursuit of hesychia, according to the Fathers, necessitated flight from the world, but the true journey was inward to the heart. Benedict advocates "short and pure prayer" which conjures up the notion of *hesychia* or rest in God. That he adds to his formula of prayer over that of Cassian "the influence of divine grace" suggests that short prayer is not only to fulfill the injunction to "pray unceasingly" (I Thess 5:17) but may also lead, by the grace of the Holy Spirit, to the *quies contemplationis.*

The notion of "purity of heart" (*RB 20.3*) is a common expression among the Fathers of the church who spoke of the prayer of the heart (cf. Mt 5:8). Prayer of the heart means a purity of heart that is freed from images, from intermediaries and sensible things. Since

God is spirit, only the pure in spirit are able to encounter him. Purity of heart, as a liberation from all sense images and sensible things that interfere with encountering God within, is related to the whole ascetic effort. Evagrius set forth a method for attaining purity of heart through the sublimation and right ordering of the emotions, or as he referred to them, passions.

Like purity of heart and purity of prayer, compunction is an important part of prayer that can bring one closer to God. In the *Rule* Benedict states: "God regards our . . . tears of compunction, not our many words" (*RB* 20.3).[78] Irénée Hausherr defines compunction (*penthos*) as: "Mourning for lost salvation, whether one's own or that of others."[79] For the Fathers, compunction was associated with the ascetical life by which one, turning away from sin and toward God, recognized God's immense love and mercy. As a gift of the Holy Spirit, it was considered a second form of baptism. Compunction could take place at all stages of the spiritual progress, from the initial fear of punishment to the love of the perfect for things eternal, and was a sign that the heart had been touched by the word of God.

The ideal of the monk was to strive for unceasing prayer to fulfill the Lord's command to "pray always" (Lk 18:1; 21:36. cf. 1 Thess 5:17). Cassian understood the Divine Office as a means to fulfill the obligation of unceasing prayer. With the development of cenobitic monasticism, the prayer of the hours was not made in private as in early monasticism; rather, the monks gathered to celebrate it together. In the *Rule*, Benedict does not provide an explanation for the Divine Office but he indicates that it is the principal duty of the monk. As he states: "Indeed, nothing is to be preferred to the work of God" (*RB* 43.3). The term *opus Dei* in the Benedictine tradition does not actually appear in the liturgical code (*RB* 8-20). However, it is referred to under other titles such as *officium divinum* (43.1), *opus divinum* (19.2), *servitutis officia* (16.2), and *servitutis pensum* (50.4). These terms recall the idea of the ancients that the monk's prayer is a work for God. Benedict emphasized the *Opus Dei* as the ideal of unceasing prayer expressing the interpenetration between corporate psalmody and private prayer. In the *Rule* he states: "Let us stand to sing the psalms in such a way that our minds are in harmony with our voices" (*RB* 19.7). The unity of mind and heart during the recitation of the psalms is expressed by Cassian: "Who is so alert and vigilant as never, while he is singing a psalm to God, to allow his mind to wander from the meaning of Scripture?"[80] The injunction to pay attention to the words recited during the chanting of the psalms indicates that the monk's pursuit of contemplation is not limited to private prayer only but is to be sought also during prayer of the divine office.

Benedict refers to the *opus Dei* as a work which anticipates the heavenly Jerusalem where God is praised unceasingly: "Let us consider, then, how we ought to behave in the presence of God and his angels, and let us stand to sing the psalms in such a way that our minds are in harmony with our voices." (*RB* 19.7) Benedict links the Divine Office with the angelic life (*vita angelica*) indicating that monks are to seek the angelic life, that is, being continuously at prayer in the heavenly Jersualem. Like Cassian, he holds that the angelic life of the monk, made possible by a unity of heart and mind, is essentially a life of unceasing prayer before God. It is this type of prayer that anticipates contemplation in the heavenly Jerusalem.

The Role of Christ

The description of the monastic life as a restoration of paradise lost in the fall, and the notion of unceasing prayer as participation in the angelic life of the heavenly Jerusalem, indicates that contemplation is not only *theoria* or gazing upon God but is also the quiet (*quies*) and freedom (*otium*) of seeking God. As Gregory reminds us, Adam was created to contemplate God but lost this ability through sin. Christ restores contemplation to humanity but more as the object of desire rather than achievement in this life.[81]

The focus on the eschatological nature of contemplation in the monastic life raises the question of the role of Christ in the ascent to God. There is no doubt that for Christian writers Christ is essential to attain the fullness of life in God. As Augustine states, one cannot enjoy God unless s/he accepts the incarnation of Christ as mediator between God and humanity.[82] Although the Fathers of the Church recognize the importance of the humanity of Christ, that is, the earthly life of Christ, in coming to know God, the emphasis on the person of Christ in the early church was on the risen Christ. In the patristic era, the ascended and glorified was the object of devotion indicated by prayers to the risen Lord. The importance of the risen and glorified Christ was evident among the desert monks for whom the victory of Christ through his passion, resurrection and ascension assured participation in the divine life. To share in Christ's passion meant to share in his glory.[83] Colin Morris suggests that the Fathers of the Church had a "corporate understanding of the incarnation; an objective social content was given to the cross and the final judgment. This lasted up until the Middle Ages where, in the eleventh century, there occurred a theological shift with respect to the person of Christ—from the risen and glorified Christ to Christ as a suffering human being, particularly in the passion.[84] The movement toward a more inward and compassionate devotion was accompanied by more personal participation in which the individual strove imaginatively to share in the suffering of Christ. This became strong in the eleventh century and in the twelfth century, it governed much of the thought on the passion. The conditions or circumstances that give way to this devotion are unclear but that devotion to the humanity of Christ developed in eleventh century monastic circles is indicated by the rise of prayers and meditations devoted to the passion of Christ.[85]

According to Leclercq, the concept of pietistic devotion, or affectivity toward the humanity of Christ, was present in medieval monasticism from the eleventh century on. At Cluny the mystery of Christmas was honored in a special way, emphasizing the mystery of the incarnation.[86] Meditations on the passion were composed such as those by Drogo and Arnold; in some monasteries the hours of the day were consecrated to the passion and psalms were chanted in honor of the five wounds. A devotion to the Sacred Heart also arose within monastic circles and monks and nuns spoke of the sacred mysteries flowing from the pierced side of Christ.[87] The Cistercians of the twelfth century spoke of the Heart of Jesus as an open door through which one could enter and contemplate the infinite love of the Incarnate Word toward us. At the Benedictine Abbey of Saint Philibert de Tournus a Mass was celebrated "in memory of the humanity of the Son of God," highlighting the saving mysteries of Christ.[88]

The rise of devotion to Christ in medieval monasticism did not signify a greater inclination to emotionalism or moral transformation alone but rather stood for a whole complex of spiritual activity by which loving dedication to God was to be nourished and expressed. Patrick O'Connell states that when the term "devotion to the humanity of Christ" was used, it meant an emphasis on the earthly life, words and deeds of the incarnate Jesus, focusing on what united the believer to Jesus.[89] The ultimate purpose of devotion, therefore, was not merely observation but participation, a sharing of Jesus' relationship with his Father in this life so as to share in that relationship in eternity.

The role of the humanity of Christ in the spiritual journey to God was described with a new vitality and sensibility by spiritual writers of the Middle Ages, as a genre of spiritual literature arose that focused on the humanity of Christ. John of Fécamp, one of the first medieval writers to give expression to the devotion to the humanity of Christ, described a sentimental devotion to the humanity of Christ that foreshadowed Bernard of Clairvaux and Franciscan piety. According to Leclercq, his texts were the most widely read spiritual texts before the *Imitation of Christ* by Thomas a Kempis.[90] Although John advocated devotion to Christ, it was in the context of a God who is transcendent and yet the object of our adoration. All of Christ's human life for John is a ray of reflection of the glory which he has in eternity and of which he is clothed in heaven.[91]

A similar combination of devotion to the humanity of Christ and eschatological fulfillment can be seen in the prayers of Peter Damian, who incorporates awareness of Christ's sufferings into a traditional salvific framework. Damian combines a vivid awareness of Jesus in his passion, and the cross as the triumph and source of new life, symbolizing not only resurrection and glorification but the fullness of the Paschal mystery. His descriptive language, provoking the senses, indicates that only through the cross is the victory of salvation attained through Christ who has gone before us and leads the way.[92]

One of the bright lights of the Middle Ages who provided a theological understanding of the incarnation was Anselm of Canterbury. Although he is not regarded as a mystic, Anselm's *Prayers and*

Meditations mark a turning point in the development of devotional prayer that was important for later medieval mysticism. His meditations are characterized by a mystical attraction toward the suffering Christ and an affective note of compassion. In his "Prayer to Christ," for example, he writes:

> Why, O my soul, were you not there to be pierced by a sword of bitter sorrow when you could not bear the piercing of the side of your Savior with a lance? Why could you not bear to see the nails violate the hands and feet of your Creator? Why did you not see with horror the blood that poured out of the side of your Redeemer? Why were you not drunk with bitter tears when they gave him bitter gall to drink? Why did you not share the sufferings of the most pure virgin, his worthy mother and your gentle lady?[93]

Like Peter Damian and John of Fécamp, Anselm focuses on the saving work of Christ, moving the reader from the physical sufferings of Christ to the glorified and risen Christ. Following his expressed desire to participate in the sufferings of Christ, for example, he writes: "Would that with the blessed band of women I might have trembled at the vision of angels and have heard the news of the Lord's resurrection, news of my consolation, so much looked for, so much desired."[94] By shifting the focus from Christ's earthly life to his glorious life, Anselm indicates that he does not intend devotion to Christ to be sheer sentimentalism nor does he want to divorce the earthly life and sufferings of Christ from their soteriological significance and their fulfillment in the vision of the glorified Christ. Rather, devotion to Christ complements the contemplative ideal of the monk, namely, entrance into the eternal life of trinitarian love through participation in the paschal mystery.

Although early medieval monastic writers considered the earthly life of Christ in a more personal manner, they continued to emphasize the soteriological and eschatological significance of the life, death and resurrection of Christ, supporting the idea that contemplation begins here below in union with Christ but reaches the full vision of God in heaven. In commenting on devotion to the humanity of Christ in the medieval period, Leclercq writes: "The death of Christ is considered less as a sorrowful mystery than as a glorious mystery. It is the first act of his glorification and the gate to ours. As the cross was Jesus' own entrance into glory, so participation in the mystery of the cross is the only means to share in that glory."[95] Essentially, the role of devotion to the humanity of Christ in the monastic life reaffirms the role of prayer in the life of the monk: to lead one to the glorified Christ, the kingdom of heaven, and for those who progress spiritually, to contemplation, that is, the vision of God.

The role of devotion to Christ in pursuit of the contemplation of God is most eloquently described by the twelfth century Cistercian, Bernard of Clairvaux, who is regarded as the Father of devotion to the humanity of Christ. For Bernard, spiritual love must progress from *amor carnalis* to *amor spiritualis*; the perfection of the will takes place in love. It is on the cross that, through the wounds of Christ, the ultimate depth of God's love is revealed.[96] Such love can bring about the perfection of the will and perfection of the rational faculty which is humility. However, love is essentially restorative. This means that to come to the perfect love of God one must grow in the perfection of love, a love which is not circumscribed by the birth, passion and death of Jesus Christ but is perfected in the ascension of Christ. As Bernard states: "Only if we 'see' Christ ascend into heaven can our love be purified and changed into spiritual love."[97] Like Origen, Bernard compares the sinful soul to an unfaithful spouse. The motive of conversion is to enable the soul to return to its lawful spouse. This return to God is possible because human nature, although wounded, retains a likeness to God. The whole work of salvation consists in restoring the order of charity by which one proceeds from the region of unlikeness to the likeness of God, underscoring the process of deification.[98] The notion of deification and participation in the divine life is essentially Platonic indicating a movement toward greater resemblance of God.

The problem with fallen humanity, according to Bernard, is that we no longer appreciate why God is the only reason for loving God, nor do we understand how to love without measure. He considers sensitive affection for the humanity of Christ as love of a relatively inferior order. Yet, it is a necessary beginning for loving God. It is a starting point which must be transcended to love fully and maturely. In Sermon six he writes:

Notice that the love of the heart is, in a certain sense, carnal, because our hearts are attracted most toward the humanity of Christ and the things he did or commanded while in the flesh. The heart that is filled with this love is quickly touched by every word on this subject. . . . The soul at prayer should have before it a sacred image of the God-man, in his birth or infancy or as he was teaching, or dying, or rising, or ascending. Whatever form it takes this image must bind the soul with the love of virtue and expel carnal vices, eliminate temptations and quiet desires. I think this is the principal reason why the invisible God willed to be seen in the flesh and to converse with men as a man. He wanted to recapture the affections of carnal men who were unable to love in any other way, by first drawing them to the salutary love of his own humanity, and then gradually to raise them to a spiritual love.[9]

Bernard describes how the love of Christ, at first carnal or sensible, progresses when it becomes rational love, and is perfected when it becomes spiritual love. The movement from carnal to spiritual love involves not a substitution of one form of love for another, but a deepening and perfection of what has begun. The soul should be able to enter directly into union, in virtue of its spiritual powers, with a God who is pure spirit. However, sin prevents this and so love for the person of Christ is bound up with the fall. In this way, the incarnation is "necessary" for humankind because it is God's willingness to encounter the human person as s/he is, unable to rise above the love of flesh because of the weight of original sin.

The perfection of love leads to mystical union, that is, the marriage of the bride with the bridegroom or the soul with the Word. In a sermon on mystical union, Bernard states: "So the soul returns and is converted to the Word to be reformed by him and conformed to him. . . . Such conformity weds the soul to the Word, for one who is like the Word by nature shows himself like him too in the exercise of his will, loving as she is loved."[10] Love is the power that leads the soul to God. The height of union is a vehement love or what Bernard terms a mystical marriage of the soul and the Word. Only love can attain God in this life; knowledge cannot. But knowledge plays a role in our ascension to God, both at the beginning and the end of the process, where Christ enlightens our soul through his saving mysteries, illuminating the intellect.

Bernard's devotion to Christ had widespread influence in the Middle Ages. Pierre Pourrat claims that Bernard gave a "new direction to piety," inspiring mystics of the following centuries to meditate on the earthly life of Christ.[101] Walter Principe states that Bernard's focus on the life and sufferings of the human Jesus was "a major influence in the devotion to the human Jesus that grew stronger in the twelfth century and flowered in Francis of Assisi, Franciscan piety, popular piety and art."[102] Patrick O'Connell, however, states that despite Bernard's widespread influence he stands somewhat apart from the mainstream of devotion as it develops in the twelfth century, since virtually nowhere in the large corpus of his writings do we find an extended imaginative representation of scenes from the life of Christ.[103] Moreover, Bernard's devotion to Christ must be put in its proper perspective and that is, like Origen's, in the service of contemplation. It is the first step but a necessary one to mystical union with God. Leclercq claims that Bernard's devotion to Jesus must be seen in its true light: it rests neither in a sensible love for his humanity, nor in mystic contemplation of the Word. He states:

> It would be truer to say that St. Bernard points out above all the divine condescension by which the Word, who since the fall of Adam was beyond our reach, is offered to us in the flesh, thus once more becoming accessible to us. By Christ in the flesh the treasures of loving kindness hidden in the bosom of the Father are made manifest to excite us to confidence, to give us a greater knowledge of the goodness and mercy of God and to draw us to imitate him and love him. All this is connected with Christ "according to the flesh" in his first coming. The Ascension leads us to a more spiritual love, since Christ is no longer there in the flesh to converse with us, except as the liturgical feasts bring him before us, or we meditate on him in his passion. More than this, it leads us higher still, to the contemplation of Christ in glory, and, reminding us of his second coming, to a conformity and union with his spirit.[104]

While Bernard's doctrine of affective spirituality is recognized, it must be recognized objectively: the visible reality of Christ's life is to enable the invisible reality of God's love to be attained. As the "last of the Fathers," Bernard continues the Christian Neoplatonic ascent to God inherited from the Fathers of the Church. The journey to God begins with the earthly life of Christ but concludes with the ascended and glorified Christ. Contemplation begins with the desire for God "here below" but finds its fulfillment in the vision of God in the heavenly Jerusalem. It is ultimately eschatological and is not to be limited to the level of the sensible. Rather, as in the practice of the *lectio divina*, the believer and seeker of God is to discover the hidden spiritual meanings of the events of Christ's life and ultimately to ascend to union with God.

Bernard's doctrine of mystical union, with an emphasis on interior union and contemplation of the ascended Christ, typifies the monastic quest for union with God. Although Bernard was highly influential on Bonaventure, particularly with regard to union as a nuptial relationship, Bonaventure did not entirely follow the Mellifluous doctor. Rather, he committed himself to the radical incarnational view held by Francis. The pervasive influence of Cistercian spirituality coupled with the radical poverty movements of medieval Italy enabled Francis to dwell on the overflowing love of God in the incarnation while breaking ties with the whole monastic endeavor. Francis' charism, theologically crystallized by Bonaventure, is an inversion of monasticism: the world is the cloister, contemplative union is a descent into the poverty and humility of the incarnate Word, and the goal of union is to enter into the diffusive love of God which is found at heart of the world, in the cross of Jesus Christ. The solitary flight to union with God in monasticism becomes the Franciscan embrace of humanity and creation through union with the Crucified Christ. While the journey to God in the monastic tradition reminds us that "here we have no lasting city," in the Franciscan tradition the city has come down in the incarnation, and the world is the unfolding of its glory. The traditions together form, in a sense, a coincidence of opposites, reminding us that the kingdom has already come but is not yet complete. It is left to the Franciscan tradition, however, to preach the Gospel to the ends of the earth, and this makes the journey to God not simply a goal for the individual but a transforming spirituality for the world.

Selected Bibliography

Primary Sources

CRITICAL EDITIONS

Analecta Franciscana. Chronica aliaque varia documenta Legendae S. Francisci Assisiensis. Edited by PP. Collegii Sancti Bonaventurae. Vol. 10. Quaracchi: Collegii Sancti Bonaventurae, 1926–1941.

Bonaventure, Saint. *Doctoris Seraphici S. Bonaventurae Opera Omnia.* Edited by PP. Collegii Sancti Bonaventurae. 10 Vols. Quaracchi: Collegii Sancti Bonaventurae, 1882–1902.

_____. *Legenda maior S. Francisci Assisiensis et eiusdem Legenda minor.* Edited by PP. Collegii Sancti Bonaventurae. (Editio minor.) Quaracchi: Collegii Sancti Bonaventurae, 1941.

Works

Bonaventure, Saint. *De reductione artium ad theologiam.* Commentary, introduction and translation by Emma Thérèse Healy. St. Bonaventure: St. Bonaventure College, 1939.

_____. *Itinerarium Mentis in Deum.* Introduction, translation and commentary by Philotheus Boehner. Vol. 2, *Works of St. Bonaventure.* Edited by Philotheus Boehner and M. Frances Laughlin. St. Bonaventure: Franciscan Institute, 1956.

_____. *Disputed Questions on the Mystery of the Trinity.* Introduction and translation by Zachary Hayes. Vol. 3, *Works of Saint Bonaventure.* Edited by George Marcil. St. Bonaventure: Franciscan Institute, 1979.

_____. *Bringing Forth Christ, the Son of God: Five Feasts of the Child Jesus.* Translation and introduction by Eric Doyle. Oxford: SLG Press, 1984.

_____. *Disputed Questions on the Knowledge of Christ.* Introduction and translation by Zachary Hayes. Vol. 4, *Works of Saint Bonaventure.* Edited by George Marcil. St. Bonaventure: Franciscan Institute, 1992.

Bonaventure: The Soul's Journey into God, The Tree of Life, The Life of St. Francis. Translated by Ewert Cousins. New York: Paulist, 1978.

Die Schriften des heiligen Franziskus von Assisi. Edited by Lothar Hardick and Engelbert Grau. Werl/Westphalia: Dietrich-Coele Verlag, 1984.

Disciple and the Master: St. Bonaventure's Sermons on St. Francis of Assisi. Translated and edited by Eric Doyle. Chicago: Franciscan Herald Press, 1983.

Essential Plotinus. Introduction and translation by Elmer O'Brien. Indianopolis: Hackett, 1964.

Francis and Clare: The Complete Works. Translated by Regis J. Armstrong and Ignatius Brady. New York: Paulist, 1982.

François d'Assise. Écrits. Introduction and translation by Théophile Desbonnets, Thaddée Matura, Jean-François Godet, Damien Vorreux. Vol. 285, *Sources Chrétiennes.* Paris: Éditions Franciscaines, 1981.

Lexique Saint Bonaventure. Edited by Jacques-Guy Bougerol. Paris: Éditions Franciscaines, 1969.

Meditations on the Life of Christ: An Illustrated Manuscript of the Fourteenth Century. Edited and translated by Isa Ragusa and Rosalie B. Green. Princeton: Princeton University Press, 1961.

Origen: On First Principles. Translated by G. W. Butterworth. Gloucester: Peter Smith, 1973.

_____. *Spirit and Fire. A Thematic Anthology of His Writings.* Edited by Hans Urs von Balthasar. Translated by Robert J. Daly. Washington DC: Catholic University America Press, 1984.

Origen: An Exhortation to Martyrdom, Prayer, First Principles: book IV, Prologue to the Commentary on the Song of Songs, Homily XXVII on Numbers. Translation and introduction by Rowan Greer. Preface by Hans Urs von Balthasar. New York: Paulist, 1979.

Plotinus. *The Enneads.* Translated by Stephen Mackenna. 2nd edition. Revised by B. S. Page. New York: Pantheon Books, 1957.

Pseudo-Dionysius: The Complete Works. Translated by Colm Luibheid. New York: Paulist, 1987.

Richard of St. Victor. *The Mystical Ark.* Translated by Grover Zinn. *Richard of St. Victor. The Twelve Patriarchs, The Mystical Ark, Book Three of the Trinity.* New York: Paulist, 1979.

_____. *Selected Writings on Contemplation.* Translation and introduction by Clare Kirchberger. London: Faber and Faber, 1957.

Rooted in Faith: Homilies to a Contemporary World. Translation and introduction by Marigwen Schumacher. Chicago: Franciscan Herald Press, 1973.

St. Bonaventure's Writings Concerning the Franciscan Order. Introduction and translation by Dominic Monti. Vol 5, *Works of Saint Bonaventure.* Edited by George Marcil. St. Bonaventure: Franciscan Institute, 1994.

St. Bonaventure: Bringing Forth Christ, the Son of God. Five Feasts of the Child Jesus. Translated by Eric Doyle. Oxford: SLG Press, 1984.

St. Francis of Assisi: Writings and Early Biographies, English Omnibus of the Sources for the Life of St. Francis. Edited by Marion Habig. Chicago: Franciscan Herald Press, 1973.

What Manner of Man: Sermons on Christ by St. Bonaventure. Introduction and translation by Zachary Hayes. Chicago: Franciscan Herald Press, 1974.

Works of Bonaventure. Translated by José de Vinck. 5 Vols. Paterson: St. Anthony Guild Press, 1960–1970.

Secondary Works

BOOKS

Balthasar, Hans Urs von. *Studies in Theological Style: Clerical Styles.* Translated by Andrew Louth, Francis McDonagh and Brian McNeil. Vol. 2. *The Glory of the Lord. A Theological Aesthetics.* Edited by Joseph Fessio. San Francisco: Ignatius, 1984.

Bonaventuriana. Miscellanea in onore di Jacques Guy Bougerol. Edited by Francisco de Asis Chavero Blanco. 2 Vols. Rome: Edizioni Antonianum, 1988.

Bonaventura, Sancti. 1274–1974. Edited by Jacques-Guy Bougerol. 4 Vols. Grottaferrata: Collegii S. Bonaventurae, 1973–74.

Bonnefoy, Jean-François. *Une somme bonaventurienne de théologie mystique: Le De triplici via.* Paris: Éditions de la Libraire Saint-François, 1934.

Bougerol, Jacques-Guy. *Introduction to the Works of Bonaventure.* Translated by José de Vinck. Paterson: St. Anthony Guild Press, 1964.

Bouyer, Louis. *A History of Christian Spirituality.* Vol. 1, *The Spirituality of the New Testament and the Fathers.* Translated by Mary P. Ryan. New York: Desclée Company, 1963.

Brooke, Rosalind. *The Coming of the Friars.* London: George Allen and Unwin, 1975.

Butler, Cuthbert Dom. *Benedictine Monachism.* London: Longmans, Green & Company, 1919.

____. *Western Mysticism.* 3rd edition. London: Constable, 1967.

Christian Spirituality: Origins to the Twelfth Century. Edited by Bernard McGinn and John Meyendorff. Vol. 16, *World Spirituality: An Encyclopedic History of the Religious Quest.* New York: Crossroad, 1987.

Cousins, Ewert. *Bonaventure and the Coincidence of Opposites.* Chicago: Franciscan Herald Press, 1978.

Daniel, E. Randolph. *The Franciscan Concept of Mission in the High Middle Ages.* Lexington: University of Kentucky Press, 1975.

Divine Representations: Postmodern Spirituality. Edited by Ann Askell. New York: Paulist Press, 1994.

Doyle, Eric. *St. Francis and the Song of Brotherhood.* New York: Seabury Press, 1981.

Esser, Kajetan., and Hardick, F. Lothar. *The Marrow of the Gospel.* Translated and edited by Ignatius C. Brady. Chicago: Franciscan Herald Press, 1958.

Esser, Kajetan. *Studien zu den Opuscula des hl. Franziskus von Assisi.* Rome: Historisches Institut der Kapuziner, 1973.

Fleming, John V. *An Introduction to the Franciscan Literature of the Middle Ages.* Chicago: Franciscan Herald Press, 1977.

Flood, David and Matura, Thadée. *The Birth of a Movement: A Study of the First Rule of St. Francis.* Translated by Paul LaChance and Paul Schwartz. Chicago: Franciscan Herald Press, 1975.

Gerken, Alexander. *Théologie du Verbe: La relation entre l'incarnation et la création selon S. Bonaventure.* Translated by Jacqueline Gréal. Paris: Éditions Franciscaines, 1970.

Gilson, Etienne. *The Philosophy of Saint Bonaventure.* Translated by Dom Illtyd Tethowan. New York: Sheed and Ward, 1938.

González, Justo Luis. "The Christology of Saint Bonaventure: A Study in the Relationship between Scholastic Theology and Franciscan Spirituality in the High Middle Ages." Ph. D. dissertation, Yale University, 1961.

Hayes, Zachary. *The Hidden Center: Spirituality and Speculative Christology in St. Bonaventure.* St. Bonaventure: Franciscan Institute, 1992.

Hellman, A. J. Wayne. *Ordo: Untersuchung eines Grundgedankens in der Theologie Bonaventuras.* München: Verlag Ferdinand Schöningh, 1974.

Hülsbusch, Werner. *Elemente einer Kreuzestheologie in den Spätschriften Bonaventuras.* Düsseldorf: Patmos Verlag, 1968.

Johnson, Timothy. *Iste pauper clamavit: Saint Bonaventure's Mendicant Theology of Prayer.* Vol. 390. European University Studies. Frankfurt am Main: Peter Lang, 1990.

Knowles, David. *The Evolution of Medieval Thought.* New York: Vintage Books, 1962.

Lakers, John J. *Christian Ethics: An Ethics of Intimacy.* Quincy, IL: Franciscan Press, 1996.

Leclercq, Jean, Vandenbroucke, François, and Louis Bouyer. *A History of Christian Spirituality.* Vol. 2, *The Spirituality of the Middle Ages.* Translated by the Benedictines of Holme Eden Abbey, Carl. New York: Seabury, 1968.

Leclercq, Jean. *The Love of Learning and the Desire for God.* Translated by Catharine Misrahi. 3rd edition. New York: Fordham University Press, 1982.

Lehmann, Leonhard. *Tiefe und Weite: Der universale Grundzug in den Gebeten des Franziskus von Assisi.* Werl: Dietrich-Coelde-Verlag, 1984.

Louth, Andrew. *The Origins of the Christian Mystical Tradition: From Plato to Denys.* Oxford: Clarendon, 1981.

_____. *Denys the Areopagite.* Outstanding Christian Thinkers Series. Edited by Brian Davies. Wilton: Morehouse-Barlow, 1989.

Manselli, Raoul. "San Bonaventura e la storia francescana." In *1274, Année charnière: Mutations et continuitiés. Lyon-Paris 30 Septembre – 5 Octobre 1974. Colloques internationaux du centre national de la recherche scientifique,* 863–872. Paris: Centre National de la Recherche Scientifique, 1977.

Marion, Jean-Luc. *God Without Being.* Translated by Thomas A. Carlson. Chicago: University of Chicago Press, 1991.

McGinn, Bernard. *The Foundations of Mysticism: Origins to the Fifth Century.* Vol. 1, *The Presence of God. A History of Western Christian Mysticism.* New York: Crossroad, 1994.

_____. *The Growth of Mysticism.* Vol. 2, *The Presence of God: A History of Western Christian Mysticism.* New York: Crossroad, 1994.

Moltmann, Jürgen. *The Crucified God: The Cross of Christ as the Foundation and Criticism of Christian Theology.* Translated by R. A. Wilson and John Bowden. San Francisco: Harper, 1991.

Muscat, Noel. *The Life of Saint Francis in the Light of Saint Bonaventure's Theology on the "Verbum Crucifixum."* Rome: Editrice Antonianum, 1989.

O'Connell, Patrick. "The Lignum Vitae of Saint Bonaventure and the Medieval Devotional Tradition." Ph. D. dissertation, Fordham University, 1985.

Prentice, Robert P. *The Psychology of Love According to St. Bonaventure.* St. Bonaventure: Franciscan Institute, 1951.

Ratzinger, Joseph. *The Theology of History in St. Bonaventure.* Translated by Zachary Hayes. Chicago: Franciscan Herald Press, 1971.

Schmucki, Octavian. *The Stigmata of St. Francis of Assisi: A Critical Investigation in the Light of Thirteenth Century Sources.* Translated by Canisius Connors. St. Bonaventure: Franciscan Institute, 1991.

Turner, Denys. *The Darkness of God: Negativity in Christian Mysticism.* Cambridge: Cambridge University Press, 1995.

Van-Khanh, Norbert Nguyên. *The Teacher of His Heart: Jesus Christ in the Thought and Writings of St. Francis.* Translated by Ed Hagman. St. Bonaventure: Franciscan Institute, 1994.

Vauchez, André. *La spiritualité du moyen âge occidental: VIII–XII siècles.* Paris: Presses Universitaires de France, 1975.

Articles

Asseldonk, Optatus van. "Altri aspetti Giovannei negli scritti di S. Francesco." *Antonianum* 54 (1979): 447–86.

_____. "San Giovanni Evangelista negli scritti di S. Francesco." *Laurentianum* 18 (1977): 225–55.

_____. "The Spirit of the Lord and Its Holy Activity." Translated by Edward Hagman. *Greyfriars Review* 5 (1991): 105–58.

Black, Alvin. "The Doctrine of the Image and Similitude in Saint Bonaventure." *Cord* 12 (1962): 269–75.

Bowman, Leonard J. "The Cosmic Exemplarism of Bonaventure." *Journal of Religion* 55 (1975): 181–98.

Bougerol, Jacques-Guy. "Saint Bonaventure et le Pseudo-Denys l'Aréopagite." *Études Franciscaines* 18 (1968, Supplement): 33–123.

_____. "Saint Bonaventure et Saint Bernard." *Antonianum* 46 (1971): 3–79.

_____. "Saint Bonaventure et la hiérarchie dionysienne." In *Saint Bonaventure: Études sur les sources de sa pensée.* 131–67. Northampton: Variorium, 1989.

Brady, Ignatius. "The Opera Omnia of St. Bonaventure Revisted." *Proceedings of the Seventh Centenary Celebration of the Death of Saint Bonaventure.* Edited by Pascal F. Foley, 47–59. St. Bonaventure: Franciscan Institute: 1975.

_____. "St. Bonaventure's Theology of the Imitation of Christ." *Proceedings of the Seventh Centenary Celebration of the Death of Saint Bonaventure.* Edited by Pascal F. Foley, 61–72. St. Bonaventure: Franciscan Institute: 1975.

Cousins, Ewert. "Christ and the Cosmos: Teilhard de Chardin and Bonaventure." *Cord* 16 (1966): 99–105.

_____. "The Coincidence of Opposites in the Christology of Saint Bonaventure." *Franciscan Studies* 28 (1968): 27–45.

_____. "Bonaventure's Mysticism of Language." In *Mysticism and Language.* Edited by Stephen Katz, 236–57. New York: Oxford University Press, 1992.

_____. "Francis of Assisi: Christian Mysticism at the Crossroads." *Mysticism and Religious Traditions.* Edited by Stephen T. Katz, 163–90. New York: Oxford University Press, 1983.

_____. "Franciscan Roots of Ignatian Meditation." *Ignatian Spirituality in a Secular Age.* Edited by George P. Schner, 51–63. Toronto: Wilfrid Laurier University Press, 1984.

_____. "Language as Metaphysics in Bonaventure." *Sprache und Erkenntnis im Mittelalter.* Edited by Jan P. Beckmann. Vol. 2, 946–51. *Miscellanea Mediaevalia.* Edited by Albert Zimmerman. Berlin: Walter de Gruyter, 1981.

_____. "Teilhard de Chardin et Saint Bonaventure. " *Études Franciscaines* 19 (1969): 175–86.

_____. "The Evolving Cosmos: Teilhard de Chardin and Bonaventure." *Cord* 16 (1966): 131–36.

_____. "The Two Poles of Bonaventure's Thought." *Sancta Bonaventura 1274–1974.* Edited by Jacques-Guy Bougerol. Vol. 4, 153–76. Grottaferatta: Collegii S. Bonaventurae, 1974.

Daniel, E. Randolph. "A Re-Examination of the Origins of Franciscan Joachitism." In *Joachim of Fiore in Christian Thought: Essays on the Influence of the Calabrian Prophet.* Edited by Delno C. West. Vol. 1, 143–48. New York: Burt Franklin, 1975.

_____. "St. Bonaventure: Defender of Franciscan Eschatology." *Sancta Bonaventura 1274–1974.* Vol. 2, 793–806. Grottaferatta: Collegii S. Bonaventurae, 1973.

_____. "Bonaventure's Debt to Joachim." In *Medievalia et Humanistica.* Edited by Paul Maurice Colgan, 61–74. New Series: Number 11. Totowa: Rowman and Littlefield, 1982.

_____. "Symbol or Model? Bonaventure's Use of St. Francis." *Bonaventuriana: Miscellanea in onore di Jacques Guy Bougerol.* Edited by Francisco de Asis Chavero Blanco. Vol. 1, 55–62. Roma: Edizioni Antonianum, 1988.

_____. "St. Bonaventure a Faithful Disciple of St. Francis? A Reexamination of the Question." *Sancta Bonaventura 1274–1974.* Edited by Jacques Guy Bougerol. Vol. 2, 170–87. Grottaferatta: Collegii S. Bonaventurae, 1973.

_____. "The Desire for Martyrdom: A *Leitmotiv* of St. Bonaventure." *Franciscan Studies* 30 (1972): 74–87.

Daniélou, Jean. "Saint Bernard et les père grecs." In *Saint Bernard Théologien: Actes du Congrès de Dijon 15–19 Septembre 1953.* 2nd edition, 46–55. Rome: Editiones Cistercienses, 1953.

Déchanet, Jean-Marie. "Contemplation au XIIe Siècle," *Dictionnaire de Spiritualité* 2 (1953): 1934–366.

_____. "Les mystères du salut: La christologie de S. Bernard." In *Saint Bernard Théologien: Actes du Congrès de Dijon 15–19 Septembre 1953.* 2nd edition, 78–91. Rome: Editiones Cistercienses, 1953.

Esser, Kajetan. "Studium und Wissenschaft im Geiste des hl. Franziskus von Assisi." *Wissenschaft und Weisheit* 39 (1976): 26–41.

Gagnan, Dominique. "La croix et la nature chez Saint François d'Assise." *Antonianum* 57 (1982): 609–705.

Gerken, Alexander. "Theological Intuition of St. Francis of Assisi." Translated by Ignatius McCormick. *Greyfriars Review* 7 (1993): 71–94.

Gonzalez, Justo L. " The Work of Christ in Saint Bonaventure's Systematic Works." *Sancta Bonaventura 1274–1974.* Edited by Jacques-Guy Bougerol. Vol. 4, 371–85. Grottaferatta: Collegii S. Bonaventurae, 1974.

Hayes, Zachary. "Bonaventure: Mystery of the Triune God." In *The History of Franciscan Theology.* Edited by Kenan B. Osborne, 39–125. St. Bonaventure: Franciscan Institute, 1994.

_____. "The Theological Image of St. Francis of Assisi in the Sermons of St. Bonaventure." In *Bonaventuriana: Miscellanea in onore di Jacques Guy Bougerol.* Edited by Francisco de Asis Chavero Blanco. Vol. 1, 323–345. Roma: Edizioni Antonianum, 1988.

_____. "Incarnation and Creation in St. Bonaventure." *Studies Honoring Ignatius Brady, Friar Minor.* Edited by Romano Stephen Almagno and Conrad L. Harkins, 309–29. St. Bonaventure: Franciscan Institute, 1976.

_____. "The Meaning of *Convenientia* in the Metaphysics of St. Bonaventure." *Franciscan Studies* 34 (1974): 74–100.

Hellman, A. J. Wayne. "The Seraph in the Legends of Thomas of Celano and St. Bonaventure: The Victorine Transition." In *Bonaventuriana: Miscellanea in onore di Jacques Guy Bougerol.* Edited by Francsico de Asis Chavero Blanco. Vol. 1, 347–56. Roma: Edizioni Antonianum, 1988.

_____. "Poverty: The Franciscan Way to God," *Theology Digest* 22 (1974): 339–45.

Matura, Thadée. "'My Holy Father!' God as Father in the Writings of St. Francis." Translated by Cyprian Rosen. *Greyfriars Review* 1 (1987): 105–29.

Mc Evoy, James. "Microcosm and Macrocosm in the Writings of St. Bonaventure." *Sancta Bonaventura 1274–1974.* Vol. 2, 309–43. Grottaferatta: Collegii S. Bonaventurae, 1973.

McGinn, Bernard. "The Significance of Bonaventure's Theology of History." *Journal of Religion* 58 (Supplement, 1978): 64–81.

_____. "The Influence of St. Francis on the Theology of the High Middle Ages." *Bonaventuriana: Miscellanea in onore di Jacques Guy Bougerol.* Edited by Francisco de Asis Chavero Blanco, Vol. 1, 96–117. Roma: Edizioni Antonianum, 1988.

_____. "Ascension and Introversion in the *Itinerarium Mentis in Deum.*" *Sancta Bonaventura 1274–1974.* Vol. 3, 535–52. Grottaferrata: Collegii S. Bonaventurae, 1973.

Rahner, Karl. "Der Begriff der ecstasis bei Bonaventura." *Zeitschrift für Aszese und Mystik* 9 (1934): 1–19.

_____. "The Doctrine of the 'Spiritual Senses' in the Middle Ages." In *Theological Investigations*. Vol. 16, 104–34. *Experience of the Spirit. Source of Theology*. Translated by David Morland. New York: Seabury, 1979.

Rorem, Paul. "The Uplifting Spirituality of the Pseudo-Dionysius." *World Spirituality: An Encyclopedic History of the Religious Quest*. Vol. 16, 132–151. *Christian Spirituality: Origins to the Twelfth Century*. Edited by Bernard McGinn and John Meyendorff. New York: Crossroad, 1987.

Sandor, Monica. "Lectio Divina and the Monastic Spirituality of Reading." *American Benedictine Review* 40 (1989): 82–114.

Schaeffer, Alexander. "The Position and Function of Man in the Created World According to Bonaventure." *Franciscan Studies* 20 (1960): 261–316; 21 (1961): 233–382.

Schalück, Hermann. "Die theologischen Implikationen des Armutsgedankens bei Bonaventura." *Franziskanische Studien* 54 (1972): 184–91.

Schmucki, Octavian. "Mentis Silentium: Contemplation in the Early Franciscan Order." Translated by Ignatius McCormick. *Greyfriars Review* 4 (1990): 35–69.

_____. "Place of Solitude: An Essay on the External Circumstances of the Prayer Life of St. Francis of Assisi." Translated by Sebastian Holland. *Greyfriars Review* 2 (1988): 77–132.

_____. "Gli Scritti Legislativi di San Francesco." In *Approccio Storico-Critico alle Fonti Francescane*. A cura di G. C. e M. C., 73–98. Rome: Editrice Antonianum, 1979.

_____. "Divine Praise and Meditation according to the Teaching and Example of St. Francis of Assisi." Translated by Ignatius McCormick. *Greyfriars Review* 4 (1990): 23–73.

_____. "The Passion of Christ in the Life of St. Francis of Assisi: A Comparative Study of the Sources in the Light of Devotion to the Passion Practiced in his Time." Translated by Ignatius McCormick. *Greyfriars Review* 4 (Supplement, 1990): 1–101.

_____. "The Spirit of Prayer and the Active Life According to the Mind of St. Francis." Translated by Paul Barrett. *Greyfriars Review* 8 (1994): 31–55.

Strack, Bonifatius. "Christusleid im Christenleben: Ein Beitrag zur Theologie des christlichen Lebens nach dem heiligen Bonaventura." In *Franziskanische Forschungen.* Herausgegeben von Philotheus Boehner und Julian Kaup. Heft 13, 1–150. Werl/Westfallen: Dietrich-Coelde-Verlag, 1960.

Endnotes

INTRODUCTION

1. Since my study highlights the *mysticism* of the Crucified as the center of
    Bonaventure's theology, it is set apart from previous studies on
    Bonaventure's theology of the cross. For some earlier studies see Werner
    Hülsbusch, *Elemente einer Kreuzestheologie in den Spätschriften Bonaventuras*
    (Düsseldorf: Patmos Verlag, 1968); Bonifatius Strack, "Christusleid im
    Christenleben: Ein Beitrag zur Theologie des christlichen Lebens nach
    dem heiligen Bonaventura" in *Franziskanische Forschungen*, hars. Philotheus
    Boehner und Julian Kaup, heft 13 (Werl/Westfallen: Verlag, 1960), 1–150;
    Hans Peter Heinz, "Dreifaltige Liebe-Gekreuzigte Liebe," *Wissenschaft und
    Weisheit* 47 (1984): 12–22.
2. For a critical analysis of the Stigmata see Octavian Schmucki, *The Stigmata
    of St. Francis of Assisi*, trans. Canisius F. Connors, Franciscan Institute
    Publications History Series no. 6, ed. Jason M. Miskuly (St. Bonaventure,
    NY: The Franciscan Institute, 1991).
3. *Itinerarium Mentis in Deum (Itin.)* prologue 3 (V, 295). "Via autem non est
    nisi per ardentissimum amorem crucifixi." Engl. trans. Ewert Cousins,
    *Bonaventure: The Soul's Journey into God, The Tree of life, The Life of St.
    Francis* (New York: Paulist, 1978), 54. The critical edition of Bonaventure's
    writings is the *Opera Omnia*, ed. PP. Collegii a S. Bonaventura, 10 vols.
    (Quaracchi: Collegii Sancti Bonaventurae, 1881–1902). References are listed
    in parentheses according to volume and page number.
4. *Itin.* prol., 2 (V, 295). Engl. trans. Cousins, *Bonaventure*, 54.
5. Ewert Cousins, *Bonaventure and the Coincidence of Opposites* (Chicago:
    Franciscan Herald Press, 1978), 65.
6. *Itin.* 1, 7 (V, 298); *Brev.* 3, 4 (V, 233).
7. I *Sent.* d. 27, p. 2, a.u., q. 2, resp. (I, 485); *Itin.* 6, 2 (V, 311); III *Sent.* d. 19, a. 2, q.
    2 (III, 410). The concepts of *medium* and *mediator* are fundamental to

Bonaventure's doctrine. He defines *medium* as that which communicates between two extremes: "*Medium* namque dicit communicantiam cum extremis"; cf. *Hex.* 1, 14 (V, 331–332) where Bonaventure explains the uniqueness of the Word as *medium*: "Istud est *medium* personarum necessario: quia, si persona est, quae producit et non producitur, et persona, quae producitur et non producit, necessario est media, quae producitur et producit." Christ as mediator, however, performs the task of reconciliation: "*Mediator* autem non tantum dicit communicantiam, sed etiam dicit *officium* reconciliationis." Bonaventure maintains that Christ is mediator not according to his divine nature but according to his human nature; cf. III *Sent.* d. 20, q. 2, concl. (III, 410) where he writes: " . . . non potest esse mediator secundum divinam naturam, sed secundum humanam." Justo L. González ("The Work of Christ in Saint Bonaventure's Systematic Works," in *S. Bonaventura*, vol. 4 [Grottaferatta: Collegii S. Bonaventurae, 1974], 385) states that an affirmation of the independent value of Christ's human nature can be made in the distinction between *medium* and *mediator*, which is wholly compatible with his work as satisfaction, example, exemplar and end.

8. Ewert Cousins, "Francis of Assisi: Christian Mysticism at the Crossroads," in *Mysticism and Religious Traditions*, ed. Stephen T. Katz (New York: Oxford University Press, 1983), 163–90. In the early 1980s Ewert Cousins identified a type of mysticism based on his studies of Francis of Assisi, indicating that Francis' imitation of and devotion to the humanity of Christ led him to the height of mystical union with God. He referred to this mystical experience as "mysticism of the historical event" stating: "In this type of consciousness, one recalls a significant event in the past, enters into its drama and draws from it spiritual energy." He argued that this is a distinct type of mystical consciousness whereby the mysticism of the event is predicated on participation: "Just as in nature mysticism we feel united to the material world, so in this form of mysticism we feel part of the historical event—as if we were there, as an eye-witness, participating in the action, absorbing its energy." According to Cousins, it is through participation in the historical event that one experiences the mystical "power" of the event. This type of mysticism finds a theological expression in Francis of Assisi whose imitation of and devotion to Christ enabled him to participate in the life of Christ, drawing him into the mystical life of God.

9. See Francis's *Admonition 6* in *Francis and Clare: The Complete Works*, trans. Regis J. Armstrong and Ignatius Brady (New York: Paulist, 1982), 29.

10. The Franciscan Question refers to a search for original documents of the life of Francis and those that are dependent on them. The question was first raised by the Protestant theologian, Paul Sabatier, at the turn of the century. Sabatier dismissed Bonaventure's biography of Francis with cynicism and contempt stating that it was not a true biography but rather polit-

ically motivated. For a good summary see Luigi Pellegrini, "A Century of Reading the Sources for the Life of Francis of Assisi," trans. Edward Hagman, *Greyfriars Review* 7 (1993): 323–46.

11. For the dating of these works see Jacques-Guy Bougerol, *Introduction to the Works of Bonaventure*, trans. José de Vinck (Paterson: St. Anthony Guild Press, 1964), 153–60; Cousins, introduction to *Bonaventure*, 18–37. The approximate dates are: *Itinerarium*, 1259; *De triplici via*, 1259; *Lignum vitae*, 1259/60; *Legenda Major*, 1260.

12. Bonaventure *Legenda maior* (*LM*) 8, 1 (EM, 64). Engl. trans. Ewert Cousins, *Bonaventure*, 250. The Latin text of the *Legenda maior* used in this study is the *Legenda maior S. Francisci Assisiensis*, ed. PP. Collegii a Sancti Bonaventurae (editio minor) (Quaracchi: Collegii Sancti Bonaventurae, 1941), 2–125. References are cited by the abbrevition *LM* followed by chapter number and section number. Unless otherwise indicated, all references to Bonaventure's Latin text will be to this critical edition of the *Legenda* listed in parentheses as EM and page number.

13. See, for example, Fernand Van Steenberghen, *The Philosophical Movement in the Thirteenth Century* (London: Nelson, 1955), 56–74; Paul Vigneaux, *Philosophy in the Middle Ages: An Introduction*, trans. E. C. Hall (Westport, Conn.: Greenwood Press, 1959), 104–15.

14. Ellen Ross makes a similar point in her fine study on the passion in late medieval England. See Ellen M. Ross, *The Grief of God: Images of the Suffering Jesus in Late Medieval England* (New York: Oxford, 97), 134, 137–38.

15. Etienne Gilson, *The Philosophy of Saint Bonaventure*, trans. Dom Illtyd Tethowan (New York: Sheed and Ward, 1938), 480–81. Gilson writes: "The totality of [Bonaventure's] system means so much that the mere notion of fragments has no meaning at all. You can either see the general economy of his doctrine in its totality, or see none of it. . . . The fragments are quite literally meaningless by themselves, since each part reaches out into all the rest of the system and is affected by the ramifications leading to it from the system as a whole. . . . Paradoxical as the assertion may seem, I hold that it is the extreme unification of Bonaventure's doctrine which has made it look incomplete and unsystematized; it is easier to deny that the details form part of a system, than to grasp the system in its entirety and think out each detail in function of the whole."

CHAPTER ONE
FRANCIS OF ASSISI: MYSTIC IN THE WORLD

1. *The Disciple and the Master: St. Bonaventure's Sermons on St. Francis of Assisi*, trans. and intro. Eric Doyle (Chicago: Franciscan Herald Press, 1983).

2. Paul Rout, *Francis and Bonaventure* (London: Fount, 1996), 1–75.

3. For contemporary biographies of Francis see Arnaldo Fortini, *Francis of Assisi*, trans. Helen Moak (New York: Seabury Press, 1981); Raoul Manselli, *St. Francis of Assisi*, trans. Paul Duggan (Chicago: Franciscan Herald Press, 1988).

4. Rosalind Brooke, *The Coming of the Friars* (London: George Allen and Unwin, 1975), 47–58; cf. Berard Marthaler, "Forerunners of the Franciscans: The Waldenses," *Franciscan Studies* 18 (1958): 133–42; Antoine Dondaine, "Aux origines du Valdéisme. Une profession de foi de Valdes," *Archivum Fratrum Praedicatorum* 16 (1946): 190–235; Herbert Grundmann, *Religiöse Bewegungen im Mittelalter,* 2nd ed. (Hildesheim: Olms, 1961), 157–69.

5. The two principal biographers of the life of Francis are Thomas of Celano and Bonaventure. The work of the third biographer, Julian of Speyer, is not considered among the major sources. In this study the biographies of both Celano and Bonaventure are employed. The critical edition of Celano's biographies is the *Analecta Franciscana: Chronica aliaque varia documenta Legendae S. Francisci Assisiensis*, ed. PP. Collegii S. Bonaventurae, vol. 10 (Quaracchi: Collegii Sancti Bonaventurae, 1926–1941). English translations of Celano's *First and Second Lives of Saint Francis* as well as the legendary accounts, *Legend of Perugia, The Three Companions, The Mirror of Perfection, Sacrum Commercium*, used in this study are from *St. Francis of Assisi: Writings and Early Biographies, English Omnibus of the Sources for the Life of St. Francis*, ed. Marion Habig (Chicago: Franciscan Herald Press, 1973) hereafter referred to as *Omnibus*. References to the critical edition are listed in parentheses as AF and page number. References are cited by the abbreviation *Cel.* with first or second life indicated before abbreviation followed by section number. It was thought that Bonaventure's *Legenda Major* was commissioned by the General Chapter of the Friars Minor held at Narbonne in 1260; however, this has been questioned recently by Dominic Monti (*St. Bonaventure's Writings Concerning the Franciscan Order,* intro. and trans. Dominic Monti, vol. 5, *Works of Saint Bonaventure*, ed. George Marcil [St. Bonaventure: The Franciscan Institute, 1994], 137) since there is no such decree found among the acts of this chapter. Bonaventure does indicate that he wrote his *Legenda* at the "unanimous urging of the General Chapter" (*LM* prol., 3) but he does not specify which chapter. Monti suggests that it may have been the Chapter of Rome in 1257. Bonaventure himself was Minister General of the Order at that time. The text was approved in 1263 and in 1266 it was prescribed as the only canonical, definitive, and exclusive text, with the Order's injunction that all earlier biographies were to be deleted. For the historical background to both Bonaventure's and Celano's biographies see Albert Hasse, "Bonventure's 'Legenda maior': A redaction critical approach" (Ph. D. dissertation, Fordham University, 1990), 12–166.

6. Regis Armstrong cites thirty-eight writings either composed or dictated by

Francis. See Regis Armstrong, *St. Francis of Assisi: Writings for a Gospel Life* (New York: Crossroad, 1994), 26; ibid., introduction to *Francis and Clare*, 7–10.

7. Bernard McGinn, "Was Francis of Assisi a Mystic?" in *Doors of Understanding: Conversations in Global Spirituality*, ed. Steven L. Chase (Quincy, IL: Franciscan Press, 1997), 148.

8. McGinn, "Was Francis a Mystic?", 148–49.

9. *LM* 10, 3 (EM, 83); 1 *Cel* 71 (AF, 73); *Legenda perugina* 9.

10. 2 *Cel* 19 (AF, 142); *LM* 12, 1 (EM, 97).

11. *LM* 12, 2 (EM, 99); *Actus*, 16. The author of the *Legenda perugina* (93) states: "He asked prayers of those who to him seemed to be friends of God, so that the Lord would make it known to him whether to fulfill his will he ought to go and preach to the people or withdraw himself to this solitary place to pray." Engl. trans. *Omnibus*, 1070.

12. The earlier Rule, the *Regula non bullata* (*RegNB*) was written in 1221, developed from the primitive rule of 1210, and gave rise to the later Rule, the *Regula bullata* (*RegB*) of 1223. For a discussion on the genesis of the Rule see David Flood and Thadée Matura, *The Birth of a Movement: A Study of the First Rule of St. Francis*, trans. Paul LaChance and Paul Schwartz (Chicago: Franciscan Herald Press, 1975), 3–56. A critical study on the Rules of St. Francis has been done by Octavian Schmucki, "Gli Scritti Legislativi de San Francesco," in *Approccio Storico-Critico alle Fonti Francescane*, a cura di G. C. e M. C. (Rome: Editrice Antonianum, 1979), 73–98.

13. *RH* 2 (Écrits, 200).

14. Thadée Matura, "'My Holy Father!' God as Father in the Writings of St. Francis," trans. Cyprian Rosen, *Greyfriars Review* 1 (1987): 129.

15. Francis of Assisi, "Compline: Psalm 1," in *Francis and Clare*, 81.

16. Matura, "My Holy Father," 123.

17. *RNB* 23, 1, 5. Engl. trans. *Francis and Clare*, 130–31. The critical edition of Francis's writings used in this study is *Francois d'Assise: Écrits*, intro. and trans. Théophile Desbonnets, Thaddée Matura, Jean-François Godet, Damien Vorreux, vol. 285, *Source Chrétiennes* (Paris: Editions Franciscaines, 1981).

18. Francis of Assisi,"Our Father," in *Francis and Clare*, 106.

19. Francis of Assisi *Oratio ante crucifixum*. Engl. trans. *Francis and Clare*, 103.

20. Francis of Assisi *Laudes ad omnes horas dicendae* (Écrits, 282). Engl. trans. *Francis and Clare*, 99.

21. 2 *Ep Fid* 4 (Écrits, 228). Engl. trans. *Francis and Clare*, 67.

22. Norbert Nguyên-Van-Khanh, *The Teacher of His Heart: Jesus Christ in the Thought and Writings of St. Francis*, trans. Ed Hagman (St. Bonaventure, NY: The Franciscan Institute, 1994), 102–02.

23. Van-Khanh, *Teacher of His Heart*, 32.

24. Ibid., 141.

25. *2 EpFid* 3 (Écrits, 228). Engl. trans. *Francis and Clare*, 67; Alexander Gerken, "Theological Intuition of St. Francis of Assisi," trans. Ignatius McCormick, *Greyfriars Review* 7 (1993): 72. Gerken states that the second version of the *Letter to the Faithful* is the most comprehensive presentation of Francis' theology.

26. *2 EpFid* 4 (Écrits, 228). Engl. trans. *Francis and Clare*, 67.

27. *Adm.* 1, 16–18 (Écrits, 92). Engl. trans. *Francis and Clare*, 26–7.

28. *EpOrd* 29 (Écrits, 250). Engl. trans. *Francis and Clare*, 58.

29. Alexander Gerken, *Théologie du Verbe: La relation entre l'incarnation et la création selon S. Bonaventure*, trans. Jacqueline Gréal (Paris: Éditions Franciscaines, 1970), 362–63. "Car on voit clairement maintenant pourquoi la décision prise par Dieu de s'incarner ne se voit pas conférer chez Bonaventure simplement le charactère de l'amour, mais le caractère d'un amour qui s'adresse au vide, à l'inférieur, à l'autre, en un mot: de l'humilité. . . . Dans l'incarnation, l' humilité agissant dans son éternité comme motif et signification de sa volonté de se donner *ad extra*. La vie tout entière de Jésus, dans son obscurité et sa pauvreté, est une manifestation de cet humble amour qui vit en Dieu et qui s'abaisse. C'est de François que Bonaventure a reçu cette conception de l'incarnation, et elle est à proprement parler la raison pour laquelle il rejette la distinction entre une Incarnation quant à sa substance et une Incarnation sous la forme de la pauvreté et de la croix."

30. *2 EpFid* 50. Engl. trans. *Francis and Clare*, 70.

31. Kajetan Esser, "Studium und Wissenschaft im Geiste des hl. Franziskus von Assisi," *Wissenschaft und Weisheit* 39 (1976): 28. "Dabei kommt es dem hl. Franziskus nicht nur auf eine äußere Nachahmung des Lebens Jesu an, sondern vor allem darauf, daß im Nachfolger Christi auch der Geist Christi lebendig und wirksam wird. Man kann diese Lehre vom Geist des Herrn (*spiritus Domini*) . . . das Herzstück im Denken und in der christlichen Haltung des hl. Franziskus nennen. Von ihm spricht er immer wieder: in seinen Regeln und Briefen, in seinen Ermahnungen für die Brüder."

32. Sebastián López, "La Regla de los Hermanos Menores, Pacto de Eterna Alianza," *Selecciones de Franciscanismo* 4 (1976): 47–49.

33. *EpOrd* 50–52 (Écrits, 254). Engl. trans. *Francis and Clare*, 61.

34. *RB* 20.3–4. Engl.tran. *Rule*, 217.

35. *RegB* 10, 8–9 (Écrits, 196).

36. Ibid. Engl. trans. *Francis and Clare*, 144.

37. *RegNB* 22, 26–27 (Écrits, 166).

38. *Reg NB* 22, 7; 17; 25 (Écrits, 162–165). Engl. trans. *Francis and Clare*, 127–28.

39. *RegB* 10, 7–9 (Écrits, 196). Engl. trans. *Francis and Clare*, 144.

40. *RegNB* 5, 4 (Écrits, 130); *2EpFid* 69 (Écrits, 238).

41. *RegB* 10, 7 (Écrits, 196). Engl. trans. *Francis and Clare*, 144.

42. *RegNB* 22, 26, 31 (Écrits, 165). Engl. trans. *Francis and Clare*, 128–29.

43. *EpOrd* 40–42 (Écrits, 252). Engl. trans. *Francis and Clare*, 59–60.
44. *RB* 19.6–7. Engl. trans. *Rule*, 217.
45. *RegNB* 22, 25 (Écrits, 162–165). Engl. trans. *Francis and Clare*, 128. On purity of heart see also *RegB* 10, 8–9; *RegNB* 22, 26–27; *RegNB* 22, 26, 31.
46. Eric Doyle and Damian McElrath,"St. Francis of Assisi and the Christocentric Character of Franciscan Life and Doctrine," in *Franciscan Christology*, ed. Damian McElrath (St. Bonaventure, NY: The Franciscan Institute, 1980), 10.
47. 2 *EpFid* 34 (Écrits, 234). Engl. trans. *Francis and Clare*, 69.
48. 1 *Ep Cust* 4 (Écrits, 256). Engl. trans. *Francis and Clare*, 53.
49. See *RegNB* 22, 46–41.
50. *EpCler* 11 (Écrits, 218), *EpOrd* 12 (Écrits, 246), 1 *EpFid* 1–5 (Écrits, 222), 2 *EpFid* 22–23 (Écrits, 232), 1 *EpCust* 2–4 (Écrits, 256), 2 *EpCust* 4 (Écrits, 258) and *EpRul* 6 (Écrits, 260).
51. Van-Khanh, *Teacher of His Heart*, 165. It is worthwhile to note that Eucharistic devotion among the Beguines was a source of mystical union. McDonnell (*Beguines and Beghards*, 311) states that ardent love for the humanity and passion of Christ explains this intense devotion. See also Jacques de Vitry, *The Life of Marie d'Oignes*, trans. Margot H. King (Toronto: Peregrina, 1989), 22,129 n. 23. Moreover, several Beguines received the Stigmata and there seems to be a link between union with Christ in the Eucharist and reception of the mystical wounds, not unlike that found in Francis. McDonnell recounts the Stigmata in Ida of Louvain and Mary of Oignies, both of whom had a passionate devotion to the humanity of Christ and the Eucharist (pp. 314, 418).
52. *LOrd* 27. Engl trans. *Francis and Clare*, 58.
53. *Adm* 1, 1–4 (Écrits, 192). Engl. trans. *Francis and Clare*, 25.
54. *Adm* 1, 8 (Écrits, 90). Engl. trans. *Francis and Clare*, 26. Emphasis added.
55. Van-Khanh, *Teacher of His Heart*, 162.
56. 1 *EpFid* 8 (Écrits, 220). Engl. trans. *Francis and Clare*, 63.
57. *EpOrd* 51–52 (Écrits, 254). Engl. trans. *Francis and Clare*, 61.
58. *Adm.* 1, 8 (Écrits, 90). "Unde omnes qui viderunt Dominum Jesum secundum humanitatem et non viderunt et crediderunt secundum spiritum et divinitatem, ipsum esse verum Filium Dei, damnati sunt."
59. *Adm.* 1, 20 (Écrits, 92). Engl. trans. *Francis and Clare*, 27.
60. *Adm.* 6 (Écrits, 100). Engl. trans. *Francis and Clare*, 29.
61. *RegNB* 22, 32–35; 41; 48; 53 (Écrits, 166–168). See also Flood and Matura, *Birth of a Movement*, 45.
62. *EpOrd* 9 (Écrits, 246). Engl. trans. *Francis and Clare*, 56.
63. See Schmucki, *Stigmata of St. Francis of Assisi*, 71–325.
64. *LM* 13, 3 (EM, 107–08). Engl. trans. Cousins, *Bonaventure*, 305.
65. Noel Muscat, *The Life of Saint Francis in the Light of Saint Bonaventure's Theology on the "Verbum Crucifixum"* (Rome: Editrice Antonianum, 1989), 238.

66. *Itin.* 7, 3–4, 6 (V, 312, 313). Engl. trans. Cousins, *Bonaventure*, 112–13.

67. Bonaventure, "Sermon 3 on St. Francis," in *Disciple and Master*, 101–02.

68. *Itin.*, prol., 3 (V, 295). See also Muscat, *Verbum crucifixum*, 242.

69. *LM* 13, 3 (EM, 108). Engl. trans. Cousins, *Bonaventure*, 305.

70. E. Randolph Daniel, *The Franciscan Concept of Mission in the High Middle Ages* (Lexington: University of Kentucky Press, 1975), 88.

CHAPTER TWO
BONAVENTURE: THEOLOGIAN AND MYSTIC

1. For details of Bonaventure's life see Jacques Guy Bougerol, *Introduction to the Works of Bonaventure*, trans. José de Vinck (Paterson, NJ: St. Anthony Guild Press, 1963), 171–77.

2. See *LM* prol., 3 (EM, 5). Bonaventure writes: "For when I was a boy, as I still vividly remember, I was snatched from the jaws of death by his invocation and merits. So if I remained silent and did not sing his praises, I fear that I would be rightly accused of the crime of ingratitude." Engl. trans. Cousins, *Bonaventure*, 182.

3. Bonaventure describes the problems of the Order in *Epistola ad amones Ministros provinciales et Custodes Ordinis Fratrum Minorum* (VIII, 468a–469b) which he wrote as a new Minister General on 23 April 1257. For a discussion of Bonaventure's role as Minister General and the problems of the Order, see Dominic Monti, introduction to *Writings Concerning the Franciscan Order*, vol. 5, *Works of St. Bonaventure*, ed. George Marcil (St. Bonaventure: Franciscan Institute, 1994), 1–36; J. R. H. Moorman, *A History of the Franciscan Order: From its Origins to the Year 1517* (Oxford: Clarendon, 1968), 105–204; Decima Douie, "St. Bonaventure's Part in the Conflict between Seculars and Mendicants at Paris," in *S. Bonaventura 1274–1974*, 5 vols. (Grottaferatta: Collegii S. Bonaventurae, 1973), 2:585–612].

4. Ewert Cousins, introduction to *Bonaventure*, 8–11.

5. Hans Urs von Balthasar, *The Glory of the Lord: A Theological Aesthetics*, vol. 2, *Studies in Theological Style: Clerical Styles*, trans. Andrew Louth, Francis McDonagh and Brian McNeil (San Francisco: Ignatius, 1984), 263.

6. Doyle, introduction to *Disciple and Master*, 2.

7. *Itin.* prol., 2 (V, 295). Engl. trans. Cousins, *Bonaventure*, 54.

8. *Itin.* prol., 3 (V, 295). "Via autem non est nisi per ardentissimum amorem Crucifixi."

9. Doyle, introduction to *Disciple and Master*, 13.

10. Joseph Ratzinger, *The Theology of History in St. Bonaventure*, trans. Zachary Hayes (Chicago: Franciscan Herald Press, 1971), 3.

11. Muscat, *Verbum crucifixum*, 112.

12. Marigwen Schumacher, "Mysticism in Metaphor," in *S. Bonaventura*, 2:384–85.

13. Zachary Hayes, "The Theological Image of St. Francis of Assisi in the Sermons of St. Bonaventure," in *Bonaventuriana: Miscellanea in onore di Jacques Guy Bougerol*, 2 vols. (Rome: Edizioni Antonianum, 1988), 1:334–45.

14. Hugh of St. Victor *Soliloquium de arrha animae* (Migne *PL* 176.954). "Ea vis amoris est, ut talem esse necesse sit, quale illud est quod amas, et qui per affectum conjungeris, in ipsius similtudinem ipsa quodammodo dilectionis societate transformaris."

15. See *LM* 4, 11 (EM, 37).

16. E. Randolph Daniel, "Symbol or Model? St. Bonaventure's Use of St. Francis," in *Bonaventuriana*, 1:61.

17. Hayes, "Theological Image," 338.

18. Gilson, *Philosophy of St. Bonaventure*, 480.

19. Ewert Cousins, "The Two Poles of Bonaventure's Thought," in *S. Bonaventura*, 4:154, 164

20. I *Sent.* d. 27, p. 1, a.u., q. 2, ad 3 (I, 470).

21. I *Sent.* d. 27, p. 1, a. u., q. 2 ad 3 (I, 471). When Bonaventure applies this principle, he cites Aritstotle as his source. The Quaracchi editors point out that Bonaventure is drawing from propositions 1, 16, 17, and 20 of the *Liber de causis*. Like his contemporaries, Bonaventure thought the *Liber de causis* was by Aristotle. However shortly after 1268 Thomas Aquinas read William of Moerbeke's Latin translation of Proclus' *Elements of Theology* and concluded that the author of the *Liber de causis* was an Arabian philosopher familiar with Proclus' treatise. See Cousins, *Coincidence of Opposites*, 103.

22. I *Sent.* d. 27, p. 1, a.u., q. 2, ad 3 (I, 471).

23. Cousins, *Coincidence of Opposites*, 103.

24. Zachary Hayes, introduction to *Disputed Questions on the Mystery of the Trinity*, vol. 3, *Works of Saint Bonaventure*, ed. George Marcil (St. Bonaventure: The Franciscan Institute, 1979), 53.

25. *Hex.* 1, 14 (V, 331–332),. Engl. trans. José De Vinck, *On the Six Days of Creation* (Paterson, NJ: 1966), 8.

26. I *Sent.* d. 6, q. 2 (I, 128a).

27. *Hex.* 1, 13 (V, 331). Engl. trans. De Vinck, *Six Days of Creation*, 8.

28. Zachary Hayes, introduction to *Disputed Questions on the Mystery of the Trinity*, 47.

29. *Brev.* 1, 3 (V, 212). See also Zachary Hayes, "The Meaning of *Convenientia* in the Metaphysics of St. Bonaventure," *Franciscan Studies* 34 (1974): 90.

30. *Hex.* 1, 16 (V, 332). Bonaventure writes: "The Father begot his own likeness, that is, the Word coeternal with himself, and expressed a similitude of himself, and in so doing he expressed all that he could." Engl. trans. De Vinck, *Six Days of Creation*, 9.

31. *Comm. in Joan.* c. 1, p. 1, q. 1 (VI, 247). Engl. trans. Hayes, introduction to *Mystery of Trinity*, 51.

32. See I *Sent.* d. 8, p. 1, q. 1, ad 4, 7 (I, 151b).

33. I *Sent.* d. 6, a.u., q. 2, resp. (I, 128).

34. Hayes, introduction to *Mystery of Trinity*, 47, 58.

35. Cousins, *Coincidence of Opposites*, 57.

36. On the theme of exemplarism in Bonaventure's theology see Jean-Marie Bissen, *L'exemplarisme divin selon saint Bonaventure* (Paris: J. Vrin, 1929); Gerken, *La théologie du verbe*, 135–39; Hayes, introduction to *Mystery of Trinity*, 47–54.

37. Cousins, *Coincidence of Opposites*, 99.

38. *Brev.* 2, 12 (V, 230).

39. The theme of Christ as book of wisdom is important in Bonaventure's theology. See *Lig. vit.* 46; *Brev*, 2, 9 (V, 229).

40. Bonaventure *De reductione artium* 16 (V, 323). Engl. trans. José de Vinck, "On Retracing the Arts," in *St. Bonaventure: Opuscula*, vol. 3, *The Works of Bonaventure* (Paterson, NJ: St. Anthony Guild Press, 1966), 26.

41. Hayes, introduction to *Mystery of Trinity*, 51.

42. *Vig. nat. Dom.* 1 (IX, 89b). "Si, ergo Pater diligit Filium et omnia dedit in manu eius, nihil sibi reservans; cum dat nobis Filium, omnia quae habuit nobis dedit in illo et in hoc mirabiliter nos ditavit."

43. I *Sent.* d. 31, p. 2, q. 2, concl. (I, 542a). "Dicendum, quod imago in divinis non tantum dicit expressionem personae, sed etiam expressionem in summo."

44. I *Sent.* d. 39, p. 1, q. 1 ad 4 (I, 686b). "Et quoniam divina veritas una et summa expressione exprimit se et alia."

45. Von Balthasar, *Clerical Styles*, 299.

46. I *Sent.* d. 8, p. 1, q. 1 ad 4, 7 (I, 151b). "Omnia enim vera sunt et nata sunt se exprimere per expressionem illius summi luminis."

47. Peter Casarella, "The Expression and Form of the Word: Trinitarian Hermeneutics and the Sacramentality of Language in Hans Urs von Balthasar's Theology," *Renascence* 48.2 (Winter, 1996): 114–15.

48. Ibid., "Experience as a Theological Category: Hans Urs von Balthasar on the Christian Encounter with God's Image," *Communio* 20 (Spring, 1993): 124.

49. Casarella, "Expression and Form," 128.

50. *Itin.* 2, 7 (V, 301).

51. *Itin.* 6, 7 (V, 312).

52. See Francis Xavier Pancheri, *The Universal Primacy of Christ*, trans. Juniper B. Carol (Front Royal, VA: Christendom Publications, 1984), 19–20. For Bonaventure, the reasons of the incarnation are: 1) God's infinite power, wisdom and goodness are manifested in a perfect manner; 2) Since the first should be joined with the last, it is fitting that the divine Word be united to man for perfection of the universe; 3) In God there are three divine persons in one nature. Thus it was fitting that there be also a divine person in more than one nature; 4) God is the infinite remunerator. Thus it was fitting that he should render man blessed according his whole nature—body and soul;

5) In order to overcome the infirmity of man's sin it was necessary to have a God-man as mediator.

53. *Dom. 2 Adv.* 9 (IX, 56ab).

54. *Itin.* 1, 7 (V, 298).

55. *Brev.* 4, 2 (V, 242); *Solil.* 1, 30 (VIII, 39). See Gregory Nazianzus *Oratio* 38.20 (Migne *PL* 36.333).

56. *Brev.* 4, 2 (V, 242). ". . . quod opus illud non inanimatio, sed incarnatio nominatur."

57. *Brev.* 5, 6 (V, 259); *Itin.* 2, 7 (V, 301).

58. *Hex.* 1, 13 (V, 331).

59. *Hex.* 1, 27 (V, 334).

60. *Brev.* 4, 2 (V, 242). "De opere incarnationis haec tenenda sunt secundum fidem Christianam, quod incarnatio est operatio Trinitatis, per quam fit assumtio carnis a Deitate et unio Deitatis cum carne."

61. Zachary Hayes, introduction to *Saint Bonaventure's Disputed Questions on the Knowledge of Christ*, vol. 4, *Works of Saint Bonaventure*, ed. George Marcil (St. Bonaventure: Franciscan Institute, 1992), 49.

62. *Brev.* 6, 3 (V, 267).

63. Ibid.

64. *Brev.* 6, 4 (V, 268).

65. III *Sent.* d. 1, a. 2, q. 3, resp. (III, 29). See Hayes, "*Convenientia* in the Metaphysics of St. Bonaventure," 89–90.

66. *De perf. vit.* 5, 10 (VIII, 120).

67. *Brev.* 1, 2 (V, 211). ". . . quia fides, cum sit principium cultus Dei et fundamentum eius quae secundum pietatem est doctrinae, dictat, de Deo esse sentiendum *altissime* et *piissime*. Non autem sentiret *altissime*, si non crederet, quod Deus posset se summe communicare; non sentiret *piissime*, si crederet, quod posset et nollet; et ideo, ut *altissime* et *piissime* sentiat, dicit, Deum se summe communicare, aeternaliter habendo dilectum et condilectum, ac per hoc Deum unum et trinum."

68. *Vig. nat. Dom.* 2 (IX, 106). "*Verbum caro factum est*, Ioannis primo. Exprimitur in hic verbis istud caeleste mysterium et admirabile sacramentum, istud opus magnificum et beneficium infinitum, quod Deus aeternus, humiliter se inclinans, limum nostrae naturae in suae assumsit unitatem personae." For the Gospel citation see Jn 1:14 (RSV).

69. *Brev.* 4, 1 (V, 245). "Decentissimum fuit, rerum principium reparativum esse Deum summum, ut, sicut omnia creaverat Deus per Verbum increatum, sic omnia creaverat Deus per Verbum incarnatum."

70. *Dom. III Adv. Serm II* (IX, 66–67). "Calceamentum tegit pedem, ita natura humana tegit naturam divinam, tamen est extranea a natura divina, sicut calceamentum a pede. Ligatura vero tantae sublimitatis est, quod *non sum dignus solvere*, id est explicare istud mysterium. Videte, quare non vult solvere? Dico, quod coniunctio Divinitatis cum humanitate est coniunctio

primi cum ultimo, summi cum infirmo, scilicet Dei cum terra, et simplicissimi cum compositissimo, quia Verbum aeternum simplicissimum est, et natura humana compositissima, Quae convenientia inter ista? . . . Hoc enim mysterium factum est sine ulla mutatione facta in Deo."

71. *Brev.* 4, 1 (V, 241); *Hex.* 8, 11 (V, 371a). Bonaventure insists that the incarnation cannot be known unless one is aware of the distinction of persons [of the Trinity]. He states that "if you acknowledge the Trinity but not the incarnation, you have a witnessing in heaven, but you do not receive it on earth." (Engl. trans. De Vinck, *Six Days of Creation*, 127). In the Crucified Word, the Spirit, the water, and the blood bear witness to God's presence (*Sermo* 1 (V, 536). The Spirit refers to the Godhead, the water to the body, and the blood, wherein is the life of the soul, to the soul. Through his blood, Christ united the Spirit with the water, for by means of the soul, the Godhead was joined to a body.

72. *Vig. nat. Dom.* (IX, 103a). "Verbum incarnatum ante nativitatem est inintelligibile, sed post nativitatem, per modum verbi voce expressi, carne inductum fit nobis sensibile . . . Et sic factum est Verbum visibile, non solum audibile . . . sed illud Verbum Patris, quod audiri non poterat nec videri, in sua nativitate, factum est visibile et audibile."

73. Gerken, *Théologie du verbe*, 182.

74. *Vig. nat. Dom.* 1 (IX, 103). "A Domino factum est istud et est mirabile in oculis nostris."

75. Ibid. (IX, 90b). "Et ideo necesse fuit, carne obumbrari, ut homines possent videre et imitari."

76. III *Sent.* d. 3, p. 1, dub. 2 (III, 79 ab); *Comm. Lc*, c. 9, n. 64 (VII, 237b); *Vig. nat. Dom.* 1 (IX, 90b). The theme of "obumbratio Christi" is also found in Bernard of Clairvaux *Serm.* 20.7 (OB 1:119).

78. *Vig. nat. Dom.* 1 (IX, 90b).

78. *De perf. vit.* 3, 3 (VIII, 12b–13a).

79. Zachary Hayes, "Bonaventure: Mystery of the Triune God," in *The History of Franciscan Theology*, ed. Kenan B. Osborne (St. Bonaventure: The Franciscan Institute, 1994), 84.

CHAPTER THREE
THE JOURNEY INTO GOD

1. *Hex.* 1, 17 (V, 332).

2. *Itin.* prol., 3 (V, 295). Engl. trans. Cousins, *Bonaventure*, 54–5.

3. Hugh of St. Victor, *Selected Writings*, intro. Aelred Squires, trans. Community of St. Mary the Virgin (New York: Harper and Row, 1963), 54.

4. *LM* 13, 2 (EM, 107). Engl. trans. Cousins, *Bonaventure*, 305.

5. *Sermo* 4, 16 (V, 571b); *Q. Sci. Chri.* q. 4 (V, 24a).

6. Plotinus *Enneads* 1. 6. 8–9. Plotinus views introversion and ascent as a "turn-

ing away forever from the material" in order for the soul, by its superior nature, to ascend to the One. The material world weighs the soul down and prevents it from returning to the Fatherland. Conversely, for Bonaventure, creation has spiritual potency and bears an imprint of the Trinity so that one like Francis, conformed to Christ, views creation as a ladder by which s/he can climb up and "embrace him who is utterly desirable." See *LM* 9, 1 (EM, 74).

7.   *Itin.* 3, 1 (V, 303). Engl. trans. Cousins, *Bonaventure*, 83.

8.   *Itin.* 3, 4 (V, 305). Engl. trans. Cousins, *Bonaventure*, 84.

9.   *M. Trin.* q. 1, concl. (V, 55). Engl. trans. Hayes, *Disputed Questions on Mystery of Trinity*, 129; cf. *Itin.* 3, 5 (V, 305). In I *Sent.* d. 3, p. 2, a. 1, q. 1 (I, 80) Bonaventure states: "Ratio imaginis consistit in perfecta capacitate, quia secundum Augustinum 'eo est mens imago, quo potest esse capax et participes Dei'; sed Deus non capitur ab anima plene nisi ametur, neque ametur nisi intelligatur, nec intelligatur nisi praesens ad animam habeatur; sed primum est per voluntatem secundum per intelligentiam, tertium per memoriam."

10. 1 *Sent.* d. 3, p. 2, a. 2, q.1, concl. (I, 89); *Brev.* 5, 4 (V, 256).

11. Hayes, "*Convenientia,*" 89; III *Sent.* d. 1, a. 2, q. 3, resp. (III, 29–30).

12. *Itin.* 6, 7 (V, 312); *Brev.* 4, 1 (V, 241). See Hayes, "Bonaventure: Mystery of Triune God," 86.

13. *Itin.* 3, 5 (V, 305).

14. This is essentially the meaning of "convenientia" that Bonaventure describes whereby the human person is immediately ordered to God and thus has the potency to receive the mystery of divine self-communication. See Hayes, "Convenientia," 89; III *Sent.* d. 1, a. 2, q. 3 resp. (III, 29–30).

15. II *Sent.*, prooem. (II, 4). Engl. trans. Gregory Shanahan, "Prologue to the Second Book of Sentences," *Cord* 35 (1985): 120.

16. *Brev.* 2, 11 (V, 229).

17. *Brev.* 3, 1 (V, 231); II *Sent.* prooem. (II,).

18. III *Sent.* d. 1, a.2, q.3, ad resp. (III, 29); Wayne Hellman, "The Franciscan Poverty of God," *Theology Digest* 20 (1975): 341.

19. *Itin.* 1, 7 (V, 298).

20. *Brev.* 2, 4 (V, 221).

21. See *Brev.* 2, 4 (V, 221).

22. *Itin.* 4, 2 (V, 306). See Cousins, *Coincidence of Opposites*, 83.

23. "Prologue to the Second Book of Sentences," trans. Gregory Shanahan, *Cord* (1985): 123.

24. *Itin.* 4, 2 (V, 306). The symbol of the ladder is discussed by Bernard McGinn, *The Golden Chain: A Study in the Theological Anthropology of Isaac of Stella* (Washington D.C.: Consortium, 1972), 94–7.

25. *Hex.* 1, 17 (V, 332b); *Hex.* 10, 12–14 (V, 378); *Red. art.* 7 (V, 322). In the drama of creation Bonaventure distinguishes three main phases: the *emanatio*, the

exemplaritas, and the *consummatio*, which is also called *reductio*. The meaning of these three phases is that the created world as a whole and all creatures in this world have their origin in God *from* whom they proceed; having been created, they *reflect* God, their divine model or exemplar, according to which they were made; they finally *return* to God for whom they were created and who is their ultimate end. These three phases are closely connected with one another and form one continuous line or process. Since this line returns to the same point from which it began, if forms a circular movement. However, if the line of creation does not bend back and close on its beginning, it has not found its perfection. In I *Sent.* d. 45, q. 2, p. 1, concl. (I, 804b–805a) Bonaventure attributes the idea of a circular movement to the Pseudo-Dionysius (*De divinis nominibus* 4.14 [Migne *PL* 122.1136–1137]). See also Zacharay Hayes (*What Manner of Man: Sermons on Christ by St. Bonaventure* [Chicago: Franciscan Herald Press, 1974, repr. 1989], 92 nn. 45–6) who writes: "The completion of creation is in the fact that the first and last have come together through a union in the human person who is the last work of creation. As a being in whom God has united the extremes of spirit and corporeality, the human is the crowning work of the first creation; but as the *ultimum* the human is the last work of God. The principle of correspondence leads to an historical parallel between the work of the first creation and that of the recreation. What appears in Adam appears also in Christ, but more firmly for in Christ is the Word of God himself. Therefore, in the fall of the first Adam the line of *egressio* is carried out in a destructive way; in the obedience of the second Adam, the movement of *egressio* bends into *reditus* and the circle closes."

26. "Sermon II Nativity," in *What Manner of Man*, 74.

27. I *Sent.* d. 3, p. 1, a. u., q. 1, fund. (I, 68b). "Eo mens est imagine Dei, quo capax Dei est et particeps esse potest. Capere autem non est secundum substantiam vel essentiam, quia sic est in omnibus creaturis: ergo per cognitionem et amorem: ergo Deus potest cognosci a creatura."

28. Alvin Black, "The Doctrine of the Image and Similitude in Saint Bonaventure: A translation of pages fifty-six to ninety-nine inclusive of *De SS. Trinitate in Creaturis Refulgente. Doctrina S. Bonaventurae*," by Titus Szabo (master's thesis, St. Bonaventure University, 1962), 40.

29. *Solil.* 1, 6 (VIII, 31).

30. *Itin.* 3, 3 (V, 305). Here Bonaventure refers to the doctrine of illumination whereby the divine light present in the soul imparts a certitude to the knowledge it conceives. See M. Hurley, "Illumination According to Bonaventure," *Gregorianum* 32 (1951): 388–404; Hayes, introduction to *Disputed Questions on the Knowledge of Christ*, vol. 4, *Works of Saint Bonaventure* (St. Bonaventure, NY: The Franciscan Institute, 1992), 57.

31. "Contuitio," in *Lexique Saint Bonaventure*, ed. Jacques-Guy Bougerol (Paris: Editions Franciscaines, 1969), 41–44. Contuition means to express the simul-

taneity of form in the created thing or mirror and in the original or eternal exemplar. It is an intuitive-type of knowledge of God whereby God is perceived in the created world without the aid of the exterior senses; cf. *Q. Sc. Chr.* q. 4, concl. (V, 23); II *Sent.* d. 23, a. 2, q. 3, concl. (II, 544).

32. "Christ, One Teacher," in *What Manner of Man*, 36; cf. Hayes, introduction to *Questions on Knowledge of Christ*, 57.

33. Ibid., 37.

34. *Red. art.* 18 (V, 324).

35. I *Sent.* d. 31, p. 2, q. 1, fund. 4 (I, 540a).

36. *Q. Sc. Chr.* 4 (V, 24a).

37. "Christ, One Teacher," in *What Manner of Man*, 21.

38. "Sermon II Nativity," in *What Manner of Man*, 98.

39. "Sermon Third Sunday Advent," in *What Manner of Man*, 97.

40. *Hex.* 12, 5 (V, 385). Engl. trans. de Vinck, *Six Days of Creation*, 174–75; cf. Bissen, *L'exemplarisme selon Saint Bonaventure*, 183.

41. "Christ, One Teacher," in *What Manner of Man*, 34–5.

42. Ibid., 37.

43. *Brev.* 4, 9 (V, 249).

44. III *Sent.* d. 14, a. 1, q. 2, resp. (III, 300). Bonaventure speaks of the human mind of Christ knowing God *totum* but not *totaliter.* See Zachary Hayes, *The Hidden Center: Spirituality and Speculative Christology in St. Bonaventure* (St. Bonaventure: The Franciscan Institute, 1992), 108–09, 155.

45. "Sermon Third Sunday Advent," in *What Manner of Man*, 97.

46. "Christ, One Teacher," in *What Manner of Man*, 40.

47. "Sermon II Nativity," in *What Manner of Man*, 100–01; cf. Caroline Walker Bynum, *Docere verbo et exemplo: An Aspect of Twelfth-Century Spirituality* (Missoula: Scholars Press, 1979), 77–87.

48. *Itin.* 7, 4 (V, 312); *Brev.* 5, 6 (V, 259).

49. *Itin.* 4, 4 (V, 306). " . . . our spirit is made hierarchical in order to mount upward, according to its conformity to the heavenly Jerusalem which no man enters unless it first descend into his heart through grace, as John saw in the Apocalypse." Engl. trans. Cousins, *Bonaventure*, 90.

50 . Pseudo-Dionysius *De coelesti hierarchia* 3.1 (Migne *PG* 3.166). The Pseudo-Dionysius describes hierarchy as "a sacred order, a state of understanding and an activity approximating as closely as possible to the divine." Engl. trans. Luibheid, *Pseudo-Dionysius*, 153. The Dionysian concept of hierarchy is derived from the Neoplatonist, Proclus. See Meyendorff, *Christ in Eastern Christian Thought*, 101–02; Bouyer, *Spirituality of New Testament*, 402–03.

51. *Hex.* 21, 17 (V, 434). Engl. trans. De Vinck, *Six Days of Creation*, 329.

52. *Itin.* 4, 5 (V, 307).

53. *Hex.* 3, 12 (V, 345); *Lig. vit.* 40 (VIII, 84); *De trans. S. Franc.* (IX, 534b). "Christus est scala secundum humanitatem terram tangens, secundum Deitatem super caelos eminens." See Bernard McGinn, "The Influence of

St. Francis on the Theology of the High Middle Ages," in *Bonaventuriana*, 1:114.

54. Ibid. Engl. trans. De Vinck, *Six Days of Creation*, 48.

55. *Hex.* 12, 3 (V, 385).

56. *Red. art.* 8, 23 (V, 322; 325); *Brev.* 4, 2 (V, 243).

57. *Itin.* 4, 5 (V, 307); *Hex.* 3, 12–21 (V, 345–347). See Hayes, *Hidden Center*, 183.

58. *Hex.* 20, 12 (V, 427).

59. *Hex.* 20, 22 (V, 429).

60. *Hex.* 20, 23–25 (V, 441).

61. *Hex.* 21, 19–20 (V, 434).

62. *Itin.* 4, 4 (V, 307).

63. *Hex.* 23, 5 (V, 445).

64. *Hex.* 23, 7 (V, 445).

65. Ibid.

66. *Hex.* 23, 9–10 (V, 446).

67. *Itin.* 4, 7–8 (V, 308). Engl. trans. Cousins, *Bonaventure*, 93.

68. *Brev.* 5, 1 (V, 253).

69. *De tripl. via* 3, 1 (VIII, 12).

70. *Hex.* 23, 12, 14 (V, 446–447).

71. See *Itin.* 5, 1 (V, 308). Bonaventure also speaks of the cherubim facing the mercy seat in the *Hexaëmeron* where they represent the two testaments. Between the two cherubim is Christ upon whom they gaze.

72. *Itin.* 6, 2 (V, 310). "See, then, and observe that the highest good is without qualification that than which no greater can be thought. And it is such that it cannot rightly be though not to be, since to be is in all ways better than not to be." Engl. trans. Cousins, *Bonaventure*, 102.

73. Rist, *Eros and Psyche*, 207. Although the idea of the self-diffusive good is a Platonic concept, Bonaventure adopts it from the Pseudo-Dionysius. See Pseudo-Dionysius *De coelesti hierarchia* 4.1 (Migne *PG* 3.178); *De divinis nominibus* 4.1.20 (Migne *PG* 3.694–695); cf. Bougerol ("Saint Bonaventure et le Pseudo-Denys l'Aréopagite," 33–123) who made an extensive study of the concept of the self-diffusive good in Bonaventure's writings, indicating sources of influence and analysis of texts in which it is found. The most frequent use of it is in the first book of the *Sentences* where Bonaventure discusses, among other things, diffusion in the Trinity. The problem inherent in this concept is that of the one and the many, a problem which, according to Anthony Murphy, is overcome by Bonaventure by rooting the self-diffusive good in the primacy of the Father. See Anthony Murphy, "Bonaventure's Synthesis of Augustinian and Dionysian Mysticism: A New Look at the Problem of the One and the Many," *Collectanea Franciscana* 63 (1994): 385–98.

74. Von Balthasar, *Clerical Styles*, 285.

75. *Itin.* 6, 2 (V, 311). Engl. trans. Cousins, *Bonaventure*, 104.

76. *Itin.* 6, 3 (V, 311). Engl. trans. Cousins, *Bonaventure*, 103.

77. *Itin.* 6, 4 (V, 311). Engl. trans. Cousins, *Bonaventure*, 106.

78. *Itin.* 6, 6 (V, 311–312). Engl. trans. Cousins, *Bonaventure*, 108.

CHAPTER FOUR
ECSTATIC UNION

1. *Itin.* 7, 6 (V, 313).

2. *Itin.* 7, 4 (V, 312). Engl. trans. Cousins, *Bonaventure*, 113.

3. Ephrem Longpré, "La théologie mystique de Saint Bonaventure," *Archivum Franciscanum Historicum* 14 (1921): 76; Jean-Francois Bonnefoy, *Une somme bonaventurienne de theologie mystique: Le De triplici via* (Paris: Editions de la Libraire Saint-François, 1934), 21.

4. *Sabbato sancto. Sermo* 1 (IX, 269b); *Itin.* prol., 1 (V, 295).

5. *Hex.* 3, 30 (V, 348). Engl. trans. De Vinck, *Six Days of Creation*, 56–7.

6. *Itin.* 7, 4 (V, 312); *Hex.* 2, 30 (V, 341b); *Serm. 4 in Epiph.* (IX, 162b); III *Sent.* d. 24, dub. 4 (III, 531b).

7. *Hex.* 2, 32. (V, 342). Engl. trans. De Vinck, *Six Days of Creation*, 38–9.

8. *Comm. Joan.* c. 1, n. 43 (VI, 255–256); III *Sent.* d. 24, dub. 4 (III, 531).

9. Longpré, "La théologie mystique," 92.

10. Ibid., 94; Gilson, *Philosophy of Bonaventure*, 462.

11. Dunstan Dobbins, *Franciscan Mysticism: A Critical Examination of the Mystical Theology of the Seraphic Doctor with Special Reference to the Sources of His Doctrine*, in *Franciscan Studies*, ed. Felix M. Kirsch (New York: Joseph F. Wagner, 1927), 158–49; Bonnefoy, *Une somme bonaventurienne*, 86; In III *Sent.* d. 23, a. 2, q. 3 (II, 546) Bonaventure states: "Haec enim est (contemplatio) in qua mirabiliter inflammatur affectio."

12. Von Balthasar, *Clerical Styles*, 269.

13. Karl Rahner, "The Doctrine of the 'Spiritual Senses,' in the Middle Ages," in *Theological Investigations*, vol. 16, *Experience of the Spirit: Source of Theology*, trans. David Morland (New York: Seabury, 1979), 118–19. A longer version of this article by Rahner ("Der Begriff der ecstasis bei Bonaventura") first appeared in *Zeitschrift für Aszese und Mystik* 9 (1934): 1–19.

14. Rahner, "Doctrine of Spiritual Senses," 118.

15. III *Sent.* d. 24, dub. 4 (III, 531b). "Cognitio viae multos habet gradus; cognoscitur enim Deus in vestigio, cognoscitur in imagine, cognoscitur et in effectu gratiae, cognoscitur etiam per intimam unionem Dei et animae, iuxta quod dicit Apostolus: Qui adhaeret Deo unus spiritus est. Et haec cognitio est excellectissima, quam docet Dionysius quae quidem est in ecstatico amore et elevat supra cognitionem fidei secundum statum communem."

16. II *Sent.* d. 23, a. 2, q. 3, concl. (II, 544b). "Dicit enim Dionysius in libro de Mystica theologia quod excellentissimus modus contemplandi est ignote

ascendere, quia nec ipse Moyses Deum valuit videre, et ideo introductus dicitur fuisse in caliginem."

17. *II Sent.* d. 23, a. 2, q. 3, ad 6 (II, 546a). " . . . et vocat istam cognitionem doctam ignorantiam."

18. *Comm. Joan.* c. 1, n. 43 (VI, 256a). "Alio modo cognoscitur Deus in se; et hoc dupliciter: aut clare, et hoc modo a solo Filio et a Beatis; alio modo in caligine, sicut dicit beatus Dionysius de Mystica theologia; et sic vidit Moyses, et sublimiter contemplantes, in quorum aspectu nulla figitur imago creaturae, tunc revera magis sentiunt, quam cognoscant."

19. *Brev.* 5, 6 (V, 260a). Engl. trans. De Vinck, *Breviloquium*, 206.

20. III *Sent.* d. 35, a.u., 1, concl. (III, 774); *De perf. evang.* 1 (V, 120); cf. Gilson, *Philosophy of Bonaventure*, 462.

21. *Hex.* 2, 30 (V, 341). "This is the highest union through love."

22. *Brev.* 5, 6 (V, 260a). "verum etiam quadam ignorantia docta supra se ipsum rapitur in caliginem et excessum." In the obscurity of the experience of union, the divine incomprehensibility is grasped more fully as the mystery of God (Dobbins, *Franciscan Mysticism*, 163). Gilson (*Philosophy of Bonaventure*, 462) describes it as illumined darkness.

23. For the Pseudo-Dionysius, mystical darkness is part of his negative theology whereby the soul ascends to God in the darkness of unknowing: "The darkness of unknowing is where he renounces all the apprehensions of his understanding and is . . . united by his highest faculty to him that is wholly unknowable of whom thus, by a rejection of all knowledge, he possesses a knowledge that exceeds his understanding." See *De mystica theologia* 1 (Migne *PG* 3.1054). Engl. trans. Rosemary Ann Lees, *The Negative Language of the Dionysian School of Mystical Theology: An Approach to the Cloud of Unknowing*, vol. 1, *Analecta Cartusiana*, ed. James Hogg (Salzburg: Institut fürAnglistik und Amerikanistik, Universität Salzburg, 1983), 141.

24. *Hex.* 2, 30–31 (V, 341). Engl. trans. De Vinck, *Six Days of Creation*, 37.

25. Karl Rahner, "The 'Spiritual Senses' According to Origen," in *Experience of the Spirit*, 81–103. Origen states that through the spiritual senses Christ is grasped by every faculty of the soul. He is the true light which illuminates the eyes of the soul. He is the word who is heard, the bread of life who is tasted, the oil of anointing and nard and thus the sweet aroma of the Logos, and he became flesh which can be expressed and comprehend so that the inner man may know the Word of life. Rahner states that it is unclear whether or not Origen's doctrine of the spiritual senses elucidates the psychology of mystical experience although they are means of mystical knowledge and prophetic inspiration (pp. 96–7). See Hans Urs von Balthasar, *Parole et mystère chez Origène* (Paris: Éditions du Cerf, 1957), 65–71.

26. Bouyer, *Spirituality of the New Testament*, 363.

27. *Itin.* 4, 4 (V, 307).

28. *Brev.* 5, 6 (V, 259); cf. Rahner ("Doctrine of Spiritual Senses," 112) who holds

that the gifts of the Holy Spirit are secondary whereas von Balthasar (*Clerical Styles*, 320) states that the spiritual senses are bestowed with grace in the gifts of the indwelling Holy Spirit.

29. Pseudo-Dionysius *De mystica theologia* 3 (Migne *PG* 3.1054). See Lees, *Negative Language of Dionysian School*, 106–15.
30. *Hex.* 3, 2 (V, 343).
31. *Brev.* 5, 6 (V, 259b). Engl. trans. De Vinck, *Breviloquium*, 205.
32. Ibid., 322.
33. Von Balthasar, *Clerical Styles*, 321.
34. Muscat, *Verbum crucifixum*, 129.
35. *Itin.* 7, 6 (V, 313). Engl. trans. Cousins, *Bonaventure*, 116.
36. Ibid.
37. *Hex.* 3, 7 (V, 344).
38. Bonaventure, *Solilquium de quatuor mentalibus exercitiis.* 1, 38 (VIII, 41). Engl. trans. José de Vinck, "Soliloguey on the Four Spiritual Exercises," in *St. Bonaventure: Opuscula Second Series*, vol. 3, *The Works of Bonaventure* (Paterson, NJ: St. Anthony Guild Press, 1966), 69
39. *Itin.* 7, 6 (V, 313). Engl. trans. Cousins, *Bonaventure*, 115.
40. Wayne Hellmann, "The Seraph in the Legends of Thomas of Celano and St. Bonaventure: The Victorine Transition," in *Bonaventuriana*, 1:355.
41. *De tripl. via* 2, 8 (VIII, 9).
42. *LM* 8, 1 (EM, 64).
43. Richard of St. Victor, "Four Degrees of Passionate Charity," in *Selected Writings on Contemplation*, trans. and intro. Clare Kirchberger (London: Faber and Faber, 1957), 230.
44. Ibid., 224.
45. *Comm. Lc.* c. 23, n. 40 (VII, 576).
46. *Lig vit.* 48 (VIII, 86).
47. See Daniel, "Symbol or Model," 61.
48. Ibid.,
49. Zachary Hayes, "Christology and Metaphysics in the Thought of Bonaventure," *Journal of Religion* 58 (Supplement, 1978): 93.
50. Ibid.
51. *Hex.* 1, 10,13 (V, 330–331).
52. *Hex.* 1, 17 (V, 332).
53. Cousins, "Mysticism at the Crossroads," 167.
54. Denys Turner, *Darkness of God: Negativity in Christian Mysticism*, (Cambridge: Cambridge University Press, 1995), 132.
55. Ibid., 131.
56. Ibid., 132.
57. Hayes, "Christology and Metaphysics," 95.
58. *Itin.* 5, 7 (V, 309).
59. Ibid.

60. Ibid. Engl. trans. Cousins, *Bonaventure*, 100.
61. *Itin.* 5, 8 (V, 310).
62. Pseudo Dionysius *De divinis nominibus* 4.2 (Migne *PG* 696c). Engl. trans. Lubheid, *Pseudo-Dionysius*, 73.
63. Pseudo Dionysius *De divinis nominibus* 5.5 (Migne *PG* 820d). Engl. trans. Lubheid, *Pseudo-Dionysius*, 99.
64. Jean-Luc Marion, *God Without Being*, trans. Thomas A. Carlson (Chicago: University of Chicago Press, 1991), 75.
65. Marion, *God Without Being*, 75–6.
66. *Itin.* 6, 2 (V, 310).
67. Ibid.
68. Ibid.
69. Marion, *God Without Being*, xxiv.
70. *Itin.* 6, 3 (V, 311).
71. *Itin.* 6, 4 (V, 311).
72. *Itin.* 6, 5 (V, 311).
73. Ibid.
74. Anders Nygren, *Agape and Eros*, trans. Philip S. Watson (Philadelphia: Westminster, 1953), 353.
75. *LM* 8, 1 (EM, 64). Engl. trans. Cousins, *Bonaventure*, 250.

CHAPTER FIVE
CONFORMITY TO CHRIST

1. Daniel, "Symbol or model," 56.
2. *LM* 13, 10 (EM, 114). Engl. trans. Cousins, *Bonaventure*, 307.
3. *Brev.* 2, 11 (V, 229).
4. *Brev.* 2, 11 (V, 229).
5. *Itin.* 1, 7 (V, 297–298). Engl. trans. Cousins, *Bonaventure*, 62.
6. *Brev.* 2, 12 (V, 230); Hugh St. Victor *De sacramentis christianae fidei* 1.10.2 (Migne *PL* 176. 330).
7. *Brev.* 2, 11 (V, 229); *M. Trin.* q. 1, a. 2, concl. (V, 54).
8. *Brev.* 2, 12 (V, 230). The idea that creation was a book consisting of signs that pointed to its dependence on the Creator was a common theme in the Middle Ages. See Richard of St. Victor *De trinitate* 1.9 (Migne *PL* 196.895a). "In natura creata legimus, quid de natura increata pensare vel aestimare debeamus"; Alan de Lille *De incarnatione Christi rhythmus perelegans* (Migne *PL* 210.579a); cf. Hugh of St. Victor, *Eruditiones didascalicae* 7.1 (Migne *PL* 176.814) who states: "Universus enim mundus iste sensibilis quasi quidam liber scriptus digito Dei, hoc est virtute divina creatus, et singulae creaturae quasi figurae quaedam sunt non humano placito inventae, sed divino arbitrio institutae ad manifestandam invisibilium Dei sapientiam . . . ita stultus et animalis homo, qui non percipit ea quae Dei sunt (1 Cor 2:14);

in visibilibus istis creaturis foris videt speciem, sed intus non intelligit rationem."

9. *Brev.* 2, 10 (V, 228). The idea of the human being as the work of perfection is found in the early church in the writings of Gregory Nazianzus *Oratio* 38.9–11 (Migne *PG* 36.320–324) and John Damascene *De fide orthodoxa* 2.12 (Migne *PG* 94.919, 922–923).

10. II *Sent.* d. 1, p. 2, a. 1, q. 2 concl. (II, 42a). "Dicendum, quod ad perfectionem universi hoc triplex genus substantiae requiritur; et hoc propter triplicem perfectionem universi, quae attenditur in amplitudine ambitus, sufficientia ordinis, influentia bonitatis, in quibus tribus exprimit in causa triplicem perfectionem, videlicet potentiae, sapientiae et bonitatis." See Alexander Schaeffer, "The Position and Function of Man in the Created World According to Bonaventure," *Franciscan Studies* 20 (1960): 295.

11. *Brev.* 7, 7 (V, 289a).

12. *Brev.* 2, 4 (V, 221).

13. Ibid.

14. *Brev.* 7, 7 (V, 290).

15. Schaeffer, "Position and Function of Man in the Created World ," 309–10.

16. Ibid.

17. *Brev.* 7, 7 (V, 290).

18. *Brev.* 2, 10 (V, 228ab).

19. II *Sent.* d. 1, p. 3, q. 2 concl. (II, 50b).

20. *Hex.* 7, 5 (V, 366).

21. *Brev.* 2, 4 (V, 221). Engl. trans. De Vinck, *Breviloquium*, 80.

22. *Solil.* 4, 21 (VIII, 63). Engl. trans. De Vinck, *Soliloquium*, 122.

23. Ibid.

24. "Sermon II Nativity," in *What Manner of Man*, 67.

25. *Hex.* 1, 37–38 (V, 335); "Sermon II Nativity," in *What Manner of Man*, 68.

26. "Sermon II Nativity," in *What Manner of Man*, 69; "Christ, One Teacher," in *What Manner of Man*, 33.

27. "Sermon II Nativity of the Lord," in *What Manner of Man*, 65.

28. Bernard McGinn, *Foundations of Christian Mysticism: Origins to the Fifth Century*, vol. 1, *The Presence of God: A History of Western Christian Mysticism* (New York: Crossroad, 1994), 30; Andrew Louth, *The Orogins of the Christian Mystical Tradition From Plato to Denys*, (Oxford: Clarendon Press, 1981), 3–7.

29. "Christ, One Teacher," in *What Manner of Man*, 33.

30. Hayes, *Hidden Center*, 172.

31. Casarella, "Expression and Form," 116.

32. Denise Depres, *Ghostly Sights: Visual Meditation in Late-Medieval Literature* (Norman: Pilgrim Books, 1989), 24.

33. Ibid., 20.

34. George Marcil, "Contrasting St. Bonaventure's *Tree of Life* and the *Meditations on the Life of Christ*," *Cord* 32 (1982): 327. For a discussion of the

structure of the *Lignum vitae* see Patrick O' Connell, "The 'Lignum vitae' of Saint Bonaventure and the Medieval Devotional Tradition," (Ph. D. dissertation, Fordham University, 1985), 194–236.

35. Marcil, "Contrasting Bonaventure's *Tree of Life*," 323, 327. Unlike the typical gospel harmony, the *Lignum vitae* contains no glosses or interpolations as found in the *Meditations*.

36. John V. Fleming, *An Introduction to the Franciscan Literature of the Middle Ages* (Chicago: Franciscan Herald Press, 1977), 210. See also Étienne Gilson, "Saint Bonaventure et l'iconographie de la passion," *Revue d'histoire franciscaine* 1 (1924): 405–424; Harry B. Gutman, "The Rebirth of the Fine Arts and Franciscan Thought," *Franciscan Studies* 25 (1945): 215–34.

37. Sandro Sticca, "*Officium Passionis Domini:* An Unpublished Manuscript of the Fourteenth Century," *Franciscan Studies* 34 (1974): 156.

38. Ibid., 153.

39. *Hex.* 1, 17 (V, 332). "Hoc est medium metaphysicum reducens, et haec est tota nostra metaphysica: de emanatione, de exemplaritate, de consummatione, scilicet illuminari per radios spirituales et reduci ad summum."

40. *Lig vit.* 48 (VIII, 85).

41. *Lig vit.* 1, 1 (VIII, 71). Engl. trans. Cousins, *Bonaventure*, 126.

42. *Lig vit.* prol., 1 (VIII, 70). Engl. trans. Cousins, *Bonaventure*, 119.

43. *Lig vit.* 26. Engl. trans. Cousins, *Bonaventure*, 148–49.

44. *Lig vit.* 4 (VIII, 72). Engl. trans. Cousins, *Bonaventure*, 129.

45. *Lig vit.* 6 (VIII, 72). Engl. trans. Cousins, *Bonaventure*, 130.

46. Hayes, "Bonaventure " in *The History of Franciscan Theology*, 84.

47. Turner, *Darkness of God*, 132.

48. *Itin.* prol., 3 (V, 295).

49. David L. Jeffrey, *The Early English Lyric and Franciscan Spirituality* (Lincoln: University Nebraska Press, 1975), 48. The *Meditations* were published among the works of Bonaventure until the eighteenth century and continued to appear in the final volume of his complete works even after the author was reduced to an unknown "Pseudo-Bonaventure." Modern scholars now agree that the author was a Franciscan friar living in Tuscany during the second half of the thirteenth century. For a discussion of authorship of this work see Olivario Oliger, "Le *Meditationes vitae Christi* del pseudo-Bonaventura," *Studi Francescani* 7 (1921): 143–83; 8 (1922): 18–47.

50. Jeffrey, *English Lyric*, 48. The most familiar and accessible modern translation is from an Italian manuscript, *Meditations on the Life of Christ: An Illustrated Manuscript of the Fourteenth Century*, ed. and trans. Isa Ragusa and Rosalie B. Green (Princeton: Princeton University Press, 1961). See also Jaime Vidal ("The Infancy Narrative in Pseudo-Bonaventure's Meditationes vitae Christi: A Study in Medieval Franciscan Christ-piety (c. 1300)," [Ph.D. dissertation, Fordham University, 1984]) who offers a critical examination of the first part of the *Meditations*.

51. George. G. Coulton, *From St. Francis to Dante* (London: David Nutt, 1907), 303.
52. Jeffrey, *English Lyric*, 49.
53. *Vig. nat. Dom.* 1 (IX, 90b).
54. *Brev.* 5, 6 (V, 260). Engl. trans. De Vinck, *Breviloquium*, 206.
55. *Lig. vit.* prol., 2 (VIII, 68). See Murray Wright Bundy, *The Theory of Imagination in Classical and Medieval Thought* (Urbana: University of Illinois Press, 1927), 183–87; 207. Bundy discusses the role of the imagination in the Middle Ages, interpreting it in light of the senses. As he states: "Sensible impressions are preserved in the imagination, a kind of treasury and storehouse of the sensible species. When the intellect, through an act of the will, wishes to recall images for examination, as in the imaginative representation of meditation, it must necessarily depend on the imagination that preserves them. Only memory, however, can actively recall them. Unlike the imagination, memory is capable of reminiscence, that is, of recalling to consciousness."
56. *De trans. S. Franc.* (IX, 534b); *Hex.* 22, 24 (V, 442).
57. Ibid.
58. "Feast of Transferral," in *Disciple and Master*, 139.
59. Ibid., 140.
60. *Brev.* 1, 6 (V, 215); cf. *Itin.* 2, 7 (V, 301) where Bonaventure writes: "et quod ille qui est imago invisibilis Dei et splendor gloriae et figura substantiae eius."
61. "Feast of Transferral," *Disciple and Master*, 140.
62. On the theme of exemplarism in Bonaventure's theology see Gerken, *La théologie du verbe*, 135–39; Hayes, introduction to *Mystery of the Trinity*, 47–54.
63. I *Sent.* d. 6, a.u., q. 3 (I, 129a–130b).
64. *Hex.* 1, 16 (V, 332a); I *Sent.* d. 31, p. 2, a. 1, q. 2, concl. (I, 542ab); Ibid., q. 3, concl. (I, 544a).
65. *Hex.* 1, 16–17 (V, 332a).
66. *Apol. paup.* 2, 12 (VIII, 242b–243a).
67. IV *Sent.* d. 3, p. 2, a. 3, q. 1, concl. ad 3 (IV, 84b); *Apol. paup.* 2, 13 (VIII, 242–43). When discussing Jesus as the divine temporal exemplar Bonaventure says that the average Christian follows the example of Christ *in spirit* but the perfect disciple imitates his master *to the letter.* All actions of Christ are intended for our instruction but not all are intended for our imitation; cf. Dominic V. Monti ("Bonaventure's Interpretation of Scripture in His Exegetical Works" [Ph. D. dissertation, University of Chicago, 1979], 171) who states: "Bonaventure believes that many things Jesus did were not intended for imitation by the perfect, but had their own historically limited explanations. Jesus is to be imitated when his actions embody the "state of perfection" that he invited his closest disciples to follow."
68. *Apol. paup.* 2, 13 (VIII, 243 ab).

69. Ibid., 1, 10–11 (VIII, 238b–239b). See Hayes, *Hidden Center,* 134–37.

70. *Apol. paup.* 2, 13 (VIII, 243 ab). Engl. trans. Timothy Johnson, *Iste pauper clamavit: Saint Bonaventure's Mendicant Theology of Prayer,* vol. 390, European University Studies (Frankfurt: Peter Lang, 1990), 84.

71. Johnson, *Iste pauper clamavit,* 84.

72. *LM* 14, 4 (EM, 117). Engl. trans. Cousins, *Bonaventure,* 318.

73. J. A. Wayne Hellman, "Poverty: The Franciscan Way to God," *Theology Digest* 22 (1974): 339.

74. *Hex.* 4, 8 (V, 350); *Hex.* 10, 17 (V, 379); II *Sent.* d. 1, p. 1, a. 3, q. 2, ad resp. (II, 34–35).

75. III *Sent.* d. 1, a. 2, q. 3, ad resp. (III, 29–30). Engl. trans. Hayes, *Hidden Center,* 165–66. "If we reflect on the fall of man, we will see that the fall took place by desiring a false equality and similitude with God. Since equality belongs above all to the Son, it follows that man took the occasion for the fall, as it were, from the Son himself. . . . Certainly, in as far as man presumed the similitude of God, he sinned directly against the Son."

76. *Hex.* 8, 5 (V, 370a). Engl. trans. De Vinck, *Six Days of Creation,* 124.

77. Gerken, *Théologie du verbe,* 357–78. See especially pp. 365–67; cf. *Vig. nat. Dom.* 28 (IX, 128).

78. Hayes, *What Manner of Man,* 81 n. 16.

79. Hülsbusch, *Elemente einer Kreuzestheologie,* 167–68.

80. *De Sp. sti.* 1, 10 (V, 459ab). "Istam reversionem servat humilitas . . . humilis continuatur cum sua origine . . . Christus reducit se in suum originale principium per humilitatem."

81. *Vig. nat. Dom.* 2 (IX, 106b). " . . . quod Deus aeternus, humiliter se inclinans, limum nostrae naturae in suae assumsit unitatem personae."

82. *Q. evang. perf.* 1 (V, 117–124).

83. Hayes, *What Manner of Man,* 90, n. 41

84. *Vig. nat. Dom.* 2 (IX, 100). "Convertamus igitur oculos spirituales ad contemplationem Dominicae nativitatis." See also *Comm. Lc.* c. 2, n. 43 (VII, 54). "In omnibus, quae audierant et viderant; in quo ostenditur plenitudo gratitudinis."

85. *Lig vit.* 1, 4 (VIII, 72). Engl. trans. Cousins, *Bonaventure,* 129.

86. *Dom. 20 post Pent.* 1 (IX, 432b–433a); *Epiph.* 6 (IX, 165ab).

87. Ibid.

88. *Comm. Lc.* c. 2, n. 29 (VII, 51). "Nota, quod glorificandus est Deus in incarnatione, quia, ut dicit Damascenus, in hoc opere demonstratur sublimis bonitas, sapientia, potentia et iustitia Dei."

89. *Comm. Lc.* c. 2, n. 34 (VII, 52).

90. Ibid. See *Vig. nat. Dom.* 4 (IX, 113).

91. *Sermo* 4, 4 (V, 568b).

92. 1 *Sent.* d. 3, 1 q. 1, ad 5 (I, 69–70).

93. *Lig. vit.* 9 (VIII, 73). Engl. trans. Cousins, *Bonaventure,* 133.

94. Ibid., 12 (VIII, 74). Engl. trans. Cousins, *Bonaventure*, 136.

95. "Feast of Transferral," in *Disciple and Master*, 140.

CHAPTER SIX
THE MYSTERY OF CRUCIFIED LOVE

1. For the structure of Richard's argument of love see *De trinitate* 3.2 (Migne *PL* 196, 926-7).

2. Hayes, introduction to *Mystery of Trinity*, 33.

3. I *Sent.* d. 10, dub. 1 (I, 205a). "The adhesion of affection with respect to the beloved."

4. II *Sent.* d. 15, a. 1, q. 1 (II, 393b). "Amor, quia unit, transformare dicitur amantem in amantem." See Hugh of St. Victor *Soliloquium de arrha animae* (Migne *PL* 176.954). "Ea vis amoris est, ut talem esse necesse sit, quale illud est quod amas, et qui per affectum conjungeris, in ipsius similitudinem ipsa quodammodo dilectionis societate transformaris."

5. I *Sent.* d. 10, a. 1, q. 2 (I, 198a). "Quando ego amo alium amor non exit a me ita ut recipiatur in alio, sed tantum a voluntate procedit, et quia est accidens ideo non recedit sed in voluntate subsistit."

6. *Dom. XIV Post Pent. Serm* I (IX, 408a).

7. *Itin.* 6, 2, 4 (V, 310-311). Engl. trans. Cousins, *Bonaventure*, 103, 106.

8. Ibid.

9. *Hex.* 1, 19 (V, 332b); *Hex.* 12, 17 (V, 387a). For Bonaventure, the heart is the true midpoint of the human person and the cross reveals the heart of God.

10. *De perf. vit.* 6, 6 (VIII, 12). Engl. trans. de Vinck, *Perfection of Life*, 243.

11. III *Sent.* d. 1, a. 2, q. 1, resp. (III, 20); *Vig. nat. Dom. II* (IX, 107-109); *Red. art.* 20 (V, 324).

12. See Pancheri, *Universal Primacy of Christ*, 19-20.

13. I *Sent.* d. 6, a. un, q. 1, ad 4 (I, 226b). Bonaventure states that gratuitous love can be affirmed of the Father because he gives without recompense; his fecundity necessarily gives of its own nature. Yet, it is the Son whom the Father gratuitously loves, and, as the perfect Image of the Father, the Son in turn loves the Father: "Pater et Filius diligunt se, id est, Pater diligit Filium et Filius Patrem." See I *Sent.* d. 32, a. 1, q. 1, concl. (I, 558b). Their mutual love is the gift of self and this gift is expressed in the person of the Holy Spirit; cf. *Brev.* 1, 3 (V, 212a). Since the Son is center and mediator it would follow that the intratrinitarian dynamic of love is reenacted in creation and is especially manifested in Jesus' death on the cross.

14. *M. Trin.* q. 8, concl. (V, 114-115).

15. III *Sent.* d. 32, a. 1, q. 1 (III, 699a). "Amor est quaedam affectio et vinculum amicitiae quo aliqui ad invicem colligantur."

16. Bernard McGinn, *The Foundations of Mysticism: Orogins to the Fifth Century*, vol. 1, *The Presence of God: A History of Western Christina Mysticism* (New York: Crossroad, 1994), 27.

17. *De tripl. via* 3, 3 (VIII, 12). "Primo considera, quis est qui patitur, et eidem subdere per rationis assensum, ut credas firmissime, Christum veraciter esse Dei Filium, omnium rerum Principium, Salvatorem hominum, Retributorem meritorum omnium. Secundo, qualis est qui patitur, et eis coniungere per compassionis affectum, ut compatiaris innocentissimo, mitissimo, nobilissimo et amantissimo." This concept of compassion is by no means comprehensive but it is elucidated here as Bonventure uses it in his devotional works. He also uses the word "compassion" in book three of his *Commentary on the Sentences.* See III *Sent.* d. 34, p. 1, a. 2, q. 1 (III, 745); III *Sent.* d. 16, a. 2, q. 2, concl. (III, 354a). However, the word "compassion" here has more of a Christological meaning and is used primarily in discussing the sufferings of Christ. See III *Sent.* d. 16, a. 1, q. 3, concl. (III, 349b).

18. Kevin F. Lynch, "The Doctrine of Alexander of Hales on the Nature of Sacramental Grace," *Franciscan Studies* 19 (1955): 334-57.

19. *Brev.* 4, 5 (V, 245). Engl. trans. De Vinck, *Breviloquium,* 169. For the state of suffering in Christ see *Brev.* 4, 8 (V, 248-249).

20. *Lig. vit.* 26 (VIII, 77-78). Engl. trans. Cousins, *Bonaventure,* 148; cf. Dunstan Dobbins (*Franciscan Mysticism,* 77) who states that medieval piety placed a high emphasis on the actual sufferings of Christ as a subject of meditation, or as an incentive to Christian practice, giving rise to a one-sided Christianity which was impossible to imitate literally. Bonaventure's doctrine on imitation, however, is related to spiritual growth and does not call for a morbid imitation of Christ's sufferings *per se.* He emphasizes the poverty and humility of the cross which, as it is argued, are ontologically rooted in the divine nature.

21. *De perf. vit.* 6, 1 (VIII, 120). Engl. trans. De Vinck, "Perfection of Life," 239.

22. "Instructions for Novices," 155.

23. *Lig. vit.* 28 (VIII, 78-79). Engl. trans. Cousins, *Bonaventure,* 152.

24. O'Connell, "Medieval Devotional Tradition," 253.

25. Bonaventure, *Bringing Forth Christ, the Son of God: Five Feasts of the Child Jesus,* trans. and intro. Eric Doyle (Oxford: SLG Press, 1984), 3.

26. *De perf. vit.* 6, 6 (VIII, 122).

27. Ibid. "Domine Iesu Christe . . . tanta enim fuit sanguinis tui effusio, ut totum corpus tuum aspergeretur."

28. *Solil.* 1, 39 (VIII, 41b). Engl. trans. De Vinck, "Soliloquy," 69.

29. *Lig. vit.* 26 (VIII, 78). ". . . et dehinc clavis transfossus, appareret tibi dilectus tuus."

30. *De perf. vit.* 6, 10 (VIII, 123).

31. Ibid. Engl. trans. Cousins, *Bonaventure,* 149.

32. *De perf. vit.* 6 (VIII, 120a). "ideo necesse est, ut frequenter, ut semper oculis cordis sui Christum in cruce tanquam morientem videat qui devotionem in se vult inexstinguibilem conservare."

33. *LM* 13, 5 (EM, 109).

34. Joannes Scotus *Versio operum S. Dionysii Areopagitae: De caelesti Ierarchia* 13 (Migne *PL* 122.1062).

35. *LM* 13, 3 (EM, 108). Engl. trans. Cousins, *Bonaventure*, 305.

36. *LM* 13, 2 (EM, 107). Engl. trans. Cousins, *Bonaventure*, 305.

37. Richard of St. Victor, "Of the Four Degrees of Passionate Charity," 215.

38. *LM* 13, 3 (EM, 108). Engl. trans. Cousins, *Bonaventure*, 305.

39. "Sermon 2 on St. Francis," in *Disciple and Master,* 92.

40. I *Sent.* d. 10, dub. 1 (I, 205a). For the notion of the Father as the fountain full-ness, see I *Sent.* d. 27, p. 1, a. u., q. 2 (I, 468-474).

41. *Lig vit.* 49 (VIII, 86). Engl. trans. Cousins, *Bonaventure*, 174.

42. "Sermon 2 St. Francis" in *Disciple and Master,* 92, 95; *Itin.* 7, 4 (V, 312).

43. *Itin.* 7, 6 (V, 313). Engl. trans. Cousins, *Bonaventure*, 115.

44. This is the theme of the *Soliloquy* by which the soul ascends to union with God through the crucified Christ.

45. *Brev.* 5, 1 (V, 252). Engl. trans. De Vinck, *Breviloquium*, 181.

46. *Brev.* 5, 6 (V, 260); *Hex.* 2, 32 (V, 342); *Itin.* prol., 3 (V, 295).

47. *Brev.* 5, 6 (V, 260a). Engl. trans. De Vinck, *Breviloquium*, 206.

48. *LM* 13, 3 (EM, 108). Engl. trans. Cousins, *Bonaventure*, 305.

49. "Sermon 2 St. Francis," in *Disciple and Master,* 92.

50. *De perf. vit.* 6, 2 (VIII, 121). Engl. trans. De Vinck, "Perfection of Life," 239-40.

51. *Itin.* 4, 3 (V, 306); *Brev.* 5, 1 (V, 252-254); II *Sent.* d. 26, a.u., q. 2, concl. (II, 635).

52. *Brev.* 5, 5 (V, 257).

53. Peter Casarella, "Fragility of Symbolic Form in Bonaventure" (Unpublished manuscript).

54. "Sermon 1 on St. Francis," in *Disciple and Master,* 69.

55. *LM* 13, 10 (EM, 114).

56. "Sermon 2 on St. Francis," in *Disciple and Master,* 92.

57. *LM* 13, 3 (EM, 108).

58. III *Sent.* d. 1, a. 2, q. 3, resp. (III, 29); Hayes, "Meaning of *Convenientia*," 89-90; ibid., "Incarnation and Creation in St. Bonaventure," in *Studies Honoring Ignatius Brady, Friar Minor,* ed. Romano Stephen Almagno and Conrad Harkins (St. Bonaventure: The Franciscan Institute, 1976), 318.

59. *LM* 13, 5 (EM, 109). The term "finger of the living God" refers to the Holy Spirit. See *Brev.* 5, 9 (V, 263); *Hex.* 2, 30 (V, 341).

60. Hayes, "Meaning of *Convenientia*," 90.

61. *Lig vit.* prol., 1 (VIII, 68). Engl. trans. Cousins, *Bonaventure*, 119.

62. *Brev.* 5, 6 (V, 259); *Itin.* 7, 6 (V, 313); *Solil.* 2, 16 (V, 50). In the *Soliloquey* Bonaventure describes this level of union as one that encompasses both body and mind, that is, flesh and spirit. He claims that the soul is inebriated with sweetness and is lifted up so that the mind, withdrawn from earthly concerns, is raised in a mysterious way above itself, above the world, and above any creature. At this point, he states, the soul partakes of the sweet-

ness of the divinity and of the purity of humanity. It is a "chaste and holy sobriety of body and mind." It is a "divine embrace" whereby the lover holds the beloved closely. Engl. trans. De Vinck, *Soliloquey*, 90.

63. It would be interesting to compare Bonaventure's theology of the Crucified to contemporary theologies of kenosis and the cross, for example, Lucien Richard, *Christ the Self-Emptying of God* (New York: Paulist, 1997); Jürgen Moltmann, *The Crucified God*, trans R. A. Wilson and John Bowden (San Francisco: Harper Collins, 1991).

64. See Richard, *Self-Emptying of God*, 107 who writes: "In some mysterious sense God is not Father, Son, and Holy Spirit without the world, so that the triune God is in process to the extent that one may refer to the trinitarian history of God. The humility on the cross reflects the eternal humility of God."

65. Dante Aligheri, "Canto XXXIII," in *The Divine Comedy: 3 Paradiso*, trans. Dorothy Sayers and Barbara Reynolds (New York: Penguin Books, 1962), 347.

66. *De S. Andrea Apost. Serm.* 1 (IX, 469a); *Fer. sext. in para. Serm.* 2 (IX, 263-264).

67. *Brev.* 1, 8 (V, 216).

68. Ibid.

69. A. J. Wayne Hellman, *Ordo: Untersuchung eines Grundgedankens in der Theologie Bonaventuras* (München: Verlag Ferdinand Schöningh, 1974), 47-92.

70. *Serm. de S. Andrea* (IX, 466). "Verbum increatum et incarnatum est Verbum sapientiae, et illud coniunctum cruci; ideo crux est fons sapientiae, quia continet in se Christum, fontem sapientiae, thesaurum sapientiae et scientiae, quia in Christo sunt omnes thesauri sapientiae et scientiae absconditi" (Col 2:3).

71. III *Sent.* d. 27, a. 2, q. 1, concl. ad 6 (III, 604ab).

72. III *Sent.* d. 35, a. 1, q. 1, concl. (III, 774ab). "Dicitur sapientia magis proprie, et sic nominat cognitionem Dei experimentalem; et hoc modo est unum de spetem donis Spiritus Sancti, cuius actus consistit in degustando divinam suavitatem."

73. *Lig vit.* 46 (VIII, 84b); *Brev.* 2, 11 (V, 229a).

74. *LM* 13, 10 (EM, 114).

75. *LM* 13, 5 (EM, 109); *Hex.* 2, 20 (V, 339).

76. *LM* prol., 2 (EM, 5).

77. *Lig vit.* 49 (VIII, 86). Engl. trans. Cousins *Bonaventure*, 174.

78. *Hex.* 1, 11 (V, 331). Engl. trans. De Vinck, *Six Days of Creation*, 6.

79. *Red. art.* 20 (V, 324b). Engl. trans. De Vinck, "Retracing the Arts," 28.

80. Ratzinger, *Theology of History*, 100.

81. *Hex.* 1, 11 (V, 331). Engl. trans. De Vinck, *Six Days of Creation*, 6.

82. Ibid.

83. *Hex.* 1, 17 (V, 332); *Lig vit.* 12, 47 (VIII, 85); *Tract. de plant.* (V, 574-575).

84. *Hex.* 1, 16 (V, 332); *Hex.* 6, 1-5 (V, 360-361); Gilson, *Philosophy of Bonaventure*, 189-97.

85. *Itin.* 6, 7 (V, 312); cf. Cousins, *Coincidence of Opposites,* 147.

86. *Hex.* 1, 18 (V, 332).

87. *Hex.* 1, 19 (V, 332); *Itin.* 2, 2 (V, 300). The microcosm-macrocosm scheme held prominence among medieval thinkers (see Marie-Dominique Chenu, *Nature, Man, and Society in the Twelfth Century,* trans. Jerome Taylor and Lester K. Little [Chicago: University of Chicago Press, 1973], 24-37) and was particularly influential in Bonaventure's theology. For an excellent discussion of microcosm and macrocosm in Bonaventure's theology see James McEvoy, "Microcosm and Macrocosm in the Writings of St. Bonaventure," in *S. Bonaventura,* vol. 2 (Grottaferatta: Collegii S. Bonaventurae, 1974), 309-43.

88. *Hex.* 1, 19-20 (V, 332). See Muscat, *Verbum crucifixum,* 149.

89. III *Sent.* d. 2, a.1, q. 2, concl. (III, 40). See Hayes, *Hidden Center,* 88-90.

90. *Itin.* 6, 2 (V, 310). Bonaventure does not maintain a pantheist but a panentheist position. In pantheism God is contained within creation so that there is nothing in the world which is not God. Conversely, panentheism means that all things are in God and God is in all things, yet, transcending them. See F. C. Happold, *Mysticism: A Study and an Anthology,* (London: Penguin Books, 1963), 93; cf. *Itin.* 6, 2 where Bonaventure maintains that God is immanent in the world without being dependent on the world.

91. Ewert Cousins, "The Coincidence of Opposites in the Christology of Saint Bonaventure," *Franciscan Studies* 28 (1968): 41. Although Bonaventure's position approximates that of primacy, he does not explicitly hold a doctrine of absolute primacy. See Pancheri, *Universal Primacy of Christ,* 22-3. For a discussion of the primacy of Christ in Scripture see Jean-François Bonnefoy, *Christ and the Cosmos,* trans. Michael Meilach (Paterson: St. Anthony Guild Press, 1965); Michael Meilach, *The Primacy of Christ: In Doctrine and Life* (Chicago: Franciscan Herald Press, 1964).

92. *Hex.* 1, 22 (V, 333).

93. Ibid.

94. Mircea Eliade, *The Sacred and the Profane,* trans. Williard Ritrash (New York: Harcourt Brace, 1959), 36-7; *Brev.* 10, 3 (V, 251).

95. Cousins, *Coincidence of Opposites,* 149.

96. *Hex.* 1, 25 (V, 333).

97. *Hex.* 1, 28 (V, 334).

98. *Hex.* 1, 28 (V, 334). Engl. trans. de Vinck, *Six Days of Creation,* 15.

99. *Hex.* 1, 30 (V, 334). Engl. trans. de Vinck, *Six Days of Creation,* 16.

100. *Hex.* 1, 32-33 (V, 334-335).

101. *Hex.* 1, 34 (V, 335).

102. *Rooted in Faith: Homilies to a Contemporary World,* trans. and intro. Marigwen Schumacher (Chicago: Franciscan Herald Press, 1973), 42. See also "Feast of Transferral," in *Disciple and Master,* 139.

103. *Hex.* 1, 34 (V, 335).

104. *Hex.* 1, 35 (V, 335).
105. *Hex.* 1, 38 (V, 335); *Lig. vit.* 12, 47-48 (VIII, 85).
106. Turner, *Darkness of God*, 132.
107. *Hex.* 1, 10-11 (V, 331). Bonaventure indicates that Christ Crucified is the phys-ical center of the universe when he states: "Ipse enim mediator Dei et hominum est, tenens medium in omnibus ut patebit."
108. Gerken, *Théologie du Verbe*, 311-18.
109. "Sermon II Nativity," in *What Manner of Man*, 73-4; *Itin.* 6, 2 (V, 310-311); I *Sent.* d. 27, p. 1, a.u., q. 2, ad 3 (I, 470-472).
110. *Itin.* 6, 2 (V, 311); *Hex.* 3, 7 (V, 370); I *Sent.* d. 27, p. 2, a.u., q. 2, resp. (I, 485).
111. The symbol of the circle occurs frequently in Bonaventure's work and he is influenced in this respect by the Pseudo-Dionysius (*De divinis nominibus* 4.14 [Migne *PG* 122.1136-1137] as well as by Alanus de Insulis (*Theologicae regulae* 7 [Migne *PL* 210.627 ac]) who uses it to symbolize the relation of God to creation. The use of the circle for Bonaventure applies first to God, then to humankind, and finally to the entire history of creation; cf. I *Sent.* d. 37, p. 1, a. 1, q. 3, ad 3 (I, 639); *Brev.* 5, 1 (V, 253); *Red. art.* 7 (V, 322); *M. Trin.* q. 8, ad 7 (V, 115); *Hex.* 1, 18-20 (V, 332-333).
112 . Rufinus Silic, *Christus und die Kirche. Ihr Verhältnis nach der Lehre des hl. Bonaventura* (Breslau: Muller and Seiffert, 1938), 108. A copy of this text was unavailable. The reference is obtained from Gerken, *Théologie du Verbe*, 290. See also Saint Anselm *Cur Deus Homo* in *St. Anselm: Proslogium; Monologium*, 190-239.
113. Romano Guardini, *Die Lehre des hl. Bonaventura von der Erlösung* (Düsseldorf: L. Schwann, 1921), 119-36.
114. Gerken, *Théologie du Verbe*, 309.
115. II *Sent.* d. 12, a. 1, q. 2, concl. (II, 297a). "Sic cum posset statim perficere materiam, maluit tamen ipsam sub quadam informitate et imperfectione facere, ut ex sua imperfectione quasi materia ad Deum clamaret, ut ipsam perficeret. Et hoc idem voluit per senarium dierum differre, ut in perfec-tione numeri simul ostenderetur perfectio universi." See Kent Emery, "Reading the Word Rightly and Squarely: Bonaventure's Doctrine of the Cardinal Virtues," *Traditio* 39 (1983): 195.
116. II *Sent.* d. 1, p. 2, a. 1, q. 2, concl. (II, 42a); Schaeffer, "Man in Created World," 295.
117. Schaeffer, "Man in Created World," 380.
118. *Brev.* 4, 4 (V, 244-245); "Sermon II Nativity," in *What Manner of Man*, 74.
119. Hayes, "Bonaventure," 68.
120. "Sermon II Nativity," in *What Manner of Man*, 74.
121. Ewert Cousins, "Christ and the Cosmos: Teilhard de Chardin and Bonaventure," *Cord* 16 (1966): 99-105; idem, "The Evolving Cosmos: Teilhard de Chardin and Bonaventure," *Cord* 16 (1966): 131-36; idem, "Teilhard de Chardin et Saint Bonaventure," *Études Franciscaines* 19 (1969): 175-86.

122. *Hex.* 1, 10 (V, 330-331); *Red. art.* 20 (V, 324).
123. Pierre Teilhard de Chardin, *The Divine Milieu*, trans. by William Collins (New York: Harper and Row, 1960), 114-21; idem, *The Phenomenon of Man*, trans. by Bernard Wall (New York: Harper and Row, 1959), 294-97; idem, *Activation of Energy*, trans. René Hague (New York: Harcourt Brace Javanovich, 1971), 279-80.
124. Cousins, *Coincidence of Opposites*, 255.
125. Teilhard, *Phenomenon of Man*, 297–98.
126. Cousins, "The Evolving Cosmos," 134. Cousins states that Bonaventure's doctrine is more complete than Teilhard de Chardin's because it is grounded in the Trinity. Teilhard de Chardin lacks a theology of Trinity and creation.

CHAPTER SEVEN
UNION WITH CHRIST, EMBRACING THE WORLD:
BONAVENTURE'S WORLD VIEW

1. Cousins, "Two Poles of Theology," 4:171.
2. *Itin.* prol., 2 (V, 295). Engl. trans. Cousins, *Bonaventure*, 54.
3. Doyle, introduction to *Disciple and Master*, 13.
4. Ilia Delio, "From Prophecy to Mysticism: Bonaventure's Eschatology in Light of Joachim of Fiore." *Traditio* 52 (1997): 153–77.
5. See *Brev.* 5, 6 (V, 259).
6. Richard of St. Victor, "Four Degrees of Passionate Charity," 230.
7. Ibid., 224.
8. Ibid., 228.
9. *De tripl. via* 2, 9–11 (VIII, 10).
10. *De tripl. via* 2, 11 (VIII, 10). Engl.trans. De Vinck, *Triple Way*, 78.
11. Ibid.
12. *LM* 13, 3 (EM, 107–08). Engl. trans. Cousins, *Bonaventure*, 306.
13. *LM* 9, 5 (EM, 77). Engl. trans. Cousins, *Bonaventure*, 266.
14. *De tripl. via* 2, 11 (VIII, 10). Engl. trans. De Vinck, *Triple Way*, 78. See *Brev.* 5, 8 (V, 261) where Bonaventure explains the order of charity as love of God, love of our self, love of neighbor equally as our self and love of body.
15. Daniel, "Desire for Martyrdom," 81–6.
16. *Itin.* 7, 6 (V, 313). ". . . qui quidem *ignis* Deus est, et huius caminus est in Ierusalem, et Christus hunc accendit in fervore suae ardentissimae passionis."
17. *Apol. paup.* 3, 2; 4, 3 (III, 245–253).
18. See for example Caroline Walker Bynum, *Holy Feast and Holy Fast: The Religious Significance of Food to Medieval Women* (Berkeley: University of California Press, 1987), 215, 222; eadem, *Fragmentation and Redemption: Essays on Gender and the Human Body in Medieval Religion* (New York: Zone

books, 1991), 151–79; Elizabeth Petroff, *Consolation of the Blessed* (New York: Alta Gaia Society, 1979).

19. Bynum, *Holy Fast*, 121.

20. Amy Hollywood, *The Soul as Virgin Wife* (Notre Dame: University of Notre Dame Press, 1995), 40.

21. Lazaro Iriarte, "The Franciscan Spirit of St. Veronica Giuliani," trans. Edward Hagman *Greyfriars Review* 7:2 (1993): 220.

22. *De tripl. via* 2, 11 (VIII, 10). Engl. trans. De Vinck, *Triple Way*, 78. "Sextus gradus est vera et plena tranquillitas, in qua est tanta pax et requies, ut anima quodam modo sit in silentio et in somno et quasi in arca noe collocata, ubi nullo modo perturbatur."

23. *De tripl. via* 3, 11 (VIII, 17). "Pax etiam includit rexum plurium."

24. *LM* 8, 1 (EM, 64). Engl. trans. Cousins, *Bonaventure*, 250.

25. *LM* 9, 1 (EM, 74). Engl. trans. Cousins, *Bonaventure*, 262–63.

26. *LM* 8, 6 (EM, 68). Engl. trans. Cousins, *Bonaventure*, 254.

27. Daniel, "Symbol or Model," 59.

28. *LM* 5, 9 (EM, 44). Bonaventure writes: "Francis had reached such purity that his body was in remarkable harmony with his spirit and his spirit with God. As a result God ordained that creation which serves its Maker should be subject in an extraordinary way to his will and command." Engl. trans. Cousins, *Bonaventure*, 225.

29. "Sermon 2 on St. Francis," in *Disciple and Master*, 93.

30. According to the *Oxford Latin Dictionary*, the word *pietas* is defined as: an attitude of respect toward those to whom one is bound by ties of religion, consanguinity; of relationships between human beings: a. of children to parents, b. of parents to children, c. between husband and wife, d. of other relationships. See *Oxford Latin Dictionary*, ed. P.G.W. Glare (Oxford: Clarendon Press, 1982, repr. 1983), 1378.

31. The story of the *Canticle* is recounted in the *Legenda perugina* 43 (*Scripta Leonis et Angeli, sociorum S. Francisci*, ed. and trans. Rosalind B. Brooke (Oxford: Claredon, 1970), 163–69.

32. Ilia Delio, "The Canticle of Brother Sun: A Song of Christ Mysticism," *Franciscan Studies* 52 (1992): 11.

33. Leonhard Lehmann, *Tiefe und Weite: Der universale Grundzug in den Gebeten des Franziskus von Assisi* (Werl: Dietrich-Coelde-Verlag, 1984), 312.

34. *Itin.* 7, 2 (V, 312); Lk 23:43 RSV.

35. *Brev.* 7, 4 (V, 284b–285a).

36. Gregory Ahlquist, "Bonaventuran Mysticism and the Seraph: A Program for Ecstasy in the Frescoes in the Upper Church in Assisi." Paper presented at the 32nd International Congress on Medieval Studies, Kalamazoo, Michigan., May 9, 1997.

37. "Sermon 2 on St. Francis" in *Disciple and Master*, 95.

38. Ibid., 92.

39. Ibid., 96.
40. Catherine Mowry LaCugna, *God For Us: The Trinity and Christian Life* (SanFrancisco: Harper, 1991), 213; Karl Rahner, *The Trinity* (New York: Herder & Herder, 1970), 10–11.
41. Von Balthasar, *Clerical Styles*, 273.
42. "Christ, the One Teacher," in *What Manner of Man*, 74.
43. Ibid.
44. Ibid.
45. Jürgen Moltmann, *The Crucified God*, trans R. A. Wilson and John Bowden (San Francisco: Harper Collins, 1991).
46. *Solil.* 1, 39 (VIII, 41b). Engl. trans. De Vinck, "Soliloquy," 69.

CHAPTER EIGHT
THE CONTEMPORARY RELEVANCE OF BONAVENTURE

1. Marie Dominique Chenu, *Nature, Man, and Society in the Twelfth Century*, trans. Jerome Taylor and Lester K. Little (Chicago: University of Chicago Press, 1973), 8. Chenu writes: "When one considers the law proper to each being, even the antimony between matter and spirit, the universe resembles an immense zither whose strings produce an astonishing harmony for all their differences of sound."

2. See Ewert Cousins, "Language as Metaphysics in Bonaventure," in *Sprache und Erkenntnis im Mittelalter*, ed. Jan P. Beckmann, vol. 2, *Miscellanea Mediaevalia* (Berlin: Walter de Gruyter, 1981), 946–51. In his *Commentary on John*, Bonaventure identifies the Word as the center of communication between God and the world, a point that he defends at the end of his life against the Averroists who maintain the Aristotelian eternity of the world (*Hex.*7, 2).

3. John J. Lakers, *Christian Ethics: An Ethics of Intimacy* (Quincy, IL: Franciscan Press, 1996), 31. This prayer for unity lies at the heart of Franciscan spirituality. See Francis *RegNB* 22, 53–54; *Brev.* 5, 7 (V, 261).

4. In I *Sent.* d. 10, dub. (I, 205a) Bonaventure describes love as "affectus adhaesionem respectu amati."

5. Although this is a contemporary theological concept, Bonaventure's metaphysics of the good as it relates to the Crucified Christ underscores this point. According to Jon Sobrino, "the Christian belief in God as Trinity takes on a new and dynamic meaning in the light of the cross. . . . What is manifest on the cross is the internal structure of God himself." See Jon Sobrino, *Christology at the Crossroads*, trans. John Drury (Maryknoll, NY: Orbis, 1994), 226; Karl Rahner (*The Trinity*, 23) who states that the economic Trinity *is* the immanent Trinity and the immanent Trinity *is* the economic Trinity.

6. *De perf. vit.* 6, 2 (VIII, 120). Engl. trans. De Vinck, "On Perfection of Life, 245.

7. *Itin.* 6, 7 (V, 312). Engl. trans. Cousins, *Bonaventure*, 108–09.

8. *LM* 13, 5 (EM, 109). Engl. trans. Cousins, *Bonaventure*, 307.

9. *Itin.* prol., 3 (V, 295).

10. Girard's theory is more highly complex than described here and relates to the idea of sacred violence which is the core of his theory. However, that which corresponds to Bonaventure's doctrine is the discovery of the Crucified as the unique subject of history to break the spiral of violence. See René Girard, *Violence and the Sacred*, trans. Patrick Gregory (Baltimore: Johns Hopkins University Press, 1979); ibid., *The Scapegoat*, trans. Yvonne Freccero (Baltimore: Johns Hopkins University Press, 1986); ibid.,*Things Hidden Since the Foundation of the World* (Stanford: Stanford University Press, 1987); ibid., *Job: The Victim of His People* (Stanford: Stanford University Press, 1987).

11. Gil Bailie, *Violence Unveiled: Humanity at the Crossroads* (New York: Crossroad, 1995), 137–38.

12. *De perf. vit.* 6, 2 (VIII, 120).

13. *De tripl. via* 2, 3 (VIII, 9).

14. *De tripl. via* 2, 11 (VIII, 11a). Engl. trans. De Vinck, *Triple Way*, 78.

15. *Itin.* prol., 1 (V, 295). Engl. trans. Cousins, *Bonaventure*, 53–4.

16. *tin.* prol., 3 (V, 295). Engl. trans. Cousins, *Bonaventure*, 55.

17. *Lig vit.* prol 1. (VIII, 68). Engl. trans. Cousins, *Bonaventure*, 119.

18. *LM* 1, 4 (EM, 11). Engl. trans. Cousins, *Bonaventure*, 188.

19. *De perf. vit.* 7, 2, 3 (VIII, 124–125); *Itin.* 1, 4 (V, 297).

20. *Itin.* 1, 1 (V, 297). "Oratio igitur est mater et origo sursum-actionis. . . . In hac oratione orando illuminamur ad cognoscendum divinae ascensionis gradus."

21. *Circum. Dom.* 1 (IX, 137a); *Comm. Lc.* n. 15, c. 21–52 (VII, 389b–402a). The call to conversion and prayer is summed up in Bonaventure's exegesis on the parable of the prodigal son where he identifies the principle aspects of conversion: divine invitation, human assent, reception of God's gifts, and perseverance in grace.

22. *Itin.* prol., 3 (V, 295).

23. III *Sent.* d. 27, a. 2, q. 2, concl. (III, 616b).

24. *De regimine animae* 7 (VIII, 129). Engl. trans. Jose de Vinck, "The Government of the Soul," in *Opuscula: Second Series,*vol. 3, *The Works of Bonaventure* (Paterson, NJ: St. Anthony Guild Presss, 1966), 244.

25. Andrew Louth, *The Origins of the Christian Mystical Tradition: From Plato to Denys* (Oxford: Claredon Press), 96–7. Gregory's doctrine of *epektasis* means that the experience of God is inexhaustible; God can never be finally known or comprehended. There is no state of final rest for the soul: it is continually drawn out of itself in its love for God—even in eternal life.

26. David Ray Griffin, introduction to *Spirituality and Society: Postmodern Visions* (Albany: State University of New York Press, 1988), 3–8; ibid., introduction to *Sacred Interconnections: Postmodern Spirituality, Political Economy, and Art* (Albany: State University of New York Press, 1990), 1–13. In her much acclaimed book, *Saints and Postmodernism: Revisioning Moral Philosophy* (Chicago: University of Chicago Press, 1980), Edith Wyschogrod writes: "that postmodernism is fine-tuned to the apocalyptic dimension of twentieth century history" (p. xxi).

27. Personal communication.

28. Ann W. Astell, introduction to *Divine Representations: Postmodern Spirituality* (New York: Paulist Press, 1994), 3.

29. Ibid., 5.

30. Ibid.

31. Bonhoeffer, *Cost of Discipleship*, trans. by R. H. Fuller (New York: Macmillan, 1972), 106.

32. Simone Weil, *Gravity and Grace*, trans. Arthur Wills (New York: G. P. Putnam, 1952), 87; Eric O. Springsted, *Simone Weil and the Suffering of Love* (Cambridge: Cowley, 1986), 103.

33. Quoted in Astell, introduction to *Divine Representations*, 9.

34. *LM* 9, 1 (EM, 74). Bonaventure writes: "In beautiful things he saw Beauty itself and through his vestiges imprinted on creation he followed his Beloved everywhere, making from all things a ladder by which he could climb up and embrace him who is utterly desirable." Engl. trans. Cousins, *Bonaventure*, 263.

35. Ann W. Astell, "Postmodern Christian Spirituality: A *Coincidentia Oppositorum?*" *Christian Spirituality Bulletin* 4 (Summer, 1996): 5.

36. *LM* 13, 10 (EM, 113). Engl. trans. Cousins, *Bonaventure*, 314.

37. *LM* 14, 1 (EM, 115).

38. Dietrich Bonhoeffer, *Letters and Papers from Prison*, ed. Eberhard Bethge (New York: Macmillan, 1953, repr. 1971), 361.

39. Eric O. Springsted, *Simone Weil and the Suffering of Love* (Cambridge: Cowley, 1986), 46–8.

40. Chiara Lubich, *Unity and Jesus Forsaken*, trans. Julian Stead (New York: New City Press, 1985). In striving for unity with Jesus Forsaken, Lubich writes: "When you find yourself in front of a person, any person at all, remember that in that heart lives God, God who might be abandoned by that same heart" (p. 60–1).

41. Bonhoeffer, *Letters and Papers From Prison*, 360–61.

42. Moltmann, *Crucified God*, 46–50.

43. See Dorothy Söelle, *Suffering*, trans. Everett R. Kalin (Philadelphia: Fortress Press, 1975), 36–59; Lucien Richard, *What Are They Saying About the Theology of Suffering?* (New York: Paulist, 1992), 76–7.

44. *LM* 13, 3 (EM, 107). Engl. trans. Cousins, *Bonaventure*, 305.

45. *De perf. vit.* 6, 8 ((VIII, 122). Engl. trans. De Vinck, "On Perfection of Life," 244.

46. Astell, introduction, 8.

47. Johann Baptist Metz, *Faith in History and Society: Toward a Practical Fundamental Theology,* trans. David Smith (New York: Seabury Press, 1980), 34–6.

48. Ibid., *The Emergent Church: The Future of Christianity in a Postbourgeois World,* trans. Peter Mann (New Yok: Crossroad, 1981), 2.

49. Lakers, *Christian Ethics,* 31.

50. Lakers, *Christian Ethics,* xviii-xix.

51. *Lig vit.* 48 (VIII, 86).

52. *Itin.* 7, 6 (V, 313). Engl. trans. Cousins, *Bonaventure,* 116.

53. *Hex.* 1, 38 (V, 335). Bonaventure claims in this *collatio* that the Crucified Christ is the theological center in eternal beatitude. He writes: "The lamb in the midst of the waters is the Son of God, the Son I mean who is the central person, and from whom all happiness comes forth. . . For the lamb of God leads us, so that seeing the body and the soul and the divinity, we may find pastures either by going in or by going out. Here the beatifying center sheds its light on body and soul." Engl. trans. De Vinck, *Six Days of Creation,* 19.

Chapter Nine
Conclusion

1. Reinhold Seeberg, *The History of Doctrines,* vol. 2, *History of Doctrines in the Middle and Early Modern Ages,* trans. Charles E. Hay (Grand Rapids: Baker Book, 1978), 109–10.

2. Marion, *God Without Being,* xxiv.

3. Moltmann, *Crucified God,* 205.

4. This point distiguishes him from Francis who discussed the significance of the Eucharist in seven out of ten letters he composed.

5. Michael L. Gaudoin-Parker, *A Window on the Mystery of Faith: Mystical Umbria Enlivened by the Eucharist* (New York: Alba House, 1997),69.

6. Kevin P. Keane, "Why Creation? Bonaventure and Thomas Aquinas on God as Creative Good," *Downside Review* 93 (1975): 120.

7. *Itin.* prol., 2 (V, 295).

8. *LM* prol., 2 (EM, 5). Engl. trans. Cousins, *Bonaventure,* 182.

9. Keane, "Why Creation," 117.

APPENDIX
MYSTICISM: METAPHYSICAL FOUNDATIONS AND THE
MONASTIC QUEST FOR GOD

1. Michel de Certeau, "'Mystique' au XVII e siècle: Le problème du langue 'mystique,'" in *L'homme devant Dieu: Mélanges offerts au Père Henri du Lubac*, vol. 2 (Paris: Aubier, 1964), 267–70; cf. *Oxford English Dictionary*, ed. William Little, H. W. Fowler, J. Coulson (New York: Oxford University Press, 1937), 1736, which states that the term mysticism was introduced in the eighteenth century in a text by H. Conventry entitled *Philemon* wherein the author proclaimed: "How much nobler a field of exercise . . . are the seraphic entertainments of mysticism and ecstasy than the mean and ordinary practice of a more earthly and common virtue."

2. For a discussion on infused and acquired contemplation see Adolphe Tanquerey, *The Spiritual Life: A Treatise on Ascetical and Mystical Theology*, trans. Herman Brandeis, 2nd ed. (Westminster: Newman Press, 1930), 649–59; Egan, *Anthology*, xxi.

3. William Johnston, *The Inner Eye of Love: Mysticism and Religion* (San Francisco: Harper and Row, 1982), 16. See also William Ralph Inge, *Christian Mysticism*, 8th ed. (London: Methuen and Company, 1948), 4.

4. Ewert Cousins, "Bonaventure's Mysticism and Language," in *Mysticism and Language*, ed. Steven T. Katz (New York: Oxford University Press, 1992), 236.

5. Louis Bouyer, *The Spirituality of the New Testament and the Fathers*, trans. Mary P. Ryan, vol. 1, *History of Christian Spirituality* (New York: Desclee Company, 1963), 406; idem, "Mysticism: An Essay on the History of a Word," in *Mystery and Mysticism: A Symposium* (London: Blackfriars Publications, 1956), 119–37. Bouyer provides a detailed treatment of the word mysticism in this essay.

6. Johnston, *Inner Eye of Love*, 16.

7. Bouyer, *Spirituality of the New Testament*, 407.

8. Origen *Commentarii in evangelium Joannis* 1.15 (Migne *PG* 14.49b); Egan, *Christian Mysticism*, 2.

9. Bouyer, *Spirituality of the New Testament*, 407–08.

10. McGinn, *Foundations of Mysticism*, 171.

11. Robert Woods, *Mysterion* (Chicago: Thomas More Press, 1981), 32.

12. McGinn, *Foundations of Christian Mysticism*, xix.

13. Cousins, "Mysticism and Language," 237.

14. Johnston, *Inner Eye of Love*, 24. See for example, Bede the Venerable *In Lucae evangelium expositio* 1.10 (Migne *PL* 92.471); Jean Leclercq, "Contemplation chez les chrétiens occidentaux," *DS* 2:1937; Smaragdus *Commentarii in Regulam sancti Benedicti* 4.36 (Migne *PL* 102.772, 924–925).

15. McGinn, *Foundations*, 29; David Ross, *Plato's Theory of Ideas* (Oxford: Clarendon Press, 1951), 69.

16. Louth, *Origins of the Christian Mystical Tradition:*s, 5–6.

17. McGinn, *Foundations*, 27.

18. Plato *Phaedo* 80 a10–b5 cited in McGinn, *Foundations*, 38; *Later Greek And Early Medieval Philosophy*, ed. A. H. Armstrong (London: Cambridge University Press, 1967), 28.

19. Plato *Thaeatetus* 176b cited in McGinn, *Foundations*, 33.

20. Plotinus, *The Enneads* 1.6.7 (trans. Stephen Mackenna, 2nd edition, revised by B. S. Page [New York: Pantheon Books, 1957, 62], 62).

21. McGinn, *Foundations of Christian Mysticism*, 45.

22. Andrew Louth, *Denys the Areopagite*, Outstanding Christian Thinkers Series, ed. Brian Davies (Wilton: Morehouse-Barlow, 1989), 12.

23. *Enn.* 1.3.1.

24. *Enn.* 6.9.8.

25. Ibid.

26. *Enn.* 1.6.7

27. McGinn, *Foundations of Christian Mysticism*, 48.

28. Elmer O'Brien, introduction to *The Essential Plotinus* (Indianapolis: Hackett, 1964), 32.

29. *Enn.* 1.6.8.

30. Henry Chadwick, *Early Christian Thought and the Classical Tradition* (New York: Oxford University Press, 1966), 100–23; John Rist, *Eros and Psyche: Studies in Plato, Plotinus, and Origen* (Toronto: University of Toronto Press, 1964); John Meyendorff, *Christ in Early Christian Thought* (Crestwood: St. Vladimir's Seminary Press, 1987).

31. Andrew Louth, *Origins of Mystical Tradition*, 61. See Origen *De principiis* I.8, II, 8.

32. According to Robert O'Connell, Augustine held a similar view of the fallen soul. He writes: "Man, as Augustine of the *Confessions* depicts him, is a composite of soul and body—'this' body of our experience. But his true identity, the real 'I,' is soul, soul originally intended for a life spent in blissful contemplation of the divine splendor in the heavenly 'City of God.' Our souls, then, pre-existed, 'enjoyed' the vision of God's supernal Truth and Beauty, but fell from that blissful state into the life we know as human beings." See Robert O'Connell, *St. Augustine's Confessions: The Odyssey of Soul* (New York: Fordham University Press, 1996), 23–4.

33. *Origen: On First Principles*, 2.8 (trans. G. W. Butterworth [Gloucester: Peter Smith, 1973], 124–28); Inge, *Christian Mysticism*, 90.

34. Rowan A. Greer, introduction to *Origen: An Exhortation to Martyrdom, Prayer, First Principles: book IV, Prologue to the Commentary on the Song of Songs, Homily XXVII on Numbers* (New York: Paulist, 1979), 25–7.

35. Origen *Homiliae in numeros* 27 (Migne *PG* 12.780–801).

36. Ibid., *Contra Celsum* 6.68 (Migne *PG* 11.1402). For studies on Origen's Christology and devotion to Christ see Marguerite Harl, *Origène et la fonc-*

tion révélatrice du verbe incarné, Patristica Sorbonensia 2 (Paris: Éditions du Seuil, 1958), 192–204; Henri Crouzel, *Origène: et la "connaissance mystique"* (Bruges-Paris: Desclée de Brouwer, 1961), 470–74.

37. *Comm. in Joan.* 32.17 (Migne *PG* 14.817c). Engl. trans. Bouyer, *Spirituality of New Testament*, 417.

38. Charles Kannengiesser, "Origen," in *Jesus in Christian Devotion and Contemplation*, trans. Paul J. Oligny, vol. 1, Religious Experience Series (St. Meinrad: Abbey Press, 1974), 21. On Origen's understanding of Scripture see C. W. Macleod, "Allegory and Mysticism in Origen and Gregory of Nyssa," *Journal of Theological Studies* 22 (1971): 362–79.

39. Jean-Marie Déchanet, "Les mystères du salut: La christologie de S. Bernard," in *Saint Bernard Théologien* (Rome: Editiones Cistercienses, 1953), 91.

40. Irénée Noye, "The Fathers of the Church: The Formation of a Christian Sensitivity," in *Jesus in Christian Devotion*, 6.

41. Ibid. See Origen *Homilia in Luc* 18 (Migne *PG* 13.1848); Patrick O'Connell, "The Lignum Vitae of Saint Bonaventure and the Medieval Devotional Tradition" (Ph. D. dissertation, Fordham University, 1985), 19.

42. Noye, "Fathers of the Church," 5–6.

43. Origen, *Spirit and Fire: A Thematic Anthology of His Writings*, ed. Hans Urs von Balthasar, trans. Robert Daly (Washington D.C.: Catholic University of America Press, 1984), 122.

44. Henri de Lubac, introduction to *Origène: Homélies sur la Genèse*, vol. 7, Sources Chrétiennes (Paris: Éditions du Cerf, 1943), 27–8; cf. Bernard *Serm.* 2.1 (OB 1:9) who states: "I want no part with parables and figures of speech; even the very beauty of the angels can only leave me wearied. For *my Jesus* utterly surpasses these in his majesty and splendor." Engl. trans. Killian Walsh, *On the Song Songs I* (Kalamazoo: Cisterican, 1978), 9. See Charles Didier, "La dévotion à l'humanité du Christ dans la spiritualité de saint Bernard," *Vie spirituelle* 25 (1930, Supplement): 7.

45. *Spirit and Fire*, 122.

46. On love in Origen see Louth, *Christian Mystican Tradition*, 67; McGinn, *Foundations*, 119–20. Origen sees both *eros* and *agape* as love that is characteristic of God. That God chooses to go out of himself in creation is similar to *eros* (McGinn, 119). God is both passionate love (*eros/amor*) as well as charity (*agape*). Origen's mysticism centers on transformation of human eros (put in soul by God) to divine *eros* (God).

47. Origen *Cant. cant.* prol., 1 (Migne *PG* 13.62).

48. McGinn, *Foundations*, 110.

49. Louth, *Christian Mystical Tradition*, 103–09; John Eudes Bamberger, introduction to *Evagrius Ponticus: The Praktikos*, lxxxviii–xc; McGinn, *Foundations*, 151–52.

50. Ibid.

51. See Irénée Hausherr, "L'origine de la théorie orientale des huit péchés capitaux," *Orientalia Christiana* 30 (1933): 173.

52. See Louth, *Denys the Areopagite*, 1–134; Bernard McGinn, "Anagogy and Apophaticism: The Mysticism of Dionysius," in *Foundations*, 157–82.

53. Pseudo-Dionysius *De mystica theologia* 1.1 (Migne *PG* 3.998a–1000a). Engl. trans. Bouyer, *Spirituality of the New Testament*, 412.

54. Explaining this motif, Proclus states: "Every effect remains in its cause, proceeds from it, and returns to it"; Pseudo-Dionysius, *Divine Names* 4.14 in *Pseudo-Dionysius: The Complete Works*, trans. Colm Lubheid (New York: Paulist, 1987), 83. The Pseudo-Dionysius uses this idea to express the divine revelation which "descends" to its recipients and then "uplifts" them.

55. Pseudo-Dionysius *De coelesti hierarchia* 3.1 (Migne *PG* 3.166). The Pseudo-Dionysius describes hierarchy as a sacred order, a state of understanding and an activity approximating as closely as possible to the divine. The Dionysian concept of hierarchy is derived from the Neoplatonist, Proclus. See Meyendorff, *Christ in Eastern Christian Thought*, 101–02; Bouyer, *Spirituality of New Testament*, 402–03.

56. Pseudo-Dionysius *De coelesti hierarchia* 4.1 (Migne *PG* 3.178); *De divinis nominibus* 4.1.20 (Migne *PG* 3.694–695); Jacques Bougerol, "Saint Bonaventure et le Pseudo-Denys l'Aréopagite," *Études Franciscaines* 18 (Supplement, 1968): 33–123.

57. Paul Rorem, "The Uplifting Spirituality of the Pseudo-Dionysius," in *Christian Spirituality: Origins to the Twelfth Century*, eds. Bernard McGinn and John Meyendorff, vol. 16, *World Spirituality: An Encyclopedic History of the Religious Quest* (New York: Crossroad, 1987), 132–51.; McGinn, *Foundations*, 39.

58. See Pseudo-Dionysius *De divinis nominibus* 1.2 (Migne *PG* 3.692).

59. See Rorem, "Uplifting Spirituality of the Pseudo-Dionysius," 140–41.

60. See Pseudo-Dionysius *De coelesti hierarchia* 2.3 in *Complete Works*, 149; Rorem, "Uplifting of the Pseudo-Dionysius," 136.

61. Pseudo-Dionysius *De mystica theologia* 1.1 (Migne *PG* 3.998).

62. Pseudo-Dionysius *De mystica theologia* 3 (Migne *PG* 3.1033c). Engl. trans. Luibheid, *Pseudo-Dionysius*, 139.

63. The question of whether love or knowledge ultimately prevails in the Dionysian ascent to God does not seem to be entirely in agreement among scholars. McGinn, for example, (*Foundations of Mysticism*, 180) states that "both love and knowledge have essential roles, though love's is higher." Similary, Rowan Williams (*Christian Spirituality* [Atlanta: John Knox, 1979], 118–19) indicates that the originality of the Pseudo-Dionysius is his emphasis on God's desire to share himself thus rendering the whole process of emanation and return as one ultimately of love. On the other hand, Denys Turner (*The Darkness of God*, 47) claims that the mysticism of Denys is centered on its resolute "intellectualism." He states: "It is the ascent of the

mind up the scale of negations which draws it into the cloud of unknowing, where, led by its own *eros* of knowing, it passes through to the darkness of union with the light. . . . In Denys, it is the immanent dialectic of knowing and unknowing *within* intellect which governs the pattern and steps of its own self-transcendence to a union, principally, of *vision.*"

64. Jean-Marie Déchanet, "Contemplation au XII e Siècle," *DS* 2:1948–1949.

65. See Bernard McGinn, *The Presence of God : A History of Western Christian Mysticism*, vol. 2, *The Growth of Mysticism: Gregory the Great through the 12th Century* (New York: Crossroad, 1994), 74–8.

66. Gregory the Great *Hom. in Ev.* 27.4 (Migne *PL* 76, 1207a).

67. Augustine, *Conf.* 7.10.16 (Migne *PL* 32, 742); ibid., *Hom. on Ps.* 130.12 (Migne *PL* 37,1712).

68. See Etienne Gilson's chapter, "Paradis Claustralis," in *The Mystical Theology of Saint Bernard* , trans. A.H.C. Downes (New York: Sheed and Ward, 1940), 91.

69. Agnès Lamy, "Monks and the Angelic Life," *Monastic Studies* 1 (1963): 51–2; Edmond Boissard, "La Doctrine des anges chex S. Bernard," in *Saint Bernard Theologien: Actes du Congrès de Dijon 15–19 Septembre 1953*, 2nd ed. (Rome: Editiones Cietercienses, 1953), 119–35; Claude J. Pfeifer, *Monastic Spirituality* (New York: Sheed and Ward, 1966), 446–49.

70. Jean Leclercq, *Love of Learning and the Desire for God*, trans. Catharine Misrahi, 3rd edition (New York: Fordham University Press, 1982), 55–6. .

71. André Vauchez, *La spiritualité du Moyen Age occidental: VII–XII siècles* (Presses Universitaires de France, 1975), 43.

72. Leclercq, *Love of Learning,* 15.

73. Leclercq, "Contemplation," *DS* 2:1937; Jacques Rousse, "*Lectio divina* et lecture spirituelle," *DS* 9:473.

74. Guigo II, *The Ladder of Monks and Twelve Meditations,* trans. and intro. Edmund Colledge and James Walsh (Kalamazoo: Cistercian, 1981), 68.

75. Keith Egan, "Guigo II: The Theology of the Contemplative Life," in *The Spirituality of Western Christendom*, ed. E. Rozanne Elder (Kalamazoo: Cistercian, 1976), 111–12.

76. *Regula sancti Benedicti (RB)* 20.3–4. Engl. trans. *RB 1980: The Rule of St. Benedict in latin and English with notes*, ed. Timothy Fry (Collegeville: Liturgical Press, 1980), 217. English translations are made according to this edition of the *Rule.*

77. Pierre Adnès, "Hésychasme," *DS* 7:382–384; Thomas Merton, "The Spiritual Father in the Desert Tradition," (Abbey of Gethsemani, 1966, photocopy), 5. Hesychia is not only a state of repose but a whole spiritual orientation toward union with God by a complete renunciation of self and total surrender to the word and will of God in faith and love. It is exemplified in the classic anecdote about the vocation of the desert Father, Arsenius, whose vocation was to "flee, keep silent and lead a life of silent contemplation."

See *The Sayings of the Desert Fathers*, trans. Benedicta Ward (London: A. R. Mowbray and Company, 1975), 8.

78. See also RB 52.4, 4.57.

79. Irénée Hausherr, *Penthos: The Doctrine of Compunction in the Christian East*, trans. Anslem Hufstader (Kalamazoo: Cistercian, 1982), 18.

80. Cassian *Conf.* 23.5 (Migne *PL* 49.1251). Engl. trans. Cuthbert Butler, *Benedictine Monachism* (London: Longmans, Green, and Company, 1919), 68.

81. McGinn, *Growth of Mysticism*, vol. 2, *The Presence of God: A History of Western Christian Mysticism* (New York: Crossroad, 1994), 78.

82. Augustine *Hom. on Jn.* 42.8 (Migne *PL* 35, 1702).

83. Flavio Di Bernardo, "Passion (Mystique de la)," *DS* 12:1262–1264; Gregory of Nazianzus *Oratio* 38.18 (Migne *PG* 36.333A); idem, *Oratio* 7.23 (Migne *PG* 35.785B); *The Desert Fathers*, trans. and intro. Helen Waddell (Ann Arbor: University Michigan Press, 1960), 29, 48. Devotion to Christ was present in the early church, for example in the martyrdom of Ignatius of Antioch who desired to follow Christ in his passion and death (*Letter to Romans* 5–7 in *Early Christian Writings: The Apostolic Fathers*, trans. Maxwell Staniforth [Harmondsworth: Penguin Books, 1968], 105–06; *Letter to Magnesians* 5 in *Apostolic Fathers*, 88; David Fleming, *The Fire and the Cloud: An Anthology of Catholic Spirituality* [New York: Paulist, 1978], 3–6.) Irenaeus (*Against Heresies* 2.22.3–4; 3.10.2–4 in *The Apostolic Fathers with Justin Martyr and Irenaeus*, trans. A. Cleveland Coxe, vol. 1 *The Ante-Nicene Fathers*, ed. Alexander Roberts and James Donaldson [Buffalo: Christian Literature Publishing Company, 1885], 390–91, 424–26) also held that following Jesus in his earthly life was the way to victory and sanctification. See Rowan Williams, *Christian Spirituality*, 28–30. Origen held that attachment to Jesus in his earthly life was a means to attain to the invisible reality of God. See Irénée Noye, "Humanité du Christ (dévotion et contemplation)," *DS* 7:1036–1039. For references to Augustine, Chyrsostom, and the Cappadocians see Di Bernardo, "Passion," *DS* 12:323–324; Étienne Ledeur, "Imitation du Christ," *DS* 7:1563–1571

84. Colin Morris, *The Discovery of the Individual 1050–1200* (New York: Harper and Row, 1973), 139–40. Morris notes that an early and important manifestation of the new spirit was a change in the form of the crucifix. Instead of the figure of the living Christ appearing radiant with vitality, Christ appeared dead on the cross. The first surviving example is likely the great wooden cross made for Archbishop Gero of Cologne (969–976). See also Caroline Walker Bynum, *Jesus as Mother: Studies in the Spirituality of the High Middle Ages* (Berkeley: University of California Press, 1982), 17; Benedicta Ward, introduction to *The Prayers and Meditations of Saint Anselm with the Proslogion* (London: Penguin Books, 1973), 57.

85. See André Wilmart, *Auteurs spirituels et textes dévots du Moyen Age Latin* (Paris: Études Augustiniennes, 1971), 138–46, 505–14.

86. Jean Leclercq, "From St. Gregory to St. Bernard," in *The Spirituality of the Middle Ages*, vol. 2, *A History of Christian Spirituality* (New York: Seabury, 1968), 185.

87. Ibid. See Ernst McDonnell, *The Beguines and Beghards in Medieval Culture* (New York: Octagon Books, 1969), 318; Auguste Hamon, "Coeur (sacré)," *DS* 2:1026–1028; Hugo Rahner, "Ströme fließen aus seinem Leib," *Zeitschrift für Aszese und Mystik* 18 (1943): 69–73.

88. Jean Leclercq, "Sur la dévotion à l'humanitaté du Christ," *Revue Bénédictine* 63 (1953): 130. Leclercq cites several orations of this eleventh century Mass which refer to the humanity of Christ.

89. O'Connell, "Lignum Vitae of Saint Bonaventure," 11.

90. Leclercq, *Love of Learning*, 61. Leclercq writes: "Under the names of Cassian, St. Ambrose, Alcuin, St. Anselm, St. Bernard, above all under the title of *Meditations of St. Augustine*, the writings of John of Fécamp were the most widely read spiritual texts before the *Imitation of Christ*." See Jean Leclercq, "Jean de Fécamp," *DS* 8:509–11.

91. John of Fécamp *Confessio theologica* 2.6 in Leclercq and Bonnes, *Un Maître de la vie spirituelle*, 128.

92. See for example Peter Damian *Oratio* 26 (Migne *PL* 145.927a).

93. Saint Anselm, "Prayer to Christ." Engl. trans. Benedicta Ward, *Prayers and Meditations of Saint Anselm with the Proslogion* (London: Penguin Books, 1957), 95.

94. Ibid., 94.

95. Leclercq, "Sur la dévotion à l'humanité du Christ," 129.

96. Roch Kereszty, "Relation Between Anthropology and Christology: St. Bernard, a Teacher for Our Age," *Analecta Cisterciensia* (Jan–Dec, 1990): 290.

97. Ibid., 290.

98. Bernard of Clairvaux *Hum.* (OB 3:16–59); *Dil.* (OB:119–154).

99. Bernard *Serm.* 20.6–8 (OB 1:118). Engl. trans. Walsh, *Song of Songs I*, 152.

100. *Serm.* 83.3 (OB 2:299). Engl. trans. Irene Edmonds, *On the Song of Songs IV* (Kalamazoo: Cistercian, 1980), 182.

101. Pierre Pourrat, *Christian Spirituality*, trans. W. H. Mitachell and S. P. Jacques, 4 vols. (Westminster: Newmann, 1953–55), 2:50.

102. Walter Principe, "Christology," in *Dictionary of the Middle Ages*, ed. Joseph R. Strayer, vol. 3 (New York: Charles Scribner's Sons, 1983), 322.

103. O'Connell, "Medieval Devotional Literature," 47.

104. Leclercq, "From St. Gregory to St. Bernard," 199.

Index